Mastering Drupal 8

A comprehensive and advanced practical guide to master Drupal 8

Chaz Chumley
William Hurley

BIRMINGHAM - MUMBAI

Mastering Drupal 8

First published: July 2017

Production reference: 1250717

Published by Packt Publishing Ltd.
Livery Place
35 Livery Street
Birmingham
B3 2PB, UK.
ISBN 978-1-78588-597-6

www.packtpub.com

Credits

Authors
Chaz Chumley
William Hurley

Copy Editor
Safis Editing

Reviewer
Michael Drayer

Project Coordinator
Ulhas Kambali

Commissioning Editor
Amarabha Banerjee

Proofreader
Safis Editing

Acquisition Editor
Anurag Banerjee

Indexer
Mariammal Chettiyar

Content Development Editor
Onkar Wani

Graphics
Abhinash Sahu

Technical Editor
Shweta Jadhav

Production Coordinator
Shraddha Falebhai

About the Author

Chaz Chumley, ever since Chaz can remember, he has been picking up a crayon, a pencil, a pen, or a computer, whether to draw a picture, write a poem, share an article, or develop the next great website. Looking back at these qualities, it's the reason he chose to use those passions to give back to the open source community. His journey has opened doors to great experiences as a consultant, instructor, trainer, author, web developer, technical architect, Drupalist, and most importantly, a father. However, he could be none of these without first being a student and learning from life, love, and a passion for education, community development, and of course, science and technology.

The sum of these things has allowed Chaz to share his experiences as an active member of the Drupal community, having participated in developing Lynda.com Drupal training videos, authoring multiple Drupal books for Packt Publishing, and giving back his knowledge by contributing numerous articles, training, and presentations at Design4Drupal, BadCamp, DrupalGovCon, and DrupalCon, all the while bringing top-notch Drupal expertise to his clients' work.

However, his greatest journey is still in front of him as he continues to learn new creative ways to architect open source websites, write about the next best things, and laugh with his colleagues along the way.

Acknowledgments

Seeing that this is the second book I have now written; the process is becoming much easier. I still make mistakes, correct them, and then make some more. However, I welcome the feedback that I get from my family, friends, and colleagues who have helped review it all along the way. I am very surprised how fast Drupal 8 has moved and improved along the way, all for the better.

During this journey, I must reflect on the one person who instilled in me my work ethic, my father; he was a tough man, but I respected him. He has since passed away and while I know he shines down on me, I can still hear him telling me to push myself, love my family, and respect everyone. While I did not get a chance to say goodbye to him, I know he knows how much I love him.

Speaking of family, I have been blessed with two great moms, an awesome brother Josh, and a beautiful sister Carly.

However, the most important person to thank is my wife, Rebecca. She s been my biggest fan and without her, none of this would be possible. She kept me sane on long weekends and late nights of writing. She made me laugh when I wanted to scream or cry. She took me on long walks, longer hikes in the Appalachian Trail, and even to one of the Seven Wonders of the World, Machu Picchu. However, after 25 years of marriage, I still think you re the greatest wonder in the world.

Finally, a huge thank you to my colleagues at Forum One: rock star developers, awe-inspiring designers, breathtaking UX, and amazing marketing.

Hey Drupal! Come for the code, stay for the community.

About the Author

William Hurley, is the chief technology officer at Forum One. He is responsible for partnering with clients to develop technical recommendations that truly serve their organizational needs. He received a bachelor's degree from George Mason University's department of computer science. He's also a culinary aficionado, and he has a notably soft spot for curry. William has been developing for the web since 1997 using PHP, Java, Adobe Flex, JavaScript, and ColdFusion, and brings a breadth of technical expertise to clients' most difficult digital dilemmas.

William is an active member of the Drupal community. He has contributed more than 10 modules, along with patches to Drupal core and other contributed modules. With close to a hundred commits, William does his best to give back to the Drupal community.

I would like to thank Meredith Hurley, my wife, for helping me keep writing and putting up with me when I did just that.

About the Reviewer

Michael Drayer has been working with Drupal websites for 5 years, and has been building them for 3 years. He is a developer at Forum One.

Customer Feedback

Thanks for purchasing this Packt book. At Packt, quality is at the heart of our editorial process. To help us improve, please leave us an honest review on this book's Amazon page at http://www.amazon.in/Mastering-Drupal-8-Chaz-Chumley/dp/1785885979.

If you'd like to join our team of regular reviewers, you can email us at customerreviews@packtpub.com. We award our regular reviewers with free eBooks and videos in exchange for their valuable feedback. Help us be relentless in improving our products!

www.PacktPub.com

For support files and downloads related to your book, please visit www.PacktPub.com.

Did you know that Packt offers eBook versions of every book published, with PDF and ePub files available? You can upgrade to the eBook version at www.PacktPub.com and as a print book customer, you are entitled to a discount on the eBook copy. Get in touch with us at service@packtpub.com for more details.

At www.PacktPub.com, you can also read a collection of free technical articles, sign up for a range of free newsletters and receive exclusive discounts and offers on Packt books and eBooks.

https://www.packtpub.com/mapt

Get the most in-demand software skills with Mapt. Mapt gives you full access to all Packt books and video courses, as well as industry-leading tools to help you plan your personal development and advance your career.

Why subscribe?

- Fully searchable across every book published by Packt
- Copy and paste, print, and bookmark content
- On demand and accessible via a web browser

Table of Contents

Preface

Drupal is an open source content management system trusted by governments and organizations around the globe to run their websites. It brings with it extensive content authoring tools, reliable performance, and a proven track record of security. The community of more than 1,000,000 developers, designers, editors, and others have developed and maintain a wealth of modules, themes, and other add-ons to help you build a dynamic web experience.

Drupal 8 is the latest release of Drupal built on the Symfony2 framework. This is the largest change to the Drupal project in its history. The entire API of Drupal has been re-built using Symfony, and everything from the administrative UI to themes to custom module development has been affected.

This book will cover everything you need to plan and build a complete website using Drupal 8. It will provide a clear and concise walkthrough of the more than 200 new features and improvements introduced in Drupal core. You will learn advanced site building techniques, how to create and modify themes using Twig, create custom modules using the new Drupal API, explore the new REST and multilingual functionality, import and export Configuration, and how to migrate from the earlier versions of Drupal.

What this book covers

Chapter 1, *Developer Workflow*, walks you through setting up a development workflow. You will learn how to install Composer, Drush, and Drupal console to easily work with Drupal 8. We will also discuss the Git workflow and how it plays an important role in Mastering Drupal 8.

Chapter 2, *Site Configuration*, says that site configuration is probably one of the most important tasks any developer will need to perform. So, to ensure that you have a well-established baseline, we will walk through the basic site settings, performance, configuration overrides, and how to use Drush to speed up your workflow.

Chapter 3, *Managing Users, Roles, and Permissions*, provides us with the experience to configure account settings, which ensure that your next Drupal site is safe and secure. We will work with users, manage roles and permissions, and look at how Drush can help manage it all from the command line.

Chapter 4, *Content Types, Taxonomy, and Comment Types,* looks at one of the most powerful capabilities of Drupal to allow for the creation of custom content types. You will learn how to manage fields, work with Taxonomy, vocabularies, and terms to allow for tagging content. We will also look at Drupal Console, another command-line tool to speed up generating content.

Chapter 5, *Working with Blocks,* covers the basics of Blocks and Regions. We will take a deep dive into block configuration, custom blocks, and how to best manage block settings and visibility. Join us as we also look at some experimental modules that allow for placing blocks easily.

Chapter 6, *Content Authoring, HTML5, and Media,* is one of the greatest improvements to Drupal 8. In this chapter, we will learn how to work with responsive admin, manage content creation with CKEditor, text formats, and how to use image styles to display various media.

Chapter 7, *Understanding Views,* will explain how to use views to create lists of content to be displayed throughout the site. This includes using filters, relationships, and contextual filters to build new listing pages and blocks.

Chapter 8, *Theming Essentials,* explores the appearance interface and the core default themes shipped with Drupal 8. You will quickly get a better understanding of what makes up a theme, how to best manage themes, and best practices for setting up your theme's structure.

Chapter 9, *Working with Twig,* takes us through setting up our local development environment for theming and enabling Twig debug. We will then take a close look at Twig syntax, filters, control structures, and functions when working with templates. Finally, we will look at how to manage assets and preprocess variables.

Chapter 10, *Extending Drupal,* Looks at how, with the adoption of Symfony to power Drupal 8, writing of custom modules, which has changed dramatically. In this chapter, we will learn about dependency injection, how to use the new routing and menu system, adding permissions, and using events and hooks.

Chapter 11, *Working with Forms and the Form API,* will introduce the Form API. We will learn about all the new elements available in Drupal 8, and how to create new forms to capture user input and use it in your custom modules.

Chapter 12, *RESTful Services,* teaches the new REST API in Drupal 8. We will learn how to expose content via the Views REST plugin, as well as how to write our own REST API resource to provide custom functionality.

Chapter 13, *Multilingual Capabilities*, walks us through Drupal 8 and all the tools necessary to create a fully translated and localized site out of the box. In this chapter, we will learn how to enable and configure the appropriate modules, translate content, and create multilingual configurations.

Chapter 14, *Configuration Management*, Introduces the new configuration management system in Drupal 8. We will learn how to export configuration from one environment and import it into another, as well as how to use it in our own custom modules.

Chapter 15, *Site Migration*, explains how to migrate content from the previous versions of Drupal or other systems into a new Drupal 8 site. We will learn how to configure the migration process and how to modify and enhance the data before its saved.

Chapter 16, *Debugging and Profiling*, says that developing a complex Drupal site requires us to peek inside and see whats going on while its running. This chapter will describe how we can easily debug issues and profile our site to understand how each layer is performing.

What you need for this book

To follow along with this book, you need an installation of Drupal 8, preferably in a local development environment located on a Windows, Mac, or Linux-based computer. Documentation regarding setting up a local development environment is covered in Chapter 1, *Developer Workflow*, and can also be found at `https://www.drupal.org/settin g-up-development-environment`.

To follow along with each lesson, you will need a text editor or IDE. To see a list of software to consider using when developing in Drupal 8, you can refer to `https://www.drupal.org /node/147789`.

Finally, you will need to have administrative access to your Windows, Mac, or Linux-based computer, with the ability to run a Terminal window that will allow you to execute various commands and install various items.

Who this book is for

This book is ideally suited to web developers, designers, and web administrators who want to dive deep into Drupal. Previous experience with Drupal is a must to unleash the full potential of this book.

Conventions

In this book, you will find several text styles that distinguish between different kinds of information. Here are some examples of these styles and an explanation of their meaning.

Code words in text, database table names, folder names, filenames, file extensions, pathnames, dummy URLs, user input, and terminal commands as follows: "So if we changed the route URL to `mastering_drupal_8/test/{message}`, we would change the controller function to:"

A block of code is set as follows:

```
name: Test
type: theme
description: A test theme.
core: 8.x
libraries:
 - test/global
regions:
 header: Header
 content: Content # the content region is required
 sidebar_first: 'Sidebar first'
 footer: Footer
```

Any command-line input or output is written as follows:

```
# composer create-project drupal/drupal
```

New terms and **important words** are shown in bold. Words that you see on the screen, for example, in menus or dialog boxes, appear in the text like this: "Clicking the **Next** button moves you to the next screen."

Warnings or important notes appear like this.

Tips and tricks appear like this.

Reader feedback

Feedback from our readers is always welcome. Let us know what you think about this book-what you liked or disliked. Reader feedback is important for us as it helps us develop titles that you will really get the most out of.

To send us general feedback, simply email `feedback@packtpub.com`, and mention the book's title in the subject of your message.

If there is a topic that you have expertise in and you are interested in either writing or contributing to a book, see our author guide at `www.packtpub.com/authors`.

Customer support

Now that you are the proud owner of a Packt book, we have several things to help you to get the most from your purchase. You can contact the authors at `https://forumone.com/team/william-hurley`or `https://forumone.com/team/chaz-chumley`if you are facing a problem with any aspect of this book.

Downloading the example code

You can download the example code files for this book from your account at `http://www.packtpub.com`. If you purchased this book elsewhere, you can visit `http://www.packtpub.com/support`and register to have the files emailed directly to you.

You can download the code files by following these steps:

1. Log in or register to our website using your email address and password.
2. Hover the mouse pointer on the **SUPPORT** tab at the top.
3. Click on **Code Downloads & Errata**.
4. Enter the name of the book in the **Search** box.
5. Select the book for which you're looking to download the code files.
6. Choose from the drop-down menu where you purchased this book from.
7. Click on **Code Download**.

Once the file is downloaded, please make sure that you unzip or extract the folder using the latest version of:

- WinRAR / 7-Zip for Windows
- Zipeg / iZip / UnRarX for Mac
- 7-Zip / PeaZip for Linux

The code bundle for the book is also hosted on GitHub at `https://github.com/PacktPublishing/Mastering-Drupal-8`. We also have other code bundles from our rich catalog of books and videos available at `https://github.com/PacktPublishing/`. Check them out!

Downloading the color images of this book

We also provide you with a PDF file that has color images of the screenshots/diagrams used in this book. The color images will help you better understand the changes in the output. You can download this file from `https://www.packtpub.com/sites/default/files/downloads/MasteringDrupal8_ColorImages.pdf`.

Errata

Although we have taken every care to ensure the accuracy of our content, mistakes do happen. If you find a mistake in one of our books-maybe a mistake in the text or the code-we would be grateful if you could report this to us. By doing so, you can save other readers from frustration and help us improve subsequent versions of this book. If you find any errata, please report them by visiting `http://www.packtpub.com/submit-errata`, selecting your book, clicking on the **Errata Submission Form** link, and entering the details of your errata. Once your errata are verified, your submission will be accepted and the errata will be uploaded to our website or added to any list of existing errata under the Errata section of that title.

To view the previously submitted errata, go to `https://www.packtpub.com/books/content/support` and enter the name of the book in the search field. The required information will appear under the **Errata** section.

Piracy

Piracy of copyrighted material on the Internet is an ongoing problem across all media. At Packt, we take the protection of our copyright and licenses very seriously. If you come across any illegal copies of our works in any form on the Internet, please provide us with the location address or website name immediately so that we can pursue a remedy. Please contact us at copyright@packtpub.com with a link to the suspected pirated material. We appreciate your help in protecting our authors and our ability to bring you valuable content.

Questions

If you have a problem with any aspect of this book, you can contact us at questions@packtpub.com, and we will do our best to address the problem.

1
Developer Workflow

In order to fully take advantage of Drupal 8, it helps to have an established developer workflow. This can range from having a local web server to using a fully integrated, virtualized AMP (Apache, MySQL, PHP) stack that mimics the development, staging, and production servers that one may need to deploy Drupal. It also helps to establish a set of best practices to follow when it comes to installing, managing, and working with Drupal 8 on a project-by-project basis. While there are various tools to choose from, we will look at some of the most common ones available to us, including **Composer**, **Drush**, **DrupalConsole**, and **Git**.

The deeper we dive into mastering Drupal 8, the more vital it becomes to learn command-line interfaces, such as Composer, Drush, Git, and Drupal Console. These require the use of a Terminal window and a level of comfort when working with the command line. While we will not be covering the basics of Windows or Unix shell, we will explain what each command does and how each tool speeds up our developer workflow.

In this chapter, we will be covering the basics of how to use each of these tools to install, extend, and manage a typical Drupal 8 developer workflow, including the following:

- Deciding on a local AMP stack
- The role of Composer
- Speeding up tasks using Drush
- A quick look at Drupal Console
- Using Git to manage source code
- Virtualizing an environment

Deciding on a local AMP stack

A developer workflow begins with having an AMP (Apache, MySQL, PHP) stack installed and configured on a Windows, OS X, or *nix based machine. Depending on the operating system, there are a lot of different methods that one can use to set up an ideal environment. However, when it comes down to choices, there are only three:

- **Native AMP stack**: This option refers to systems that generally either come preconfigured with Apache, MySQL, and PHP, or have a generally easy installation path to download and configure these three requirements. There are plenty of great tutorials on how to achieve this workflow, but this requires familiarity with the operating system.
- **Packaged AMP stack**: This option refers to third-party solutions, such as MAMP(https://www.mamp.info/en/), WAMP(http://www.wampserver.com/en/), or Acquia Dev Desktop(https://dev.acquia.com/downloads). These solutions come with an installer that generally works on Windows and OS X, and is a self-contained AMP stack allowing for general web server development. Out of these three, only Acquia Dev Desktop is Drupal specific.
- **Virtual machine (VM)**: This option is often the best solution as it closely represents the actual development, staging, and production web servers. However, this can also be the most complex to initially set up and requires some knowledge of how to configure specific parts of the AMP stack. There are a few well-documented VMs available that can help reduce the experience needed. Two great virtual machines to look at are Drupal VM(https://www.drupalvm.com/) and **Vagrant Drupal Development (VDD)**(https://www.drupal.org/project/vdd).

In the end, my recommendation is to choose an environment that is flexible enough to quickly install, set up, and configure Drupal instances. The preceding choices are all good to start with, and by no means is any single solution a bad choice.

If you are a single person developer, a packaged AMP stack such as MAMP may be the perfect choice. However, if you are in a team environment, I would strongly recommend one of the previously mentioned VM options or consider creating your own VM environment that can be distributed to your team.

We will discuss virtualized environments in more detail, but, before we do, we need to have a basic understanding of how to work with three very important command-line interfaces: Composer, Drush, and Drupal Console.

The role of Composer

Drupal 8 and each minor version introduces new features and functionality: everything from moving the most commonly used third-party modules into its core to the introduction of an object-oriented PHP framework. These improvements also introduced the **Symfony framework** that brings in the ability to use a dependency management tool called Composer.

Composer (https://getcomposer.org/) is a dependency manager for PHP that allows us to perform a multitude of tasks: everything from creating a Drupal project to declaring libraries and even installing contributed modules, just to name a few. The advantage of using Composer is that it allows us to quickly install and update dependencies by simply running a few commands. These configurations are then stored within a composer.json file that can be shared with other developers to quickly set up identical Drupal instances.

If you are new to Composer, let's take a moment to discuss how to go about installing Composer for the first time within a local environment.

Installing Composer locally

Composer can be installed on Windows, Linux, Unix, and OS X. For this example, we will be following the install found at https://getcomposer.org/download/. Ensure that you take a look at the **Getting Started** documentation that corresponds with your operating system.

Begin by opening a new Terminal window. By default, our Terminal window should place us in the user directory. We can then continue by executing the following four commands:

1. Download Composer installer to the local directory:

   ```
   php -r "copy('https://getcomposer.org/installer', 'composer-setup.php');"
   ```

2. Verify the installer:

   Since Composer versions are often updated, it is important to refer to the date on the Download Composer page to ensure that the preceding hash file is the most current one.

3. Run the installer:

```
php composer-setup.php
```

4. Remove the installer:

```
php -r "unlink('composer-setup.php');"
```

5. Composer is now installed locally, and we can verify this by executing the following command within a Terminal window:

```
php composer.phar
```

6. Composer should now present us with a list of the available commands:

```
Available commands:
  about            Short information about Composer
  archive          Create an archive of this composer package
  browse           Opens the package's repository URL or homepage in your browser.
  clear-cache      Clears composer's internal package cache.
  clearcache       Clears composer's internal package cache.
  config           Set config options
  create-project   Create new project from a package into given directory.
```

The challenge with having Composer installed locally is that it restricts us from using it outside the current user directory. In most cases, we will be creating projects outside of our user directory, so having the ability to globally use Composer quickly becomes a necessity.

Installing Composer globally

Moving the composer.phar file from its current location to a global directory can be achieved by executing the following command within a Terminal window:

```
mv composer.phar /usr/local/bin/composer
```

We can now execute Composer commands globally by typing composer in the Terminal window.

Using Composer to create a Drupal project

One of the most common uses for Composer is the ability to create a PHP project. The `create-project` command takes several arguments, including the type of PHP project we want to build, the location where we want to install the project, and, optionally, the package version. Using this command, we no longer need to manually download Drupal and extract the contents into an install directory. We can speed up the entire process using one simple command.

Begin by opening a Terminal window and navigating to the folder where we want to install Drupal. Next, we can use Composer to execute the following command:

```
composer create-project drupal-composer/drupal-project:8.x-dev mastering --
stability dev --no-interaction
```

The `create-project` command tells Composer that we want to create a new Drupal project within a folder called `mastering`. We also tell Composer that we want the most stable development version. Once the command is executed, Composer locates the current version of Drupal and installs the project, along with any additional dependencies that it needs:

```
cchumley@forumone:~/Sandbox ⇒ composer create-project drupal-composer/drupal-project:8.x-dev mastering --stability dev --no-interaction
Installing drupal-composer/drupal-project (8.x-dev a271d50e329428529e85f473db3a55c8f5514a7e)
  - Installing drupal-composer/drupal-project (8.x-dev a271d50) Cloning a271d50e32 from cache
Created project in mastering
```

The Composer project template provides a kick-start for managing Drupal projects following best practice implementation. This includes installing both Drush and Drupal Console, which are command line tools we can use to work with Drupal outside of the typical user interface. The reason Drush and Drupal console are packaged with the Composer project is both to avoid dependency issues and to allow for different versions of these tools per project. We will explore Drush and Drupal Console in greater detail a little later.

Composer also scaffolds a new directory structure that warrants taking a moment to review:

The new directory structure places everything related to Drupal within the /web folder, including the core, modules, profiles, sites, and themes. Drush and Drupal Console along with any dependencies that Drupal needs get installed within the /vendor folder. The remaining two folders /drush and /scripts are utilized by Drush and Drupal 8 to help configure our project.

All the installation, configuration, and scaffolding that takes place is a result of the composer.json file that Composer uses to create a project. Often referred to as a package, the composer.json file allows us to distribute it to other computers, web servers, or team members to generate an identical Drupal 8 code base by simply executing, composer install.

We will be using Composer to manage every aspect of a Drupal project. This will include the ability to update Drupal core when new versions are available, install and update Modules that we may want to use to extend Drupal, and to add any additional configuration to manage installer paths and possibly patch modules. We will review these additional commands throughout the book.

For now, lets switch our focus to some of the command line tools that were installed with our Drupal project, beginning with Drush.

Speeding up tasks using Drush

Drush (`http://www.drush.org/en/master/`) is a command-line shell and Unix-scripting interface that allows us to interact with Drupal. Drush gives us the ability to use the command line to accomplish tasks quickly, without the need to rely on the Drupal admin UI. As part of the composer install, our project has the latest version of Drush installed automatically.

Executing a Drush command is typically as easy as typing the word `drush` within a Terminal window.

However, the challenge of having a per-project instance of Drush is in the way we are forced to currently execute Drush commands. Since the `drush` executable is located within the projects `/vendor/bin/drush` folder, if we are within the root of our project, we execute drush by entering the following within the Terminal window:

```
./vendor/bin/drush
```

The problem is the path can easily change; if, for instance, we are in the `/web` root, the same command would be:

```
../vendor/bin/drush
```

Notice the two dots indicating one must traverse up a level to locate the `/vendor` folder.

This is not ideal when we will be using Drush quite frequently to perform various tasks. We can resolve this in a couple of different ways.

Using Drush wrapper

The first is to use `drush.wrapper` located within the `/vendor/drush/drush/examples` folder. This file is a wrapper script that launches Drush within a project. If we open the file within an editor, we will see that it states we need to copy the file to our `/web` folder and rename it to drush.

Choosing to follow this method would then allow us from within the `/web` folder to execute drush commands by entering the following within our Terminal window:

```
./drush
```

This is a little better; however, this is not quite as nice as simply typing the word `drush` without the need to know how to run a script. We can accomplish this by globally installing Drush using Composer.

Installing Drush globally

Installing Drush globally varies based on the operating system or AMP stack, as there is a dependency on PHP 5.5.9 or higher. This dependency will be satisfied in most cases, but ensure that you verify the version of PHP that is available.

Begin by opening the Terminal window, changing into the user directory, and executing the following commands:

1. Verify that Composer is installed:

   ```
   composer
   ```

2. Add Composer's bin directory to the system path:

   ```
   export PATH="$HOME/.composer/vendor/bin:$PATH"
   ```

3. Install the latest stable release:

   ```
   composer global require drush/drush
   ```

4. Verify that Drush works:

   ```
   drush status
   ```

5. Now that Drush has been installed globally, we can easily ensure that we always have the latest version by running this:

   ```
   composer global update
   ```

6. To get our first look at the available commands that Drush provides, we can execute the following:

   ```
   drush
   ```

```
Core Drush commands: (core)
 archive-dump (ard,      Backup your code, files, and database into a single file.
 archive-backup, arb)
 archive-restore         Expand a site archive into a Drupal web site.
 (arr)
 core-cli (php)          Open an interactive shell on a Drupal site.
```

The list of Drush commands is quite long, but it does provide us with the ability to perform almost any action we may need when working on a Drupal project. Some simple commands that we will commonly use throughout the book are clearing cache, managing configurations, and even installing Drupal. For a list of all the various commands, we can browse Drush Commands at https://drushcommands.com/.

Using Drush to create a Drupal project

Some common uses of Drush are to download modules, themes, and even Drupal itself. The command to execute this task is drush dl. Since we previously installed Drush globally, we can change to a brand-new directory using the Terminal window, and download another copy of Drupal by executing the following command:

```
drush dl drupal
```

```
cchumley@forumone:~/Sandbox|⇒  drush dl drupal
Project drupal (8.3.4) downloaded to /Users/cchumley/Sandbox/drupal-8.3.4.
```

As we can see from the preceding screenshot, executing the command downloads the current version of Drupal. We can verify this by listing the contents of the current directory:

```
cchumley@forumone:~/Sandbox|⇒  ll
total 0
drwxr-xr-x  24 cchumley  staff   816B Jun 21 14:28 drupal-8.3.4
drwxr-xr-x  13 cchumley  staff   442B Jul  2 09:54 mastering
```

Now that we have a second copy of Drupal, we can use Drush to perform a quick install.

Note that, to use Drush to install Drupal without setting up or configuring an instance of an *AMP stack, we will need to at least have PHP 5.5.9 or higher installed.

Within a Terminal window, change into the drupal-8.x directory that Drush downloaded and execute the following command:

```
drush qd --use-existing --uri=http://localhost:8383 --profile=standard
```

This command tells Drush to perform a quick Drupal installation using the existing source files. Drupal will use the standard profile and, once the installation has completed, a PHP server will be started on localhost port 8383.

Ensure that you specify that you want to continue with the installation when prompted. Once the Drupal installation has finished, a browser window will open on the admin user page with the one-time login where we can then create a new password:

We will not be using this instance of Drupal, so we can terminate the PHP server that is currently running in the Terminal window by entering *Ctrl + C* on the keyboard.

Hopefully, we can begin to see how using Drush can speed up common tasks. Throughout each lesson, we will explore Drush in more detail and utilize additional commands. Now that we have a better understanding of Drush, it's time to take a look at another command-line tool that we can benefit from using when developing a Drupal website.

A quick look at Drupal Console

Drupal Console (`https://drupalconsole.com/`) is a new command-line tool that has been welcomed by the Drupal community. Like Drush, but in my opinion, much more powerful, Drupal Console allows us to perform site installs, manage configurations, create content, generate boilerplate code, and much more.

Accessing Drupal Console locally

As part of the original composer install of our Drupal project, Drupal console was installed. However, just like accessing Drush locally, we are faced with the same complexities of knowing the exact location of the Drupal console executable.

If we look within the `/vendor/drupal/console/bin` folder, we will see the executable that allows us to use Drupal console from the command line. We can enter the following command within the Terminal window to run the executable:

`./vendor/drupal/console/bin/drupal`

```
⇒    ./vendor/drupal/console/bin/drupal

Drupal Console (1.0.0-rc23)
============================
```

Installing Drupal using Drupal Console

We should all be familiar with the typical install process of Drupal: download the files, create the database, set up a localhost, open a browser, and finish the installation. As we all know, this is a necessary evil, but also a time-consuming task. Since we now have Drupal Console installed, we can achieve all this by executing one single command.

Begin by opening a Terminal window, changing into the `mastering` folder, and executing the following command:

`./vendor/drupal/console/bin/drupal site:install`

This command will begin a series of prompts that will walk us through the remaining install process, beginning with choosing an install profile:

```
⇒  ./vendor/drupal/console/bin/drupal site:install

Select Drupal profile to be installed:
  [0] minimal
  [1] standard
> 1
```

Select the **Standard** install, which is option **1**, and press *Enter*.

We will then be prompted to select the language that we want Drupal installed in:

```
Select language for your Drupal installation [English]:
> English
```

Input **English** and then press *Enter*.

Next, we will be prompted to choose the **Drupal Database type**, **Database File**, and **Database Prefix** that Drupal will use for the necessary database and tables. For the sake of demonstration, we will let Drupal Console create an SQLite database:

```
Drupal Database type:
  [0] MySQL, MariaDB, Percona Server, or equivalent
  [1] PostgreSQL
  [2] SQLite
> 2

Database File [sites/default/files/.ht.sqlite]:
> mastering.sqlite

Database Prefix [ ]:
>
```

Select option **2** and then press *Enter*. Next, we will enter a value of `mastering.sqlite` as the default name for the **Database File** and leave the default for the **Database Prefix**.

At this point, we will be prompted to provide the site name for our Drupal instance:

```
Provide your Drupal site name [Drupal 8]:
> Mastering Drupal 8
```

Input the site name as `Mastering Drupal 8` and then press *Enter*.

Drupal Console now requires us to provide a site email that will be used to notify us of any updates, users that request an account, and various other administrative notifications:

```
Provide your Drupal site mail [admin@example.com]:
> admin@example.com
```

Input the email as `admin@example.com` and then press *Enter*.

The next three values we will need to provide will be for our administrator's account and consist of the admin account name, e-mail, and password:

```
Provide your Drupal administrator account name [admin]:
> admin

Provide your Drupal administrator account password:
>

Provide your Drupal administrator account mail [admin@example.com]:
> admin@example.com
```

We will input `admin` for our administrator account name and then press *Enter*.

Next, we will add a generic administrator account email of `admin@example.com` and then press *Enter*.

Finally, we will input an administrator account password of `admin` and then press *Enter*.

At this point, Drupal Console will begin the install process and configure our new Drupal 8 instance. If everything is successful, we will be prompted with a notification that the Drupal 8 installation was completed successfully:

```
Starting Drupal 8 install process

[OK] Your Drupal 8 installation was completed successfully
```

Now that Drupal 8 is installed and configured, it would be nice to not have to always type the full path to Drupal Console the next time we want to use it. We can shorten this up to just entering `drupal` by installing Drupal console globally like we did for Drush.

Installing Drupal Console globally

Having global access to Drupal Console will allow us to execute commands regardless of our location within a project by simply typing drupal.

Begin by opening the Terminal window, changing to our user directory, and executing the following commands:

1. Install Drupal Console Launcher:

   ```
   curl https://drupalconsole.com/installer -L -o drupal.phar
   mv drupal.phar /usr/local/bin/drupal
   chmod +x /usr/local/bin/drupal
   ```

2. Update Drupal Console Launcher:

   ```
   drupal self-update
   ```

3. Run Drupal Console to list all commands:

```
drupal list
```

```
Available commands:
    about           Display basic information about Drupal Console project
    chain           Chain command execution
    check           System requirement checker
    exec            Execute an external command.
    help            Displays help for a command
    init            Copy configuration files.
    list            Lists all available commands
```

Running a built-in PHP web server

Another advantage of using Drupal Console within our project is that we can utilize the built-in PHP web server to display our new Drupal 8 site. If we take a look at the available commands listed by Drupal Console, we will notice a command called `server`.

Open a Terminal window, and enter the following command:

```
drupal server
```

Drupal Console can utilize the current version of PHP installed on our system. It identifies the document root of our Drupal installation and allows us to preview our site within the browser by navigating to `http://127.0.0.1:8088`:

```
⇒ drupal server

[OK] Executing php from "/Applications/MAMP/bin/php/php7.0.13/bin/php".

Listening on "127.0.0.1:8088".
```

If we open a browser and enter the url of `http://127.0.0.1:8088`, we will be taken to our new Drupal 8 instance.

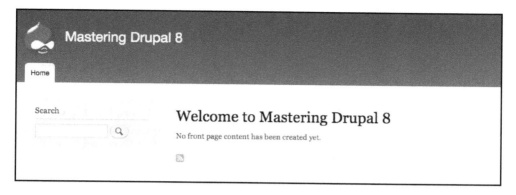

The advantages of using Drupal Console to execute a wide range of commands, including installing Drupal, is that it is a huge time saver. As we dig deeper into Mastering Drupal 8, we will discover additional commands that will allow us to manage users, roles, and content.

So far, we have looked at Composer, Drush, and Drupal Console. However, all this is of no benefit to us if we have no way to ensure that our work is protected and can be shared with other developers. In fact, managing source code is the most important tool any development workflow should embrace.

Using Git to manage source code

Git (https://git-scm.com) is probably the most popular open source software available to manage source code. Git allows us to distribute code to ourselves or other developers, and provides a robust mechanism for tracking changes, creating branches, and staging changes to software, or, in our case, web projects.

While we will not be diving deeply into all the great flexibility that this tool provides, it is important that we touch on the basics of how to use Git within a development workflow.

Generally, there are a handful of tasks that we will perform with Git:

- Creating a repository to store our code.
- Adding code to our repository.
- Tracking changes to our code.
- Pulling and pushing changes.

Installing Git

Git can be installed using a variety of methods, including browsing the Git website at `https://git-scm.com/downloads` and downloading the latest release suitable for your operating system.

For the sake of demonstration, we will be installing Git on Mac OS X. Once we click on the appropriate link, our download will start and the binary files will be copied to our designated downloads folder. All that is left to do is to extract the files and then double-click on the installer to complete the installation process.

We can validate that Git has been installed correctly by opening up a Terminal window and executing the following command:

```
which git
```

The preceding command is illustrated in the following image:

```
⇒  which git
/usr/local/bin/git
```

If at any point there is a need to refer to the Git documentation, we can browse `https://git-scm.com/doc`. The documentation covers everything from the basics to advanced topics.

Assuming that we have Git installed properly, we will need to configure it for use.

Configuring Git

Git can be configured locally per project or globally. In most cases, we will want to globally configure Git for use with all our projects. We are only concerned with a few configurations to begin with: mainly, our `user.name` and `user.email`, which are used for associating our user with commit messages when tracking code.

Begin by opening a Terminal window and executing the following commands:

```
git config --global user.name "Your Name"
git config --global user.email "your@email.com"
```

If we ever need to view what our configuration contains, we can execute the following command:

```
git config --list
```

Now that we have Git installed and configured, we will need to decide where we want to store our code.

Creating a remote repository

While we can create a local repository, it would make more sense to create a remote repository. When someone mentions Git, it is generally synonymous with GitHub (https://github.com/). To use GitHub, we will need to sign up for a free account or log in to an existing account:

Once logged into GitHub, we will create a new empty repository. For the sake of demonstration, we will call our repository `Mastering-Drupal-8`:

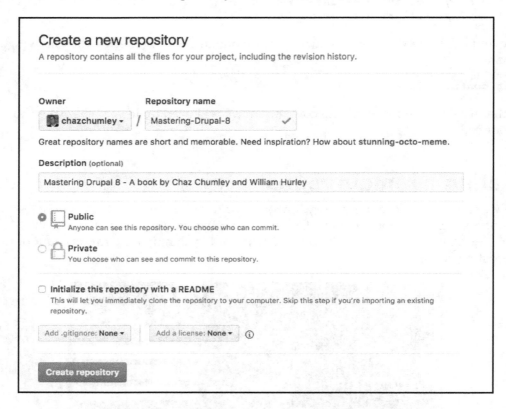

In the preceding example, the **Owner** field would be replaced with your account name and **Repository name** based on your preferences. At this point we can click on the **Create repository** button to finish the creation of our Remote repository. Next we will create a local repository and push our local file up to GitHub.

Setting up a local repository

To start a local repository, we need to ensure that we are within the folder that contains the files we want to begin tracking. Instantiating a local repository allows us to add files, commit them, and push them up to the remote repository that others can clone and work from. For our example, we will add the Drupal 8 instance we just created.

Begin by opening a Terminal window and entering the following command:

```
git init
```

The preceding command is illustrated in the following image:

```
cchumley@forumone:~/Sandbox/mastering|
⇒ git init
Initialized empty Git repository in /Users/cchumley/Sandbox/mastering/.git/
```

Tracking and committing files with Git

Now that we have initialized our `mastering` folder to be a local repository, we can add the contents of the folder to Git for tracking any changes. Adding and committing files requires two steps.

The first is adding the entire contents of the folder or specific files. In our example, we can add the entire Drupal instance by typing the following command in the Terminal window:

```
git add.
```

Second, we need to tell Git what we have added by committing the files and including a message describing what the addition contains. This can be accomplished by entering the following command in the Terminal window:

```
git commit -m 'Initial Drupal instance added to repo'
```

Adding a remote origin

With our files added and committed locally, we now need to add a remote origin that our local repository can push to. We can execute the following command in a Terminal window, remembering to replace the origin URL with your own repo path:

```
git remote add origin https://github.com/chazchumley/Mastering-Drupal-8.git
```

To find the correct origin URL, simply look at the URL within the browser after the remote repo was created.

Pushing files to the remote repository

Now that our local repository knows that we have a remote repository, we can simply push the committed files to GitHub by executing the following command in a Terminal window:

```
git push -u origin master
```

If we navigate to GitHub, we will now see that our once-empty repo contains the Drupal 8 instance that we added locally:

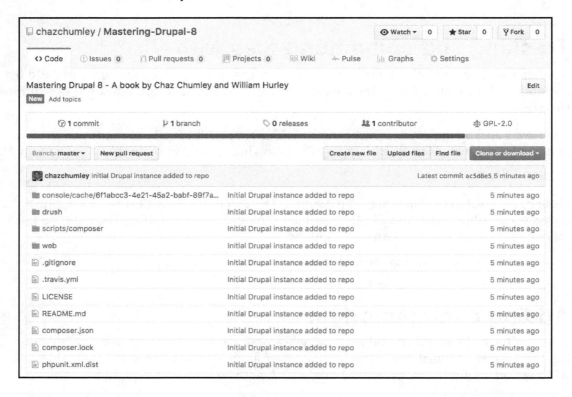

With our files now safely being tracked both locally and remotely, we can ensure that any change we make can be safely retrieved and reverted. Think of this as a snapshot of our code. If we are working in a team environment, we can share the repo with others to clone the repo to their local machines. There is a lot of great documentation on how to manage Drupal workflows using Git at `https://www.drupal.org/node/803746`.

Realize that these are the very basics of using Git, and depending on the size of your development team, there are additional strategies that may need to be implemented.

At this point, you may be thinking that there is a lot of information to remember when installing and configuring a Drupal project. While you may be right, it is also the reason why virtualizing a development environment makes perfect sense.

Virtualizing an environment

When we first began with this lesson, we mentioned the various ways to set up a local development environment. Depending on the size of your organization or team, having a repeatable and configured method for starting each Drupal project cuts down on having to manually install tools and dependencies. A VM also eliminates issues with something working locally, but not working on a remote server.

Using Drupal VM as a web starter

Depending on your skill level, it may make sense to create your own web starter by packaging and configuring Vagrant, VirtualBox, PHP, MySQL, and the list goes on. However, if some of those terms seem foreign to you, I would recommend the well-documented and easy-to-use Drupal VM (`http://www.drupalvm.com`):

Drupal VM is a virtual machine for local Drupal development, built with Vagrant and Ansible, that can be installed and run on Mac, Windows, or Linux. This package allows a consistent development experience with a robust set of tools already installed, including Composer, Drush, and Drupal Console.

Drupal VM was created and is maintained by Jeff Geerling. It is by far the best option for working with a Drupal-based web project and, while the steps involved to install it are clearly spelled out in the documentation, I would recommend starting with the *Quick Start Guide* available at `https://github.com/geerlingguy/drupal-vm#quick-start-guide`.

It is worth taking the time to learn how to work with a virtualized environment that can be configured and customized to work with any requirements your next Drupal project may have.

If at any point you experience any issues, the Drupal VM repository issue queue (`https://github.com/geerlingguy/drupal-vm/issues`)--is available to post questions for assistance.

Summary

As we progress through each lesson of Mastering Drupal 8, it is important that a local development environment has been set up with the basic tools we covered in this lesson. That includes an instance of Drupal 8 with Composer, Drush, and Drupal Console. By now, it should also be clear how each tool can expedite tasks that would manually take a lot longer to perform. These tools should be part of every Drupal project as they will help you master your skills as a developer.

In the next chapter, we will begin to walk through Drupal 8 site configuration, including changes to the administrative interface, how to manage regional settings, site information, and performance while developing.

2
Site Configuration

Site configuration is probably one of the most important tasks any developer will need to perform when first creating a Drupal project. Establishing a baseline configuration for Drupal projects ensures that, as we begin to further develop our website, we have accounted for how users will be able to upload files, how dates will be displayed, and even how content will be cached.

However, sometimes site configuration can be overlooked as a few items get configured for us during the installation process; for example, Basic site settings such as the Site name, email address, and Regional settings. Depending on the size of your Drupal project, you may think why bother with any additional site configuration?

In this chapter, we will be exploring Drupal 8 from an administrator or site builder's point of view and explain why it is important to configure your site properly. There have been a few changes in how basic site configuration is performed, where some items have been moved to, and how you interact with administrative panels. So, we will look at the following topics:

- Exploring Drupal's interface
- Basic site settings
- Managing performance while developing
- Configuration overrides
- Using Drush to manage configuration
- Working with the File system
- Regional settings

Assumptions

Mastering Drupal 8 assumes that you are already running a local AMP stack and are familiar with installing Drupal using the standard means of downloading, setting up a database, configuring a local host, and completing the browser-based install. In Chapter 1, *Developer Workflow*, we walked through quickly installing Drupal using **Composer**, **Drush**, and **Drupal Console**. Ensure that you have a working AMP stack and are comfortable working within the command-line interface using a Terminal window before continuing.

Exploring Drupal's interface

By default, Drupal has two interfaces we can work with. The first is what any visitor to our site will see, consisting of content and blocks displayed in various regions on the page. This is often referred to as the *anonymous* user's view:

The second interface, known as the administrator interface, requires us to be logged in to a Drupal instance. We can log in by clicking on the login link or by navigating to /user/login and entering the user credentials that were created when Drupal was first installed:

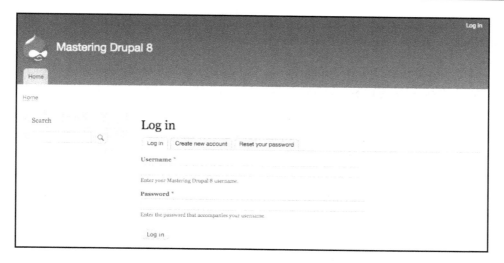

Once logged in we are considered to be authenticated and, since we are logged in as User one, which is the Super User, we are also considered to be an administrator and are presented with an Admin toolbar.

The Admin toolbar itself is separated into three different functional areas: **Manage**, **Shortcuts**, and **admin**. Each of these sections organize the functionality based on the tasks that need to be performed, which include everything from managing content, providing shortcuts to frequently performed tasks, and, finally, the ability to view and edit the user profile.

Let's quickly look at each section of the Admin toolbar keeping in mind that we will revisit these sections in greater detail in the later chapters.

Managing Drupal

The **Manage** menu of the Admin toolbar includes about 90% of the tasks that we may wish to perform at any given time. Each section allows us to manage different aspects of site building. Lets have look at those sections:

- **Content**: The **Content** section is divided into three subsections that display user generated **Content**, **Comments**, and **Files**. Any time new content is added, we can view a summary of the content that can be filtered by **Published status**, **Content type**, **Title**, and **Language**. With the introduction of Drupal 8, the Content display can be customized to add additional fields and filters as needed by simply modifying the administrative view. We will take a closer look at the Comments and Files in Chapter 04, *Content Types, Taxonomy, and Comments*:

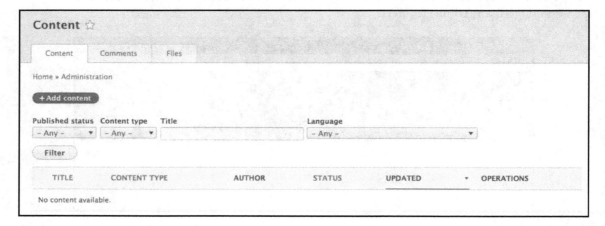

- **Structure**: The **Structure** section is divided into **Block layout**, **Comment types**, **Contact forms**, **Content types**, **Display modes**, **Menus**, **Taxonomy**, and **Views**. We will explore each of these areas in more detail as we continue to master Drupal 8:

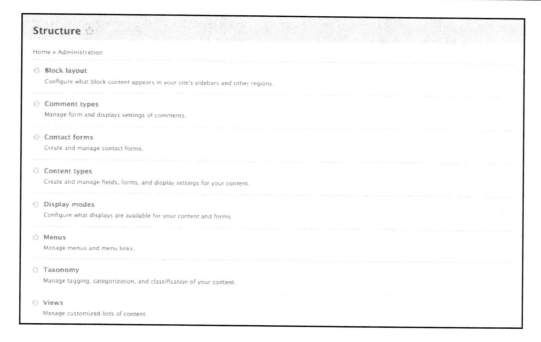

- **Appearance**: The **Appearance** section provides the interface for enabling, disabling, and configuring default themes as well as administrative themes. Any custom themes that we create will also be displayed in this area and provide additional settings that we can configure:

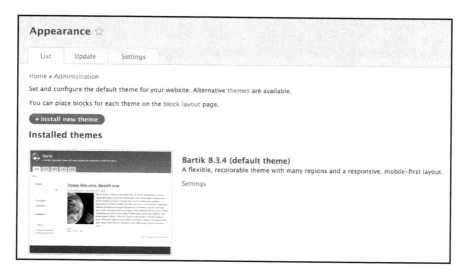

- **Extend**: Formerly known as Modules, the **Extend** section provides the listing of available modules and the ability to update and uninstall core, custom, and contributed modules. There's a new ability to search for modules using a filter. Various contributed modules have been moved into **CORE**, including Views and CKEditor:

- **Configuration**: The **Configuration** section contains the configuration for both core and contributed modules. Each area is grouped into functional areas that allow the management of various settings. This chapter will focus on some important tasks and the various ways to configure Drupal. We will be covering the **Basic site settings**, **File system**, and more a little later in the chapter:

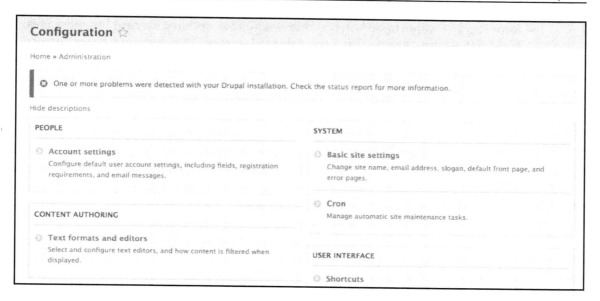

- **People**: The **People** section allows us to manage users, permissions, and roles. The display for users is now an Administrative View that can be customized to add additional fields and filters as needed. We will cover this section in depth in Chapter 03, *Managing Users, Roles, and Permissions*:

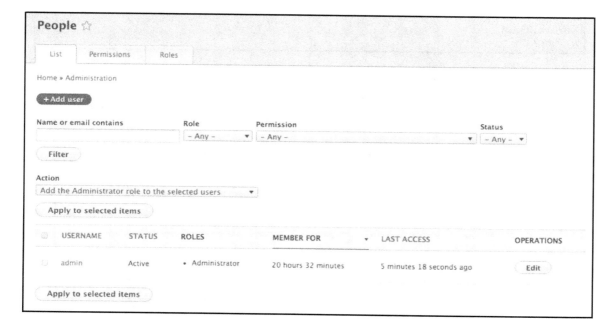

- **Reports**: The **Reports** section provides **Available updates**, **Recent log messages**, **Field list**, **Status report**, **Top 'access denied' errors**, **Top 'page not found' errors**, **Top search phrases**, and **Views plugins**:

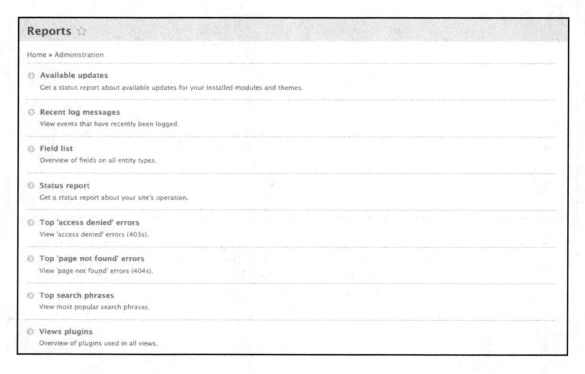

- **Help**: The **Help** section provides helpful information on the functionalities necessary to know when administering a Drupal 8 website. This includes a **Getting Started** section and Help topics on items such as Block, Views, user, and more:

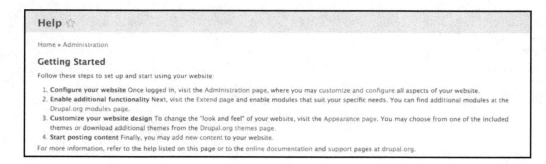

Now that we know how to navigate the various management sections of Drupal, we can focus on some of the tasks that we will need to master when first configuring a website.

Basic site settings

Changes to the Site name, Email address, default front page, and error pages can all be configured under the **Basic site settings** of Drupal. This section of Drupal can often be overlooked since both the Site name and Email address fields are configured for us during installation. However, the **Basic site settings** control more than just these two fields, and it is important to know where they are located and how to modify these values using all the tools made available to us.

We can navigate to the **Basic site settings** by directly entering the URL of `/admin/config/system/site-information`, or by using the Admin toolbar and clicking on **Manage** | **Configuration** | **Basic site settings**:

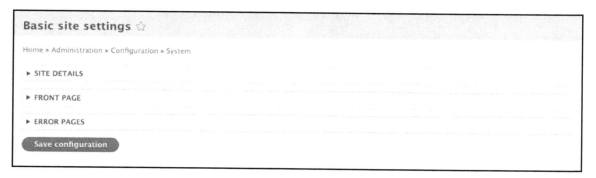

The **Basic site settings** for Drupal contain three subsections:

- **SITE DETAILS**
- **FRONT PAGE**
- **ERROR PAGES**

SITE DETAILS

The **SITE DETAILS** section contains the **Site name**, **Slogan**, and **Email address** fields. Depending on how an installation is completed, there will always be values for both **Site name** and **Email address** already filled in:

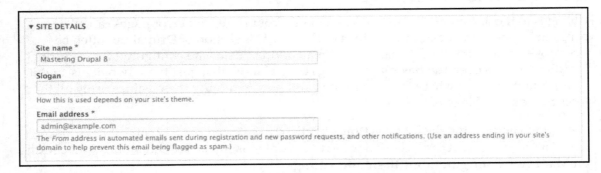

The **Site name** field is used by Drupal to display the website's name.

The **Slogan** field is used for displaying a website's tagline.

Both the **Site name** and **Slogan** can be toggled on and off from within the Site branding block used by our theme, and generally displayed within the Header region.

The **Email address** is used as the *from* address for all automated emails sent by Drupal. These emails can be for registration, retrieving passwords, and other notifications. This **Email address** is also used to notify us when an update is available for the core or contributed modules.

FRONT PAGE

The next section located under **Basic site settings** is referred to as **FRONT PAGE** and is used for managing which node or page Drupal will use as the default front page:

When a Drupal site is first created, Drupal will configure the front page to utilize a view of all the content that has been created. In almost every case, we will create a specific node or piece of content to use as our home page. Once this node has been created, we can configure the **FRONT PAGE** section to point to the specific node ID.

ERROR PAGES

The final section located under **Basic site settings** is referred to as **ERROR PAGES**, and is used for managing both the 403 (access denied) and 404 (not found) pages:

▼ ERROR PAGES

Default 403 (access denied) page

This page is displayed when the requested document is denied to the current user. Leave blank to display a generic "access denied" page.

Default 404 (not found) page

This page is displayed when no other content matches the requested document. Leave blank to display a generic "page not found" page.

This section is the most commonly missed and underutilized section of the **Basic site settings**. If analytics is important, then failing to create a basic 403 or 404 page means that new users coming to our website may not stay or come back. So, what does each page do?

Default 403 pages are displayed when either an anonymous user tries to access a portion of your site that they do not have access to or an authenticated user tries to access a section of the site that they have not been granted permission to.

Default 404 pages are displayed when a node or piece of content no longer exists when a user tries to view the URL for it. This can often happen when either some content has been deleted that Google has indexed or a user has bookmarked the path to content that has changed.

When either an access-denied or page-not-found error is triggered by Drupal, it is helpful if we specify a specific node or page that contains additional information for our user. This can easily be accomplished using these two fields.

Performance

Another important section of basic site configuration deals with performance. Performance can be considered to be how content is cached and aggregated. Drupal provides various settings that allow us to cache Blocks, Views, and Pages of content. In fact, a lot of work has been done to ensure that performance for internal page caching as well as dynamic page caching is top notch. Drupal has even added core modules to manage this.

However, unless we manage the settings for caching properly, none of these improvements will help us.

If we navigate to `/admin/config/development/performance`, or use the Admin menu and click on **Configuration** | **Performance**, we can take a look at the values we can set:

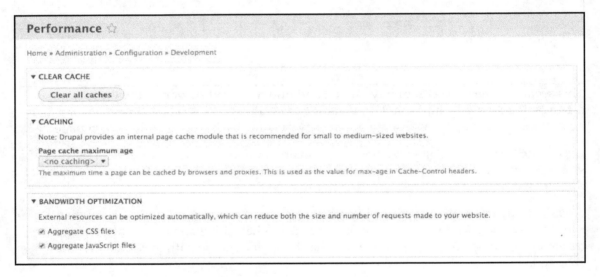

Performance can be divided into two sections:

- **CACHING**: The maximum time, a page can be cached by browsers
- **BANDWIDTH OPTIMIZATION**: How CSS and JavaScript files can be aggregated to reduce the size and number of requests

Both sections can be enabled and disabled depending on the values set for each. If we want to enable caching, we simply need to specify a **Page cache maximum age**, which can range from one minute to one day. If we want to optimize CSS and JS, we simply need to ensure that each value is checked.

Clearing cache

As Drupal tries hard to optimize a site, there are quite a few items that are cached. This requires us to know how to clear the cache to ensure that configuration changes are applied. For example, anytime we develop a theme, install a module, or work with the API, we will find ourselves needing to clear the cache. To utilize the administration panel, we simply need to click on the **Clear all caches** button located under the **CLEAR CACHE** section:

Since we will be clearing the cache quite often, it helps to know how to utilize both Drush and Drupal Console to clear the cache using the command line.

Using Drush to clear cache

As we develop a site and especially whenever we create or modify a file, whether that be the `settings.php` file, or as we begin to create themes or custom modules, we will frequently need to clear the cache. Often, it is not convenient to try to use the UI to perform such a task. In fact, we can use Drush to perform this task much more easily.

If we open a Terminal window and change to the `/web` directory, we can enter the following command to rebuild the cache:

```
drush cr
```

```
⇒ drush cr
Cache rebuild complete.
```

We can see that Drush has rebuilt the cache, and if we keep a Terminal window open while we are developing, this is much quicker to perform.

Using Drupal Console to clear the cache

In the same way we can use the command line and Drush, we can also use Drupal Console to clear or rebuild the cache. With a Terminal window still open, we can enter the following command:

```
drupal cache:rebuild all
```

```
⇒ drupal cache:rebuild all

Rebuilding cache(s), wait a moment please.


[OK] Done clearing cache(s).
```

With multiple ways to clear the cache, we should be able to perform this task regardless of whether we are within the UI or are using the command line.

Configuration overrides

Managing configuration within Drupal does not always involve changing settings within the administrative panels of a specific section. In fact, Drupal also allows various settings to be configured within the settings.php file. Configuration settings within the settings.php file act as global overrides to those in the database. Some settings, as we will see, can only be set or modified from the settings.php file.

The settings.php file can be located within the /sites/default folder of a Drupal installation.

 Keep in mind that the file permissions are set to read only; so, it is important to temporarily modify the permissions to be writeable before making any changes.

Once we have made the `settings.php` file writeable, we can open it within our favorite editor and locate the **Configuration overrides** section:

```
/**
 * Configuration overrides.
 *
 * To globally override specific configuration values for this site,
 * set them here. You usually don't need to use this feature. This is
 * useful in a configuration file for a vhost or directory, rather than
 * the default settings.php.
 *
 * Note that any values you provide in these variable overrides will not be
 * viewable from the Drupal administration interface. The administration
 * interface displays the values stored in configuration so that you can stage
 * changes to other environments that don't have the overrides.
 *
 * There are particular configuration values that are risky to override. For
 * example, overriding the list of installed modules in 'core.extension' is not
 * supported as module install or uninstall has not occurred. Other examples
 * include field storage configuration, because it has effects on database
 * structure, and 'core.menu.static_menu_link_overrides' since this is cached in
 * a way that is not config override aware. Also, note that changing
 * configuration values in settings.php will not fire any of the configuration
 * change events.
 */
# $config['system.site']['name'] = 'My Drupal site';
# $config['system.theme']['default'] = 'stark';
# $config['user.settings']['anonymous'] = 'Visitor';
```

Reading through the **Configuration overrides** documentation, we can get our first glimpse of which specific values can be overridden, which values are risky or not recommended to be changed, and the syntax to set a specific variable and value.

Currently, there are three examples commented out. Each line follows a specific convention that tells Drupal the configuration setting and value that should be used.

For example, if we wanted to override the **Site name** configuration, we would use the following syntax:

```
$config['system.site']['name'] = 'My Drupal site';
```

Let's try it now by removing the comment to enable this override, save the changes, clear Drupal's cache, and navigate back to our home page to verify that the **Site name** has changed:

One thing to note is that any global configuration completed within the settings.php file will not be reflected within the admin interface. We can see an example of this by browsing back to the **Basic site settings** page located at /admin/config/system/site-information:

Keep in mind that, once we begin using global overrides, it is easy to create confusion as to where the value of a variable is being set. This brings up the point of how important it is to document any global overrides that are being configured, especially if there are multiple developers working on a Drupal project.

If, for any reason, configuration overrides are not documented, we can take advantage of Drush to assist us with managing configuration.

Using Drush to manage configuration

Drush allows us to perform a multitude of tasks using the command line to interact with Drupal. A handful of commands that allow us to manage configuration include drush config-list, drush config-get, and drush config-set. Let's look at how we would use each of these to manage **Basic site settings**.

Listing configuration variables

If we open a Terminal window and navigate to our Drupal instance, we can enter the following command to see a list of variables:

```
drush config-list
```

```
⇒ drush config-list
automated_cron.settings
block.block.bartik_account_menu
block.block.bartik_branding
block.block.bartik_breadcrumbs
block.block.bartik_content
```

Retrieving specific variables

We can also retrieve the value of a specific variable, returned by calling `drush config-get`, followed by the variable name. Since some variables have multiple named values that can be set, this command is helpful for knowing what we can modify within our `settings.php` file.

If we open a Terminal window, we can enter the following command to see the values contained within a variable:

```
drush config-get system.site
```

```
⇒ drush config-get system.site
uuid: 6f1abcc3-4e21-45a2-babf-89f7ad960ad6
name: 'Mastering Drupal 8'
mail: admin@example.com
slogan: ''
page:
  403: ''
  404: ''
  front: /node
admin_compact_mode: false
weight_select_max: 100
langcode: en
default_langcode: en
_core:
  default_config_hash: AyT9s80UcclfALRE_imByOMgtZ19eOlqdF6zI3p7yqo
```

One thing to point out is that the site name value returned from the `system.site` variable still reflects `'Mastering Drupal 8'` when, clearly, we are overriding it within our `settings.php` file. This is a perfect example of where there may be some confusion if someone doesn't know we are overriding that value.

We can remedy this by passing an argument to `drush config-get` to include the overridden values. Within the Terminal window, enter the following command:

```
drush config-get system.site --include-overridden
```

```
⇒ drush config-get system.site --include-overridden
uuid: 6f1abcc3-4e21-45a2-babf-89f7ad960ad6
name: 'My Drupal site'
mail: admin@example.com
slogan: ''
page:
  403: ''
  404: ''
  front: /node
admin_compact_mode: false
weight_select_max: 100
langcode: en
default_langcode: en
_core:
  default_config_hash: AyT9s8OUcclfALRE_imByOMgtZ19eOlqdF6zI3p7yqo
```

The addition of the `--include-overridden` argument will allowing Drush to display any values that are being overwritten within our `settings.php` file. The combination of using `drush config-list` and `drush config-get` helps with managing configuration.

Setting configuration variables

Another command that we can use to manage variables using Drush is that of `drush config-set`. Being able to set variables using the command line can help speed up our development time as well as allow us to quickly test values without the need for navigating back and forth in the Drupal interface.

For example, we can easily change the site's email address by opening a Terminal window and entering the following command:

```
drush config-set system.site mail 'test@example.com'
```

```
⇒ drush config-set system.site mail 'test@example.com'
Do you want to update mail key in system.site config? (y/n): y
```

Unlike using global overrides placed within our `settings.php` file, any variable modified or changed using this method will be reflected in the Drupal admin. We can also easily test that the value has been changed using `drush config-get` to retrieve the `system.site` value, like we did earlier in the chapter.

Using Drupal Console to manage configuration

Drupal Console also allows us to perform a multitude of tasks using the command line to interact with Drupal. Managing configuration is just a small portion of its capabilities. Like Drush, we can use Drupal Console to list, get, and set configuration.

Listing configuration variables

If we open a Terminal window and navigate to our Drupal instance, we can enter the following command to see a list of variables:

```
drupal config:debug
```

```
⇒ drupal config:debug

Configuration name.
automated_cron.settings
block.block.bartik_account_menu
block.block.bartik_branding
block.block.bartik_breadcrumbs
block.block.bartik_content
```

Retrieving specific variables

We can also retrieve the value of a specific variable by calling `drupal config:debug`, followed by the specific configuration name.

If we open a Terminal window, we can enter the following command to see the values contained within a variable:

```
drupal config:debug system.site
```

The preceding command is illustrated in the following image:

```
⇒ drupal config:debug system.site

system.site
uuid: 6f1abcc3-4e21-45a2-babf-89f7ad960ad6
name: 'Mastering Drupal 8'
mail: 'test@example.com'
slogan: ''
page:
  403: ''
  404: ''
  front: /node
admin_compact_mode: false
weight_select_max: 100
langcode: en
default_langcode: en
_core:
  default_config_hash: AyT9s80UcclfALRE_imByOMgtZ19eOlqdF6zI3p7yqo
```

Setting configuration variables

Setting configuration variables using Drupal Console is also possible using `drupal config:edit`, followed by specifying the configuration name. However, unlike Drush, Drupal Console opens the specified configuration YAML file within the Terminal window for editing. This allows us to modify multiple values instead of single values. It also gives us a glimpse into what the configuration looks like in detail.

For example, we can edit the site settings by opening a Terminal window and entering the following command:

```
drupal config:edit system.site
```

```
uuid: 6f1abcc3-4e21-45a2-babf-89f7ad960ad6
name: 'Mastering Drupal 8'
mail: 'test@example.com'
slogan: ''
page:
  403: ''
  404: ''
  front: /node
admin_compact_mode: false
weight_select_max: 100
langcode: en
default_langcode: en
_core:
  default_config_hash: AyT9s80UcclfALRE_imByOMgtZ19eOlqdF6zI3p7yqo
```

Depending on the default editor that your Terminal window has configured, you will interact with the `system.site.yml` file. In our case, the editor is already using the insert mode, which will allow us to modify the values in the file and then save any changes. We will take a close look at the additional configuration commands that we can use with Drupal Console in `Chapter 14`, *Configuration Management*.

For now, we can exit the command-line editor window by executing the following in the Terminal window:

esc :q

Working with the File system

The next section of configuration we will look at is the **File system**. By default, Drupal creates a `/sites/default/files` folder as part of the installation process. It is this directory that Drupal will use to store the files that are uploaded as part of the content.

We can take a better look at this configuration by navigating to `/admin/config/media/file-system`, or using the Admin toolbar and clicking on **Manage | Configuration | File system**:

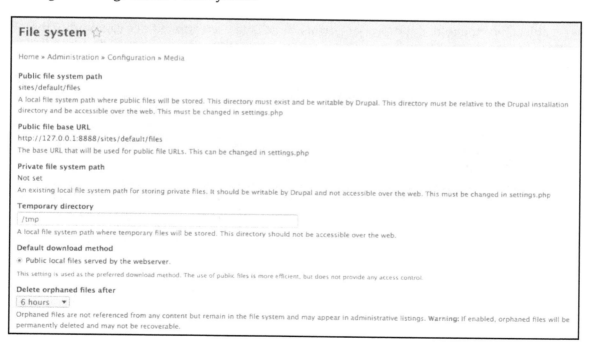

The **File system** interface is used to manage how files are stored, where they are stored, and how orphaned files should be managed. One new setting is the ability to specify an interval of time that lets Drupal know when files no longer being used can be deleted. This is known as the garbage collector and is a method of keeping your files folder from growing too large.

Unlike in the earlier version of Drupal, we can no longer change the public or private system paths from within the admin interface. We will need to use the settings.php file to switch to a private File system, or to modify the paths to both the public and private File systems.

Managing file paths

In most cases, we are fine with using the default public path for managing access to the files used in Drupal content. However, if we ever need to change the path, there are two steps involved:

1. Ensure that the new path exists.
2. Modify the path value within the settings.php file.

For example, if we want to move our files to be located within /sites/default/files/test, we would need to ensure that the new folder exists and is writeable. Once the folder and proper permissions have been applied, we can modify the settings by opening the settings.php file within an editor and locating the **Public file path** section:

```
/**
 * Public file path:
 *
 * A local file system path where public files will be stored. This directory
 * must exist and be writable by Drupal. This directory must be relative to
 * the Drupal installation directory and be accessible over the web.
 */
# $settings['file_public_path'] = 'sites/default/files';
```

Currently, Drupal is using the default path of /sites/default/files. To change this, we can uncomment the setting and then modify it to reflect the new path:

```
$settings['file_public_path'] = 'sites/default/files/test';
```

Save the changes, clear Drupal's cache, and navigate back to the **File system** page to verify that our file path has been updated:

Public file system path
sites/default/files/test
A local file system path where public files will be stored. This directory must exist and be writable by Drupal. This directory must be relative to the Drupal installation directory and be accessible over the web. This must be changed in settings.php

To follow best practices, let's comment out the **Public file path** in our `settings.php` file to ensure that our path remains `/sites/default/files`. Once commented out, ensure that you save the change and clear Drupal's cache.

By now, we should be getting comfortable managing **Basic site settings** using the admin interface, `settings.php` file, Drush, and Drupal Console. Next, we can move on to Regional settings.

Regional settings

Depending on how our website will be utilizing dates, whether for display within content, or for filtering content based on published dates or date fields, having proper Regional settings configured can make all the difference.

If we navigate to `/admin/config/regional/settings`, or use the Admin menu and click on **Configuration** | **Regional settings**, we can take a look at the values we can set:

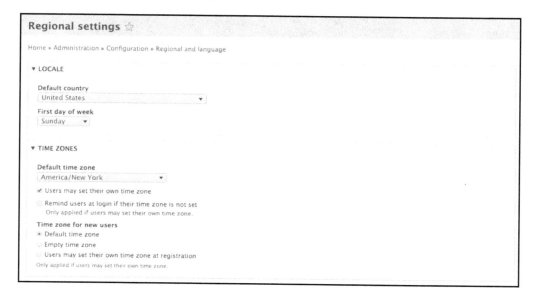

Depending on the Drupal installation process, the **Default country** and **Default time zone** fields may or may not be filled in. In any case, it is important to ensure that both these fields are set as per the country and time zone the website will be using.

Date and time formats

Drupal 8 uses **Date and time formats** for a variety of functionalities. Ranging from how Views filter content to field formatters that allow for a specific date format to be selected for use on content. As part of site building, we may want to configure the default display of dates or even add additional date formats that content can take advantage of.

If we navigate to `/admin/config/regional/date-time`, or use the Admin menu and click on **Configuration | Date and time formats**, we can look at the values we can set:

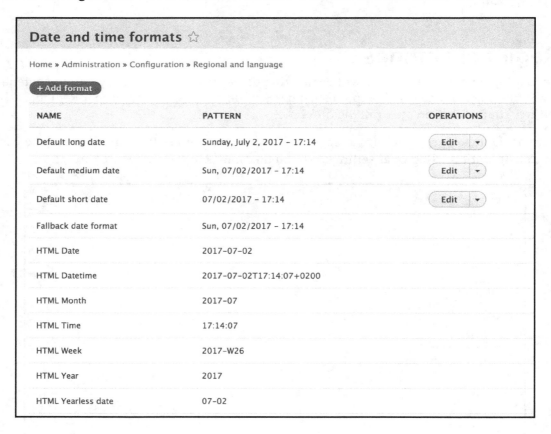

As we can see, Drupal specifies numerous date formats that can be used. However, only three can be modified: **Default long date**, **Default medium date**, and **Default short date**. Currently, they are set to use the 24-hour military time format. Let's look at changing the **Default long date** to 12-hour standard time and add the AM/PM value to the end of the date object.

Begin by clicking on the **Edit** button next to **Default long date**.

Next, we will modify the **Format string** to use the following value:

```
l, F j, Y - h:i A
```

The preceding string is illustrated in the following image:

Keep in mind that the **Format string** uses the PHP date object format. For more information on the available formats, click on the **PHP manual** link located following to the **Format string** field. There is a wide range of formatting that can be used.

Once we have modified the value, we can click on the **Save format** button to save our changes.

Go ahead and change the remaining **Default medium date** and **Default short date** formats to follow similar formatting as our **Default long date**.

However, what if we need to add additional date formats?

Adding new date formats

We can also add new date formats by clicking on the **Add format** button on the **Date and time formats** admin page. This will present us with a similar screen to the one we just used to modify default formats. However, we will need to give our new format a **Name** and provide a date object string this time.

For example, let's create a format for displaying the Day only:

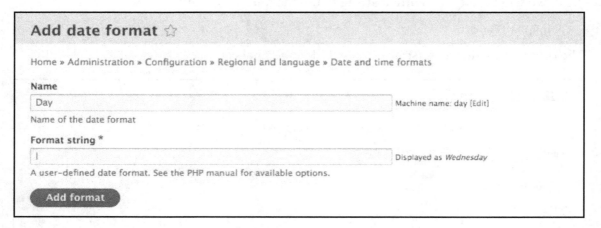

Once we enter the correct values, we can click on the **Add format** button to save our new date format to Drupal. We can now use this format wherever needed throughout the rest of our website.

Summary

At first glance, managing **Basic site settings** using the Drupal admin interface is quite simple. Knowing the importance of each section and why specific values should be configured will ensure that our Drupal website follows best practices. However, it is not enough to just know how to use the admin interface. We have learned that some configuration must be set using the settings.php file and that we can globally override settings contained in the database using this method.

Drush and Drupal Console provide us with the ability to inspect configuration variables, retrieve their values, and set them using the command line. In fact, using command-line interfaces such as Drush and Drupal Console allow us to accomplish a varied range of tasks, including clearing Drupal's cache, which is a task that will need to be done quite often during development.

In the next chapter, we will walk through managing users, roles, and permissions in Drupal 8. We will work more with both Drush and Drupal Console to learn how to log in, reset credentials, and create dummy users, all using the command line.

3
Managing Users, Roles, and Permissions

By default, Drupal 8 provides us with a single user account with administrative permissions. Often referred to as user one, this account is set up and configured for use when we first install Drupal. We could build and manage a complete site without the need to ever create another user. The benefit of using a **content management system** (**CMS**) is the ability to add additional users and assign them a role to play in creating, managing, or viewing its content.

As you will learn, **People** can be assigned **Roles** that have specific **Permissions**. We can configure these permissions to allow for very granular control or to silo off entire areas of a functionality. A typical Drupal website will deal with the following three categories of users: *anonymous*, *authenticated*, and *administrative*. To help us master users, roles, and permissions, we will look at the following:

- Exploring People
- Managing roles and permissions
- Working with users
- Configuring Account settings
- Using Drush to manage users

Assumptions

Mastering Drupal 8 assumes that you are already running a local AMP stack and have a familiarity with installing Drupal using the standard means of downloading, setting up a database, configuring a localhost, and completing the browser-based install. In Chapter 1, *Developer Workflow*, we walked through installing Drupal using Composer, Drush, and Drupal Console. Please ensure that you have a working AMP stack and are comfortable working within the command-line interface using a terminal window before continuing.

Exploring People

Managing users is an important part of any CMS, and Drupal is no different. Being able to quickly glance at a list of users along with their status and roles can help a site admin know which users have an account and what are their limitations. The process of managing users begins with **People**.

We can navigate to the **People** panel by directly entering /admin/people or using the Admin toolbar and clicking on **Manage | People**.

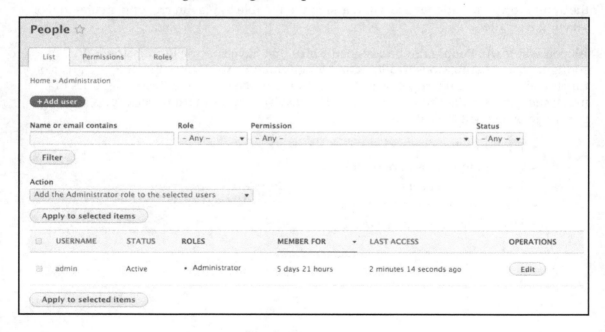

The **People** panel is divided into the following three sections:

- **List**: Displays all users within Drupal and allows to manage them individually or using bulk operations
- **Permissions**: Allows us to assign granular permissions to one or many roles that either permit or restrict a user from being able to view or perform some action
- **Roles**: Allows us to add, update, or delete roles within Drupal

All three of these tabs combined provide us the workflow to create users and assign them one or more roles with specific permissions.

By default, Drupal creates a single user during installation that allows us to log in and manage our site. This user is known as *user one* and is considered the super user. User one inherits all permissions, and these cannot be modified. While it may be tempting to use the user one account during development, it makes more sense to create an account for each person who needs to work on the site. We can then ensure that each user has only the required role and/or permissions to perform specified duties.

Managing roles and permissions

Generally, when we think about managing users in Drupal, we first think about what role the user has and what permissions they have been assigned. We don't just blindly start creating users without having an idea of what function they will perform or what limitations we may want to enforce upon them. For that reason, we need to ask ourselves what is a role?

What is a role?

A role in Drupal helps to define what a user can do. By default, a role lacks permissions and is just a named grouping that helps to identify a specific set of functionality or privileges that may be assigned.

For example, in a typical editorial workflow, you may have users who can contribute content, editors who review the content, and a publisher who schedules the content to be published at a specific time. Each of these users will have a corresponding role of a contributor, editor, and publisher and a defined set of permissions that will be assigned to each role.

We can navigate to the **Roles** panel by directly entering `/admin/people/roles` or using the Admin toolbar and clicking on **Manage | People** and then the **Roles** tab.

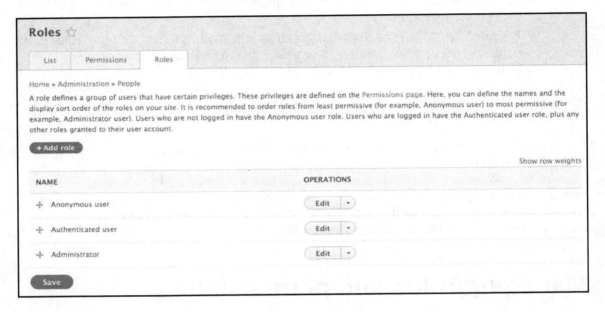

At a first glance, we see that Drupal creates three roles for us to use:

- **Anonymous user** is anyone who visits our website but is not logged in. This user generally has the least amount of permissions and can only view or interact with Drupal based on a limited set of privileges.
- **Authenticated user** is anyone who is logged in to Drupal. This user may be able to add content or perform some limited admin functionality determined by the permissions assigned to the role.
- **Administrator** is typically any user who will manage Drupal. This could be a site builder or developer. In most cases, the **Administrator** has full permissions assigned to them.

One thing to note is that the **Anonymous user** and **Authenticated user** roles cannot be deleted. These two roles are required to help identify users who are just visiting or are logged in. The third role of the **Administrator** allows for a user to be assigned the ability to perform all tasks in Drupal.

We are not limited to just these three roles. In fact, we generally find ourselves needing additional roles based on the type of website we are developing.

For the purpose of demonstration, let's add a new role called `Developer`.

Creating a role

Adding a new role is as simple as clicking on the **Add role** button, which will take us to the **Add role** panel.

Next, we will input a new **Role name** called `Developer`, as follows:

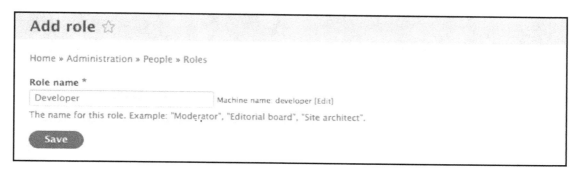

Finally, we will click on the **Save** button, which will add our new role and return us to the **Roles** panel.

Reordering roles

Roles should always be listed from least permissive to most permissive. This will ensure that the **Administrator** role inherits the functionality given to other roles without having to manually assign them. This is often overlooked, but by simply reordering roles, we can ensure that the task of assigning permissions to roles is simpler.

To reorder roles, all we need to do is drag the **Developer** role preceding the **Administrator** role using the drag icon handle located to the left of the **Role name**. Once we have completed the process, Drupal will notify us of unsaved changes. We can save our changes by clicking on the **Save** button.

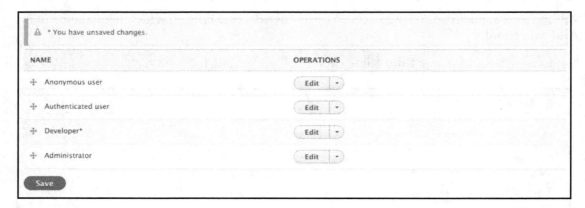

We now have our roles ordered from least permissive to most permissive.

Editing a role

Roles can also be edited or deleted from the **Roles** page by clicking on the drop-down button located to the right of each role under **OPERATIONS**. We have the following three options for managing a role:

- **Edit**: Allows us to modify the name of the role
- **Edit permissions**: Takes us to the **Permissions** admin for the specified role
- **Delete**: Allows us to delete the role

If we click on the **Edit** button next to the **Developer** role, we will be taken to the **Edit role** page; we can modify the **Role name**, save our changes, and delete the role permanently:

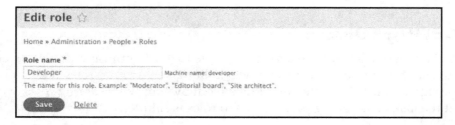

We will use the **Developer** role to help walk us through the remaining process, so we can return to the **Roles** page by simply clicking on the **Save** button.

Roles and permissions go hand in hand. Having a role by itself is meaningless unless we assign a set of privileges to the role that we can then assign to a user. So, it makes perfect sense for us to visit the **Permissions** tab next to continue the user management workflow.

We can navigate to the **Permissions** panel by directly entering /admin/people/permissions or using the Admin toolbar and clicking on **Manage** | **People** and then on the **Permissions** tab.

Setting permissions

The **Permissions** panel displays various sections of the functionality within Drupal, grouped by task with each role displayed across the top of the page. Permissions allow us to control what each role can do or see within our site. The list of functionality and the permissions we can manage for each will continue to grow, based on the number of cores or contributed modules we enable or the number of content types we create.

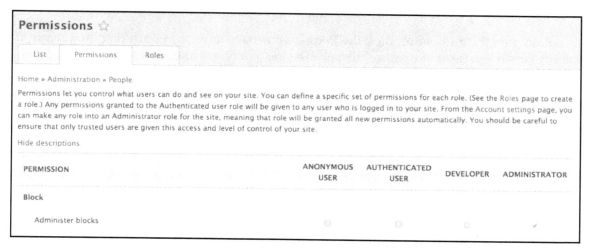

As we can see from the preceding screenshot, roles are arranged across the top of the **Permissions** page based on how they are ordered. Starting from the least permissive to the most permissive role, we can easily assign permissions to them by clicking on the checkbox next to the task or function.

Unlike Drupal 7, where we were required to constantly check off permissions for the administrator role, the administrator role automatically is assigned all permissions in Drupal 8 . This ensures that every time we add a new module or create a new content type, we don't have to revisit the **Permissions** page. The automatic assignment of permissions to the **Administrator** role is configurable from the **Account** settings page, which we will review a little later.

For now, if we want any other role to have the proper privilege, we need to first locate the functionality, then the role, and make sure that the permission is checked. To allow our **DEVELOPER** role to **Administer blocks**, all we will need to do is click on the checkbox under that role:

PERMISSION	ANONYMOUS USER	AUTHENTICATED USER	DEVELOPER	ADMINISTRATOR
Block				
Administer blocks	☐	☐	☑	☑

Keep in mind that whenever we modify permissions for a specific role, it is important to click on the **Save permissions** button located at the bottom of the **Permissions** page.

Depending on the number of roles, the **Permissions** page may become difficult to review. If for any reason we need to manage the permissions of a single role, we can always do so by returning to the **Roles** page, locating the specific role, and clicking on the **Edit permissions** button:

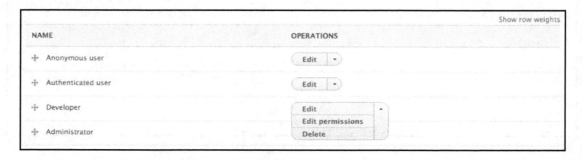

		Show row weights
NAME	OPERATIONS	
✛ Anonymous user	Edit ▾	
✛ Authenticated user	Edit ▾	
✛ Developer	Edit ▾	
	Edit permissions	
✛ Administrator	Delete	

Editing the permissions from the **Roles** page will take us back to the **Permissions** page filtered by the individual role:

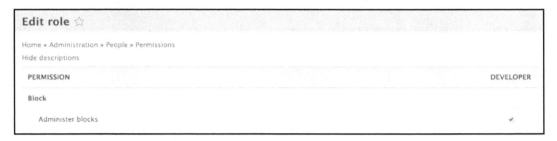

From this perspective, it is much easier to manage the permission for our role and locate the specific privilege that we need to enable or disable.

Don't forget to test the various roles and permissions when they are assigned--whether this means creating user accounts for each role that you can log in as or by using a common module such as Masquerade, `https://www.drupal.org/project/masquerade`, which allows you to switch from one user to another to test permissions.

A general rule of thumb is to fine-tune permissions closer to the end of a project to limit having to repeat these tasks.

Now that we have created our **Developer** role and assigned it the necessary permissions, it's time we create a new user and assign the **Developer** role to them.

Working with users

When we work with users in Drupal, we are generally referring to creating a user for the sake of performing some function within our website or managing an existing user. Managing a user can consist of assigning them a role, managing their access, or deleting them altogether.

Adding a user

We can navigate to the **People** panel by directly entering `/admin/people` or by using the Admin toolbar and clicking on **Manage** | **People**.

The **People** listing not only displays the existing users, but allows us to easily add new users by clicking on the **Add user** button.

The **Add user** page allows us to register new users by completing a series of fields. Some fields are required by Drupal to authenticate the user, whereas others are required to notify the user that their account has been created or to allow them to retrieve their password.

The first part of creating a user involves entering their credentials; credentials include **Email address**, **Username**, and **Password**:

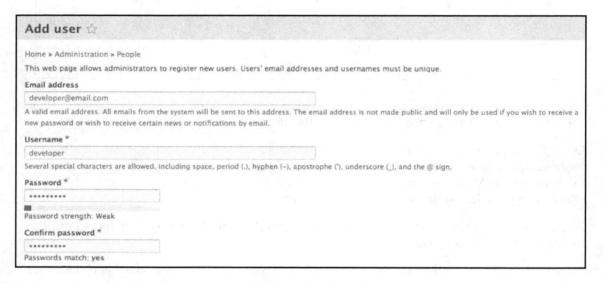

For the purpose of demonstration, we will enter a fictitious e-mail, `developer@email.com`.

Next, we will enter **Username** as `developer`, and **Password** as `developer`.

Leave the remaining default values and then click on the **Create new account** button at the bottom of the page. Once our user has been added, we can navigate back to the **People** listing page located at `/admin/people`.

Bulk updating users

Independently managing a user by clicking on the **Edit** button next to each user can often become cumbersome when dealing with multiple users. However, we can easily bulk manage users from the **People** listing page. We can add and remove roles, block users, and even cancel our user accounts:

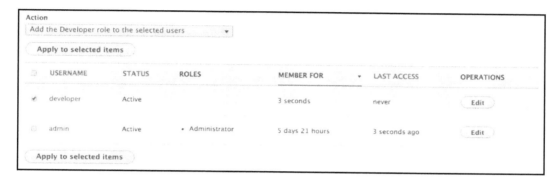

For example, let's assign the developer role to our new developer user using the bulk operations by following these steps:

1. Click on the checkbox next to **developer**.
2. Choose **Add the Developer role to the selected users** from the **Action** dropdown.
3. Click on the **Apply to selected items** button to complete the operation.

If we now look at the **ROLES** for our **developer** user, we can see that it has the **Developer** role assigned to it.

Configuring Account settings

Account configuration in Drupal 8 consists of managing various settings associated with a user, that is, anything from enabling contact settings, specifying which role will be used for administrative purposes, how a user can register for a new account, to even the ability to add additional fields to the user profile.

To see how this can be accomplished, we can begin by navigating to the **Account settings** page located at `/admin/config/people/accounts` or using the Admin toolbar and clicking on the **Manage** | **Configuration** | **Account settings**.

The **Account settings** page is arranged into various groups:

- **CONTACT SETTINGS**: Allows us to enable and disable personal contact form
- **ANONYMOUS USERS**: Allows us to specify which role will be used for anonymous users

- **ADMINISTRATOR ROLE**: Allows us to select a role that will be considered as the administrator so that permissions can be automatically assigned to it
- **REGISTRATION AND CANCELLATION**: Controls the ability to allow users to register an account and handles the user and their content when a user is deleted
- **Notification email address**: This is the from address used for sending notifications
- **Emails**: Email templates for various notifications

We will take a look at a few sections in more detail.

CONTACT SETTINGS

Before adding users or allowing users to register a new account, we may want to consider allowing each user to be able to be contacted using a personal contact form. By default, Drupal assumes that we want to allow this functionality. However, if, for some reason this functionality is not displayed to the users or we want to disable this functionality altogether, we can do so by clicking on the checkbox next to **Enable the personal contact form by default for new users**.

▼ CONTACT SETTINGS

☑ Enable the personal contact form by default for new users
Changing this setting will not affect existing users.

Enabling or disabling this functionality should be done during the initial setup of Drupal. Changing this setting after users have been added to Drupal will not affect existing users.

ADMINISTRATOR ROLE

Drupal allows us to easily manage roles, and depending on how those roles are set up, we may want to change which role is considered the Administrator. For example, when we use the Standard install profile, Drupal creates an Administrator role and assigns that role accordingly.

If, for some reason, we want to assign a different role as administrator, we can select from a list of roles using the drop-down list located under the **Administrator role** section:

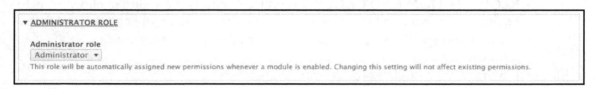

Based on our selection, this role will automatically be assigned proper permissions when a new module is enabled or a content type has been created.

Keep in mind that if we use the Minimal install profile this section may not have a role selected, and it may require both a role to be created and then for that role to be assigned as the default **Administrator**.

REGISTRATION AND CANCELLATION

The **REGISTRATION AND CANCELLATION** section determines whether a new user can register for an account, or whether an Administrator is required to create a new account. This section also determines how an existing account will be handled when a user is deleted or canceled.

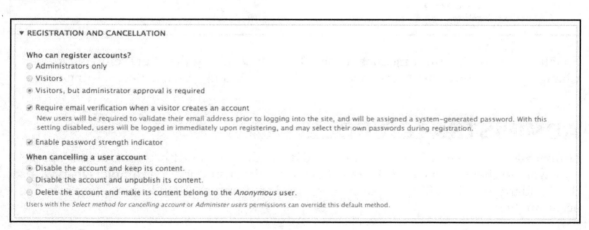

Managing user fields

Another function of **Account settings** is the ability to add additional fields to the user profile. When we created a new user, we were limited to only the minimal information that was needed to allow the user to log in. Often, there is a requirement to capture additional information such, as the user's full name or bio.

Fortunately, adding additional fields is a simple process. If we click on the **Manage fields** tab within the **Account settings** page, we will be taken to the **Manage fields** page where we can use the **Field UI**. The **Field UI** allows us to add and configure additional fields that we want to use for our user. The **Manage fields** section is something we will become quite familiar with, by using it through various sections of Drupal.

Adding fields

We can begin adding new fields by clicking on the **Add field** button. For the purpose of demonstration, we will add a field to capture the Full name of the user.

As shown in the preceding screenshot, we have selected the `Text (plain)` field from the **Add a new field** drop-down, followed by supplying a **Label** for our field called `Full name`.

Once we have chosen our field and provided a label, we can click on the **Save and continue** button.

From the **Field settings** page, we can choose a **Maximum length** of characters that our field will hold as well as the **Allowed number of values**. The **Allowed number of values** provides us with the ability to display the field one or multiple times for data entry.

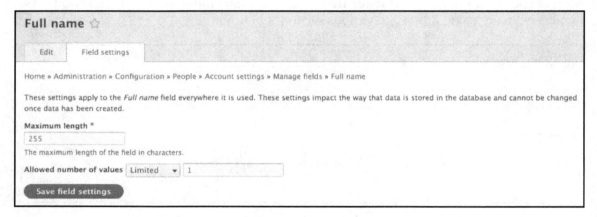

We will leave the default values as shown in the preceding screenshot, and then click on the **Save field settings** button.

We are now presented with the ability to change our **Label** if needed, provide some **Help text**, mark the field as **Required field**, and provide a **DEFAULT VALUE** that will be shown to the users when the field is displayed first.

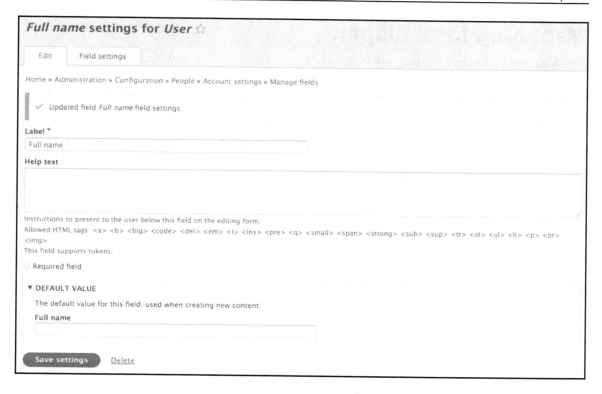

Finally, we can click on the **Save settings** button to create our new field:

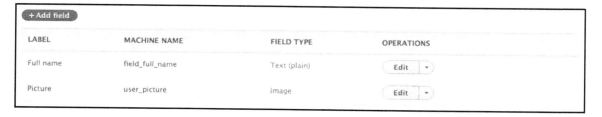

With our new field created, we can now manage how fields will be displayed on the user form by clicking on the **Manage form display** tab.

Managing form display

The **Manage form display** page allows us to reorder how fields will be displayed. Like how we reordered roles, we can easily drag and rearrange fields. Let's locate our new field and drag it to the top so that the **Full name** field will be displayed before the **User name and password**.

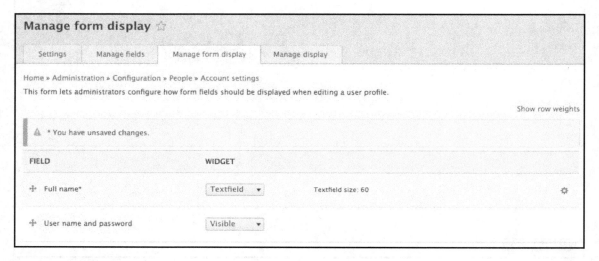

Drupal will notify us whenever we have unsaved changes. Make sure that you click on the **Save** button to complete the process. To see our new field displayed, we can navigate back to the **People** panel located at /admin/people or use the Admin toolbar and click on **Manage | People**. Next, we can click on the **Edit** button next to the **developer** user account and preview our new field:

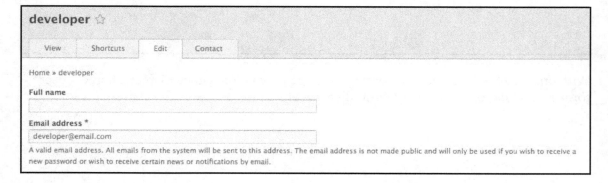

So far, we have been working solely in the Admin interface of Drupal. However, there are a handful of tasks that can be accomplished directly from the command line using Drush.

Using Drush to manage roles

If we open a terminal window and navigate to our Drupal project, we can enter the following command to retrieve a list of commands:

```
drush
```

If we scan down the list, we can locate all the `Role commands`:

```
Role commands: (role)
  role-add-perm (rap)    Grant specified permission(s) to a role.
  role-create (rcrt)     Create a new role.
  role-delete (rdel)     Delete a role.
  role-list (rls)        Display a list of all roles defined on the system.  If a role name is
                         provided as an argument, then all of the permissions of that role will be
                         listed.  If a permission name is provided as an option, then all of the roles
                         that have been granted that permission will be listed.
  role-remove-perm       Remove specified permission(s) from a role.
  (rmp)
```

In fact, we can utilize Drush to quickly perform the following tasks:

- Listing roles
- Creating roles
- Deleting roles
- Adding permissions to roles
- Removing permissions from roles

Listing roles

Using Drush to retrieve a list of roles is simple using the `drush role-list` command. Within a terminal window, we can retrieve all the current roles that exist by entering the following command:

```
drush role-list
```

```
⇒ drush role-list
  ID             Role Label
  anonymous      Anonymous user
  authenticated  Authenticated user
  developer      Developer
  administrator  Administrator
```

From the preceding list, we can see that we have roles for `Anonymous user`, `Authenticated user`, `Developer`, and `Administrator`.

Creating roles

Adding additional roles using Drush is quite simple and much faster than using the admin UI. To create a role using Drush, we only need to know the name of the role we want to create and the `drush role-create` command.

For example, if we want to create a new role for editors we would enter the following command in a terminal window:

```
drush role-create editor
```

```
⇒ drush role-create editor

Created "editor"                                                    [success]
```

We can then list our roles again to verify that our new role has been created:

```
⇒ drush role-list
  ID              Role Label
  anonymous       Anonymous user
  authenticated   Authenticated user
  developer       Developer
  administrator   Administrator
  editor          Editor
```

Deleting roles

Deleting roles using Drush is also simple when using the `drush role-delete` command with the name of the role passed as an argument.

For example, if we want to delete the editor role from Drupal, we can enter the following command in a terminal window:

```
drush role-delete editor
```

```
⇒ drush role-delete editor

Deleted "editor"                                                    [success]
```

We can then list the role information to verify that the role has been deleted:

```
⇒ drush role-list
 ID             Role Label
 anonymous      Anonymous user
 authenticated  Authenticated user
 developer      Developer
 administrator  Administrator
```

Listing permissions

In most cases, Drush can utilize arguments passed to display additional information about an object in Drupal. So far, we have used the `drush role-list` command to display all roles. However, if we pass the name of the role as an argument, Drush will return the permissions assigned to that role.

For example, to display the permissions assigned to our `developer` role, all we need to do is enter the following command in a terminal window:

```
drush role-list developer
```

```
⇒ drush role-list developer

 Permission
 administer blocks
```

Adding permissions

To add a permission to a specific role, we need to know what the permission is called, the name of the role, and the `drush role-add-perm` command. Sometimes, knowing what permission is called may be tricky. In those cases, we can always use the Drupal Admin UI to navigate to the **Permissions** page to get a better idea of what a permission may be called.

For example, if we want to allow the `developer` role to `administer comment types` and settings, that would equate it to `'administer comment types'`. Knowing this information, we can open a terminal window and enter the following command:

```
drush role-add-perm developer 'administer comment types'
```

```
⇒ drush role-add-perm developer 'administer comment types'

Added "administer comment types" to "Developer"                    [success]
Cache rebuild complete.                                            [ok]
```

To verify that our developer role has the new permission we just assigned, we can use the `drush role-list developer` command again to view the assigned permissions:

```
⇒ drush role-list developer

Permission
administer blocks
administer comment types
```

Removing permissions

We can also use Drush to remove permissions using the `drush role-remove-perm` command and pass arguments for the role and the permission name that we want to remove.

We can finish up this exercise by removing the `'administer comment types'` permissions that we previously added by executing the following command in a terminal window:

```
drush role-remove-perm developer 'administer comment types'
```

```
⇒ drush role-remove-perm developer 'administer comment types'

Removed "administer comment types" from "Developer"               [ok]
Cache rebuild complete.                                           [ok]
```

By now, we should be getting comfortable with using Drush to execute various commands against our Drupal instance without the need to use the Admin UI.

Using Drush to manage users

Another great way to speed up our development in Drupal is to use Drush to manage users.

If we open a terminal window and navigate to our Drupal project, we can enter the following command to retrieve a list of commands:

```
drush
```

If we scan down the list, we can locate all the User commands:

```
User commands: (user)
 user-add-role (urol)  Add a role to the specified user accounts.
 user-block (ublk)     Block the specified user(s).
 user-cancel (ucan)    Cancel a user account with the specified name.
 user-create (ucrt)    Create a user account with the specified name.
 user-information      Print information about the specified user(s).
 (uinf)
 user-login (uli)      Display a one time login link for the given user account (defaults to uid 1).
 user-password (upwd)  (Re)Set the password for the user account with the specified name.
 user-remove-role      Remove a role from the specified user accounts.
 (urrol)
 user-unblock (uublk)  Unblock the specified user(s).
```

We will take a deeper look at utilizing Drush to quickly perform the following tasks:

- Displaying user information
- Adding and removing roles from a user
- Blocking and unblocking a user
- Creating and deleting user accounts
- Creating a one-time login

Displaying user information

Using Drush to retrieve user information is simple. If we know the user ID associated with the user, we can use the drush user-information command to return information about that user. We can locate the user ID by navigating to the **People** panel in Drupal and hovering over the username. In our example, the developer user has an ID of 2.

We can open a terminal window and enter the following command to retrieve our developer user's information:

drush user-information 2

```
⇒ drush user-information 2

User ID       :  2
User name     :  developer
User mail     :  developer@example.com
User roles    :  authenticated
                 developer
User status   :  1
```

Assigning roles

To assign a role to a user using Drush, we simply need to know the name of the role, the user ID we want to assign the role to, and the drush user-add-role command.

For example, if we want to assign the administrator role to our developer user, we would enter the following command:

drush user-add-role 'administrator' 2

```
⇒ drush user-add-role 'administrator' 2
Added role administrator role to developer                              [success]
```

We can then list the user information to verify that the role has been assigned.

```
⇒ drush user-information 2

User ID       :  2
User name     :  developer
User mail     :  developer@example.com
User roles    :  authenticated
                 developer
                 administrator
User status   :  1
```

Removing roles

To remove a role from a user using Drush, we need to simply perform the opposite command by entering the following:

```
drush user-remove-role 'administrator' 2
```

```
⇒ drush user-remove-role 'administrator' 2
Removed administrator role from developer                              [success]
```

We can then list the user information to verify that the role has been removed.

```
⇒ drush user-information 2

   User ID      :  2
   User name    :  developer
   User mail    :  developer@example.com
   User roles   :  authenticated
                   developer
   User status  :  1
```

Blocking a user

There may be times when you need to quickly block a user from logging in. Blocking a user ensures that they can't log in, but allows the account to remain in Drupal until it needs to be deleted. All we need to know is the user ID of the account we want to block and the `drush user-block` command.

To block a user using Drush, we need to simply enter the following command in a terminal window:

```
drush user-block 2
```

```
⇒ drush user-block 2
Blocked user(s): developer                                            [success]
```

Unblocking a user

To unblock a user using Drush, we need to simply enter the following command:

```
drush user-unblock 2
```

```
⇒ drush user-unblock 2
Unblocked user(s): developer                                      [success]
```

Creating user accounts

Previously, we used the Admin interface to create a user account. However, the process can be done using the command line and Drush just as easy. All that is required is the name of the account to be added and the `drush user-create` command. We can also choose to pass optional arguments for password and e-mail.

To create a new user using Drush, we need to simply enter the following command in a terminal window:

```
drush user-create editor --mail='editor@email.com' --password='letmein'
```

```
⇒ drush user-create editor --mail='editor@email.com' --password='letmein'

User ID        :  3
User name      :  editor
User mail      :  editor@email.com
User roles     :  authenticated
User status    :  1
```

Cancelling user account

To cancel a user account, all we need to know is the name of the user, which is the equivalent to the username for the account, and the `drush user-cancel` command.

For example, to cancel the new user we created previously, open a terminal window and enter the following command:

```
drush user-cancel editor
```

```
⇒ drush user-cancel editor

Cancel user account?:  (y/n): y
Cancelled user(s): editor                                          [success]
The update has been performed.                                     [status]
editor has been deleted.                                           [status]
```

While executing this command, we will be prompted to verify that we want to cancel the account; we can choose **yes** to complete the action.

Resetting passwords

To utilize Drush to reset a password for an account, we need to know the name of the user, pass an optional value for the new password, and know the `drush user-password` command.

For example, if we need to reset the developer user's password, we would open a terminal window and enter the following command:

```
drush user-password developer --password='new-password'
```

```
⇒ drush user-password developer --password='new-password'
Changed password for developer                                    [success]
```

Creating a one-time login

One of the more common tasks when developing a Drupal site is creating a one-time login for the user 1 account. Generally, this is done when working with multiple developers and sharing a database. Instead of having to constantly ask what the password is, we can simply reset it for local use to whatever we need it to, be using the `drush user-login` command.

Sometimes, we may need to pass in an optional argument for the hostname or IP that we are using for Drush to execute the command. In this case, since I am using the built-in PHP server, I will pass in the IP being used.

Open a terminal window, and enter the following command:

```
drush user-login --uri='http://127.0.0.1:8088'
```

```
⇒ drush user-login --uri='http://127.0.0.1:8088'
http://127.0.0.1:8088/user/reset/1/1488730930/4sM6LkLojZeREIdUqJWhvn4sTJV3yZS8KfOXZxKUmzQ/login
```

Drush will also attempt to open a new browser window or tab, log you in with the one-time login link, and take you to the **admin** user page. From here, we can change the password to something we can use for local development.

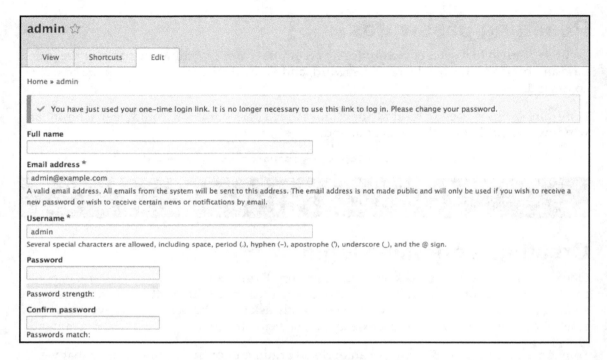

As we can see through this chapter, Drush is quite a powerful tool that allows us to perform various tasks without the need to use the browser.

Summary

Managing users in Drupal is not a trivial task. In fact, it is one of the most important aspects of developing a website. We began with exploring the **People** page to get a better understanding of how users are managed, with everything from creating roles to assigning permissions to roles and adding roles to users.

Once we understood the workflow of how users are managed, we looked at Account settings and how to best configure them for everyday use, such as the tasks that enable personal contact forms and specify which role will inherit permissions, and the ability to control user registration and cancellation.

Finally, we took a deeper look at using Drush to manage users and roles outside of the browser. Being able to quickly create and delete roles, display user information, assign roles to existing users, and even create and delete users directly from the command line.

In the next chapter, we will discuss how Content types, Taxonomy, and Comments in Drupal 8 provide for a powerful ability to create content. We will explore the Field UI along with managing form display and view modes, while understanding how to reference other pieces of content.

4
Content Types, Taxonomy, and Comment Types

One of the more powerful capabilities of Drupal is the ability to create custom content types. Often referred to as a node, we can think of Content types as containers for holding content that has been defined with specific fields, such as a title and a body. However, we are not limited to only those two fields. We can pretty much add as many fields as needed based on how the content itself has been defined.

Something new to Drupal 8 is the Comment field, which can be added to content types, allowing users to comment on the content. Drupal provides this ability out of the box as part of the core with the ability to add **Comment types** that can have fields of their own. We will look at the default configuration and how to customize comments.

We can also add fields to tag, categorize, or classify content, known as Taxonomy. Categorizing content using various terms allows us to enhance content that can then be attached to content types as a term reference.

To help us master Content types, Comment types, and Taxonomy, we will look at the following:

- Exploring content types
- Managing fields
- Creating custom content types
- Adding fields
- Taxonomy, vocabularies, and terms
- Introduction to Comment types
- Working with form and content display
- Using Drupal Console to generate content

Assumptions

Mastering Drupal 8 assumes that you are already running a local AMP stack and are familiar with installing Drupal using the standard means of downloading, setting up a database, configuring a localhost, and completing the browser-based install. In Chapter 1, *Developer Workflow*, we walked through quickly installing Drupal using Composer, Drush, and Drupal Console. Before continuing, ensure that you have a working AMP stack and are comfortable working within the command-line interface using a Terminal window.

Exploring Content types

In most cases, our first glimpse of content types comes from the two default **Content types** that Drupal configures as part of the standard install: **Article** and **Basic page**.

We can navigate to **Content types** by directly entering /admin/structure/types or by using the **Administration** toolbar and clicking on **Manage** | **Structure** | **Content types**:

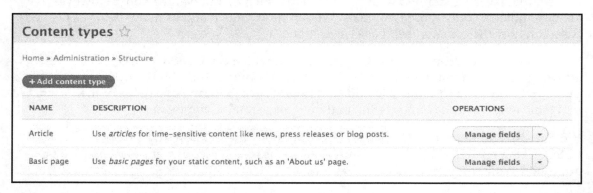

The **Content types** page lists all content types, including their name and description. From this page, we can add, edit, and manage content types along with their respective fields and displays. Currently, our **Content types** consist of **Article** and **Basic page**.

To get a better look at the makeup of a content type, we can view the **Basic page content type** by selecting the drop-down button and choosing **Edit**:

The **Edit** screen defines the configuration of a content type by providing a **Name**, a **Description**, and four subsections that handle various settings.

Submission form settings

Submission form settings allow us to define the **Title field label**, specify whether content can be previewed before saving new nodes, and specify any submission guidelines we want to provide to users:

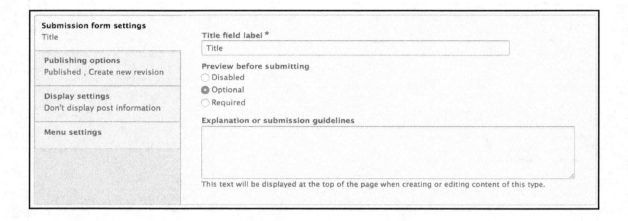

Preview before submitting

The **Preview before submitting** option provides two functions:

- Appearance of a **Preview** button when creating a new node
- Ability to switch between various displays of the content

If we navigate to the **Add content** page by entering /node/add/page or by using the Admin toolbar and clicking on **Manage** | **Content**, selecting **Add content** and then **Basic page**, we can create our first **Basic page** and preview the content in it:

On the **Create Basic page** screen, we will need to enter the following information:

- **Title***: About Us
- **Body**: Add some default Lorem Ipsum using http://www.lipsum.com/:

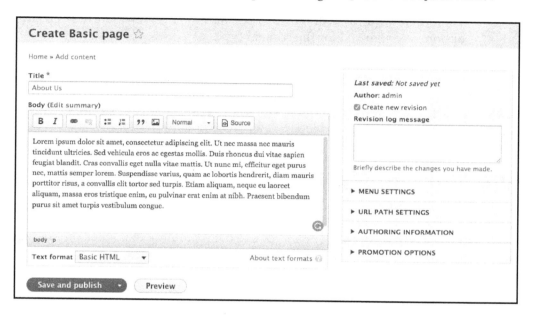

With our content added, we can select the **Preview** button to view our content with the ability to change the **View mode** of how the content is displayed:

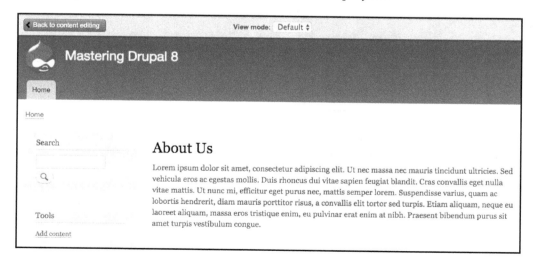

The display modes enabled on each content type will determine what choices are available in the **View mode** dropdown. For our example, we can switch between the **Default** and **Teaser** displays. Once we are done previewing the content, we can switch back to the **Add Basic** page screen by selecting the **Back to content editing** button.

 The **Preview** button will only be present if the **Preview before submitting** option is configured for the content type.

Once we are back on the **Create Basic page** screen, we can save our new page by clicking on the **Save and publish** button. We will revisit the content as we review the **Publishing options**.

Publishing options

Navigate back to the Basic page settings located at `/admin/structure/types/manage/page` or use the Admin toolbar, click on **Manage** | **Structure** | **Content types**, and select the **Edit** link from the drop-down button next to **Basic page**:

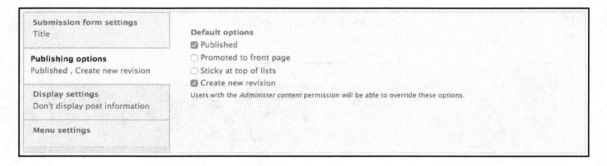

The **Publishing options** mainly control whether content is published by default and whether to create new revisions each time we edit content. If we do not want content to be published automatically, we can uncheck the **Published** option. Drupal 8 has a new ability to have revisions enabled by default. This setting allows for multiple versions of content to be saved each time content is created or edited. If we are governed by an editorial workflow, this is a great option.

Managing revisions

We can see an example of how revisions work by navigating back to the **About Us** page we created earlier by directly entering `/node/1/edit` or using the Admin toolbar, clicking on **Manage** | **Content**, and selecting the **About Us** link and then the **Edit** tab.

If we look at the right sidebar on the **Edit Basic** page screen, we will see the **Create new revision** section and the corresponding log message that allows us to add additional information about what we are changing. To test this functionality, change the **Title** from **About Us** to `About`, add a **Revision log message** of `Changed title`, and click on the **Save and keep published** button:

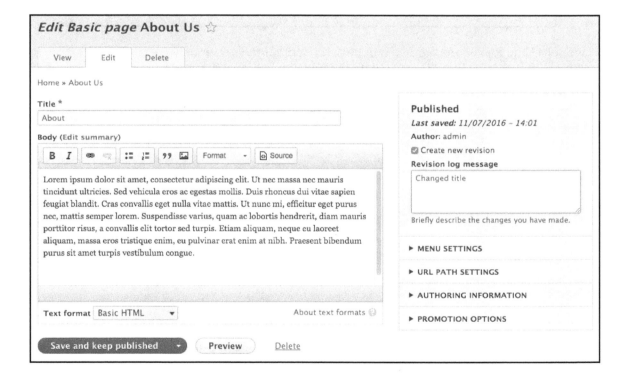

Now when we view the **About** page, we will see a new tab alerting us that we have **Revisions** available:

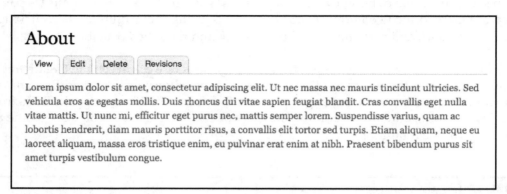

If we select the **Revisions** tab, we will have a list of all the previously created or edited versions of our page, including the date the edit was made, who made it, and any log messages that were added:

The **Revisions** functionality can be extended to provide a side-by-side comparison of differences by adding the contributed module--`https://www.drupal.org/project/diff`.

Reverting content

With revisions being tracked, we can easily revert our content back to its previous state by clicking on the **Revert** button next to the revision that we want to be active. Drupal will ask us to confirm our choice before reverting the page, and we will need to click on the **Revert** button once more:

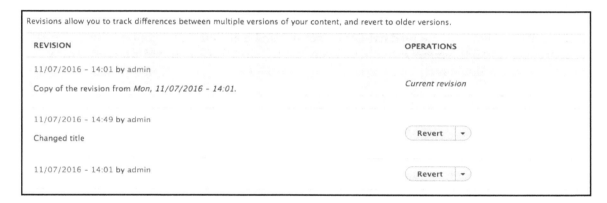

We can select the **View** tab and confirm that our **About** page displays the reverted version.

Display settings

Navigate back to the **Basic** page settings located at `/admin/structure/types/manage/page` or by using the Admin toolbar and clicking on **Manage** | **Structure** | **Content types**, and select the **Edit** link from the drop-down button next to **Basic** page:

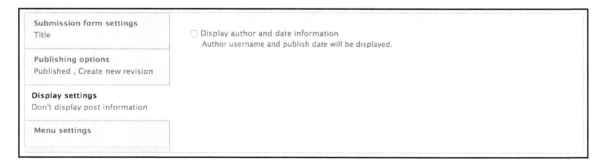

Display settings is a single configuration that triggers whether to print the author's username and the date the content was created on our page. In most cases, we would uncheck this option as it would be preferable to create actual fields to store the data that can be presented and styled in a different fashion.

Menu settings

Menu settings determine which available menus can be added to the content. By default, Drupal displays all the menus that have been created. In this case, the **Main navigation** menu will be available for content creators to choose from:

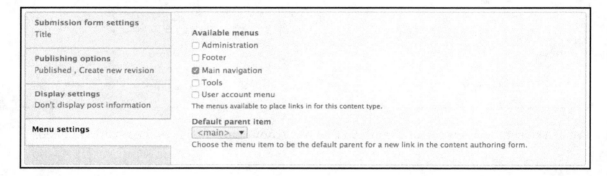

Navigate back to the **About Us** page by entering /node/1/edit or using the Admin toolbar and selecting **Manage** | **Content**, selecting the **About Us** link and then the **Edit** tab. In the right sidebar of the **Edit** page, you'll find the **Menu settings** configuration.

By selecting the **Provide a menu link**, we have the following options:

- **Menu link title**: This defaults to our page title, but can be modified accordingly
- **Description**: This is the menu description that will display on certain browsers when a user hovers their mouse over the menu link
- **Parent item**: This is the default menu that was chosen when configuring the content type
- **Weight**: This controls how menu links are ordered within the menu

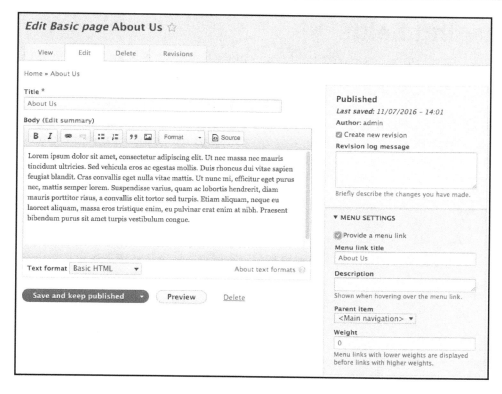

For demonstration purposes, we will leave the defaults and click on the **Save and keep published** button located at the bottom of the page. We now have a new menu item that allows us to navigate to the **About Us** page:

With a better understanding of the configuration options content types provide, it is now time to dive a little deeper and look at how we can manage fields associated with content types.

Managing fields

By default, Drupal provides a **Title** field and a **Body** field. We saw an example of this when we created our first **Basic page**. However, we can add a wide array of fields to capture just about any type of content you can imagine.

Navigate back to the **Basic page** content type by entering `/admin/structure/types/manage/page/fields` or using the Admin toolbar and selecting **Manage** | **Structure** | **Content types** and then the **Manage fields** button for the **Basic page** content type. We will get our first glimpse of what is known as the Field UI:

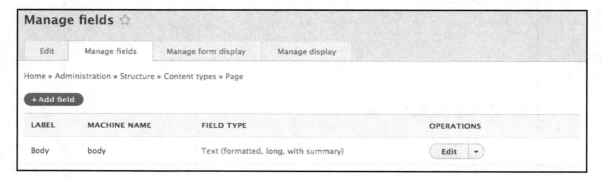

Remember I said there were two fields. Well, the Title field is a system field, so we won't see it displayed under **Manage fields**, but keep in mind that it is required by every content type.

Every new field we add will be listed here and will display the **LABEL**, **MACHINE NAME**, and **FIELD TYPE**. We can add fields, edit fields, and even delete fields from the **Manage fields** page. One caveat is that depending on the field, we may not be able to delete it if we have already added content to the content type that the field is attached to or if we have reused the field on multiple content types.

We will add fields later when we explore creating custom content types. For now, though, we will take a look at editing the **Body** field to get familiar with some of the basic configuration screens a field provides.

If we click on the **Edit** button for the **Body** field, we will see the settings page for the **Text (formatted long)** field type:

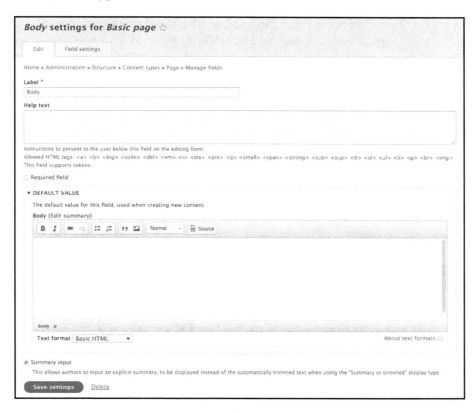

Every field type will provide a **Label**, **Help text**, **Required field**, and **DEFAULT VALUE**:

- **Label**: Provides the user with a label describing the type or name of the field
- **Help text**: Instructions to assist the user in what to enter in each field
- **Required field**: Provides the ability to enforce the field to have a value before the user can save the page
- **DEFAULT VALUE**: Allows for a default value to be used, and it varies based on the field type

As we begin creating new fields, we will look at additional settings based on the field type or additional configuration needed to properly create the field.

Field settings

Based on the type of field, there may be cases where you want to allow multiple instances of a field. Maybe you want to collect multiple images. The **Field settings** tab allows us to specify whether we want a single instance, a specific number of instances, or unlimited instances.

If we click on the **Field settings** tab, we will see that the **Body** field only allows a single instance:

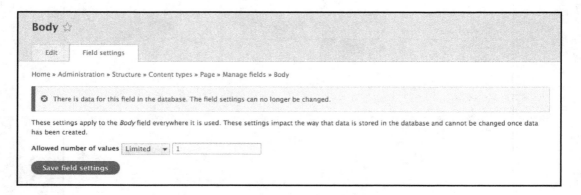

Keep in mind that **Field settings** can only be modified if we have not added content to a field that has data stored in it. So, it is important to think about how we want to use a field when we first create it. Having a clear content model will ensure that we don't run into issues where we may need to recreate a field for the sake of modifying the **Field settings**.

Now that we have a better understanding of content types and their respective fields, it's time to take a closer look by creating our first custom content type.

Creating custom content types

One of the most important steps to consider before blindly developing custom content types is to think of how content will be used. In most cases, a content audit is a preliminary step that should be taken. A *content audit* is quite easy to conduct, beginning with just asking two questions: how will the content be used and how will it be displayed?

If we look around the web, we can easily identify a common content type used on blogs, known as a **Post**. By understanding how a Post will be displayed, we can identify some of the fields we will need, such as the date the Post was created and the author of a Post. Also, most Posts contain some sort of media, generally consisting of an image or possibly a video. Using the Post as our model, we can easily create a new Post content type by following these steps:

Begin by navigating to /admin/structure/types or use the Admin toolbar and click on **Manage** | **Structure** and then **Content types**.

So far, we have only looked at content types, but by clicking on the **Add content type** button, we can begin inputting the following information to create our first custom content type:

- **Name***: Post
- **Description**: Post content type used for creating blog posts

---

Add content type ☆

Home » Administration » Structure » Content types

Individual content types can have different fields, behaviors, and permissions assigned to them.

Name *

Post   Machine name: post [Edit]

The human-readable name of this content type. This text will be displayed as part of the list on the *Add content* page. This name must be unique.

Description

Post content type used for creating blog posts

This text will be displayed on the *Add new content* page.

When working with content types, it helps to provide a detailed description about how the content type will be used. Remember that the **Description** will be shown to users when they first view content types on the Admin screen. For the remaining four subsections, we will enter the following information:

- **Submission form settings**

  Preview before submitting: Optional

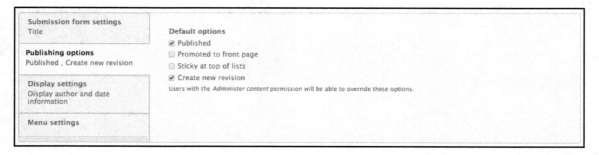

- **Publishing options**

  Default options: Published and **Create new revision**

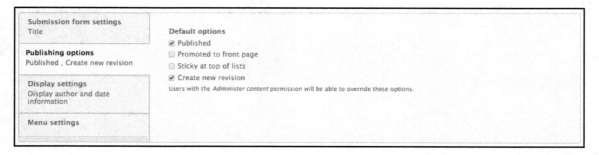

- **Display settings**

  Display author and date information: Unchecked

Submission form settings Title	☐ Display author and date information Author username and publish date will be displayed.
Publishing options Published , Create new revision	
Display settings Don't display post information	
Menu settings	

- **Menu settings**

  Available menus: No options selected

Submission form settings Title	Available menus ☐ Administration ☐ Footer ☐ Main navigation ☐ Tools ☐ User account menu The menus available to place links in for this content type.
Publishing options Published , Create new revision	
Display settings Don't display post information	
Menu settings	

With the initial configuration added, we can click on the **Save and manage fields** button to create our Post content type. Next, we will look at managing fields using the Field UI.

Managing fields using the Field UI

Managing fields in Drupal 8 is quite simple and is just a matter of choosing the type of field we want to add and configuring it. By default, Drupal adds a **Body** field for managing basic content. We can choose to use this field to capture formatted data, but since we have not created any post content, we can also choose to delete this field and create all new fields.

Deleting fields

Deleting a field using the Field UI only requires that the field is not being reused across multiple content types and that the field has no data stored in it. Since this is a new instance of our Post content type, we can delete the **Body** field by selecting **Delete** from the drop-down button next to the field name:

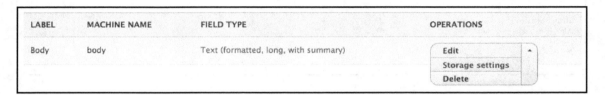

Once we choose to delete a field, we will be prompted by Drupal, asking us to confirm our selection. We can complete the process by clicking on the **Delete** button once more.

Now that we have only the Title field attached to our Post content type, we will need to add some new fields to capture the data that we want to display when users view our blog.

Adding new fields

Adding a new field consists of two steps. The first is specifying the type of field we want to use, which can vary based on the type of data the field will be holding. The second is configuring the field based on the type of field chosen. We will see this in more detail as we add various field types. Let's see how we can add the **Published Date**, **Author**, **Teaser**, **Content**, and **Featured Image** fields to our page:

- Published Date
    1. Click on the **Add field** button.
    2. Choose `Date` from the **Add a new field** drop-down.
    3. Enter `Published` in the **Label** textbox:

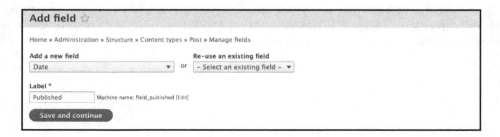

4. Click on the **Save and continue** button.

5. Choose `Date only` from the **Date type** drop-down.

6. Leave the default value of `1` for the **Allowed number of values** field:

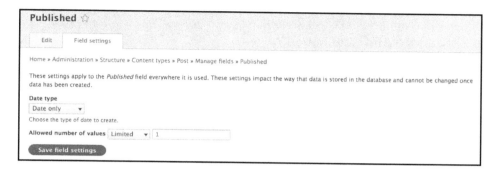

7. Click on the **Save field settings** button.

8. Choose `Current date` from the **Default date** drop-down.

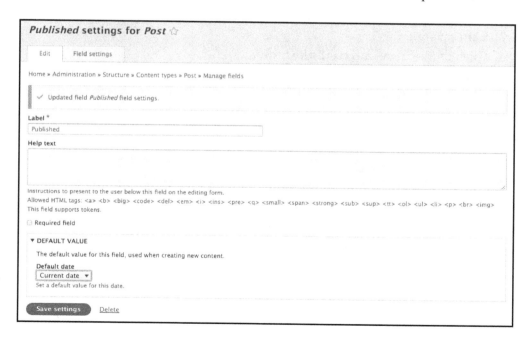

9. Click on the **Save settings** button.

We have now created our first field and can repeat the steps to add the remaining fields. Ensure that we pay close attention to the configuration settings when adding the remaining fields, as they will vary based on the field type.

Author field

1. Click on the **Add field** button.
2. Choose **Text (plain)** from the **Add a new field** dropdown.
3. **Label**: Author.
4. Click on the **Save and continue** button.
5. Click on the **Save field settings** button.
6. Click on the **Save settings** button.

Teaser field

1. Click on the **Add field** button.
2. Choose **Text (plain, long)** from the **Add a new field** dropdown.
3. **Label**: Teaser.
4. Click on the **Save and continue** button.
5. Click on the **Save field settings** button.
6. Click on the **Save settings** button.

Content field

1. Click on the **Add field** button.
2. Choose **Text (formatted, long)** from the **Add a new field** dropdown.
3. **Label**: Content.
4. Click on the **Save and continue** button.
5. Click on the **Save field settings** button.
6. Click on the **Save settings** button.

Featured Image field

1. Click on the **Add field** button.
2. Choose **Image** from the **Add a new field** dropdown.
3. **Label**: `Featured Image`.
4. Click on the **Save and continue** button.
5. Click on the **Save field settings** button.
6. Click on the **Save settings** button.

Our **Manage fields** page should now be displaying a list of all the fields we just added:

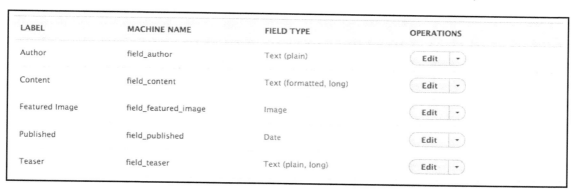

LABEL	MACHINE NAME	FIELD TYPE	OPERATIONS
Author	field_author	Text (plain)	Edit ▾
Content	field_content	Text (formatted, long)	Edit ▾
Featured Image	field_featured_image	Image	Edit ▾
Published	field_published	Date	Edit ▾
Teaser	field_teaser	Text (plain, long)	Edit ▾

Sometimes we may find ourselves wanting to use specialized fields that allow us to categorize content, reference other pieces of content, or even provide users the ability to comment on content we have added. This is where Taxonomy comes in.

Taxonomy, Vocabularies, and Terms

Categorizing content is a great way to allow users to find all content grouped by a specific term. Adding **Taxonomy** in Drupal gives us this ability by adding **Vocabularies** with **Terms** that we can add as a field to content types. However, to add a term field to our Post content type, we need to first create a Taxonomy.

We can begin by navigating to `/admin/structure/taxonomy` or using the **Admin** toolbar and clicking on **Manage - Structure**, then selecting **Taxonomy**:

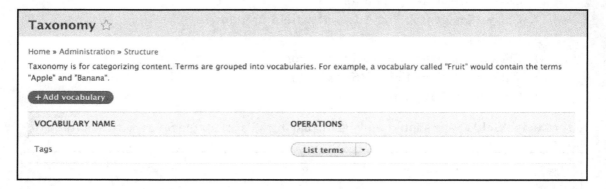

Taxonomy terms are grouped into vocabularies and by default Drupal provides us with the **Tags** vocabulary. Vocabularies contain terms, which is just the name used to identify the piece of content within that specific category.

Adding a vocabulary

We will be adding a vocabulary entitled **Category**, where we will then add terms for items such as Outdoors, Camping, Rock Climbing, and any other terms we may need in the future.

We can begin by following these steps by clicking on the **Add vocabulary** button and entering the following values:

- **Name**: Category
- **Description**: Categorize Post types

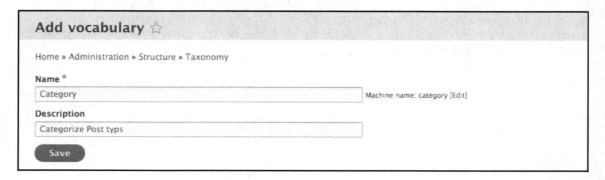

We can now click on the **Save** button to complete adding our new Taxonomy vocabulary called **Category**. Like content types, Taxonomy vocabularies are fieldable and can be presented in multiple ways. The interface for managing Taxonomy should be familiar, except for adding terms:

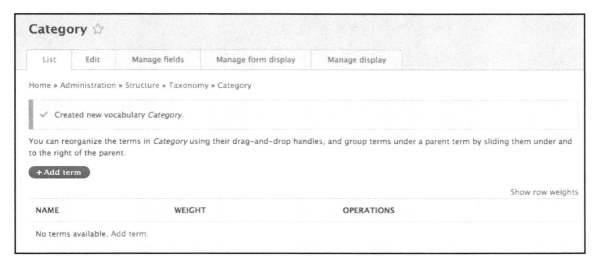

Adding terms

Adding terms to our **Category** vocabulary will enable a user to filter Posts by those terms. We can add new terms by clicking on the **Add term** button and entering the following values:

- **Outdoors term**
    - **Name**: Outdoors
    - **Description**: empty

- **URL alias**: `/category/outdoors`

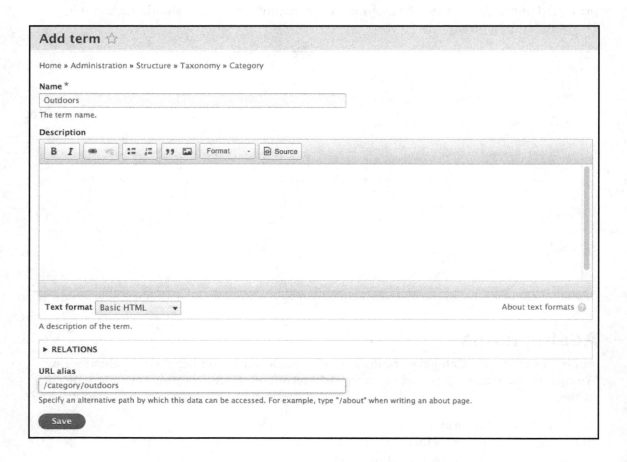

Now, click on the **Save** button to add our first term and then repeat the steps for the remaining terms:

- **Camping term**
    - **Name**: `Camping`.
    - **URL alias**: `/category/camping`.
    - Click on the **Save** button.

- **Rock climbing term**
  1. Click on the **Add term** button.
  2. **Name**: Rock climbing.
  3. **URL alias**: /category/rock-climbing.
  4. Click on the **Save** button.

If we now navigate back to our **Category** listing, we should see the three terms we added:

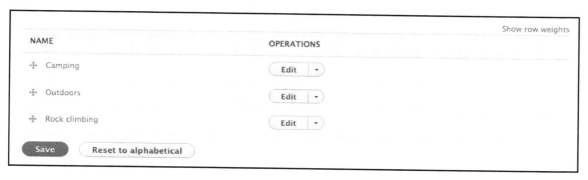

One important item to point out is that the order in which the terms appear in our list is how they will appear to users when using them from the node add/edit page, or from any filter using the Category vocab.

If we want to reorder the list manually, we can accomplish this by dragging the terms in the order we want them to appear. We can also reset them to back to display alphabetically by selecting the **Reset to alphabetical** button.

Adding a Taxonomy field

We can add taxonomies to content types as a field, like how we added fields earlier. To demonstrate adding the Category vocab as a field, navigate to /admin/structure/types/manage/post/fields or use the Admin toolbar to click on **Manage - Structure - Content types** and select the **Manage fields** button next to the Post content type.

We can now add our new Category Taxonomy vocab by performing the following steps:

1. Click on the **Add field** button.
2. Choose **Taxonomy term** from the **Add a new field** dropdown.
3. **Label**: Category.

4. Click on the **Save and continue** button.
5. Choose `Unlimited` from the **Allowed number of values** dropdown.
6. Click on the **Save field settings** button.
7. Choose `Category` from the **AvailableVocabularies** field under **REFERENCE TYPE**.
8. Click on the **Save settings** button.

We have now successfully added a Term reference field to our Post content type. We will visit adding a post in a moment. For now, we have one additional field that our content type would benefit from, and that is the ability for users to comment on each post.

Working with Comment types

The appearance of **Comment types** is new to Drupal 8. No longer are comments assumed to be part of every content type. Comment types are like content types in that they are fieldable and can have additional fields added to them to capture info outside of the normal subject, author, and comment.

We can view the Comment types screen by navigating to `/admin/structure/comment` or using the Admin toolbar and click on **Manage - Structure - Comment types**:

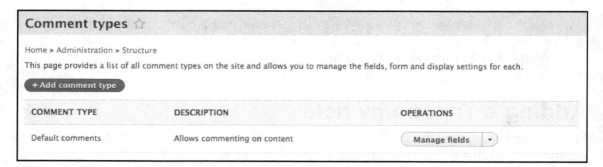

By default, Drupal provides us with a **Default comments** type that contains three fields: Author, Subject, and Comment body. Comment types can be managed exactly like content types, which we will see next by adding a new Comment type that we will add to our Post.

Adding a Comment type

We will add a new Post Comment type by first clicking on the **Add comment type** button located on the **Comment types** admin screen. Like content types, we will need to add a **Label**, a **Description**, and choose a **Target entity type** by entering the following values:

1. **Label**: Post Comment Type.
2. **Description**: Post Comment type to be added to all posts.
3. **Target entity type**: Choose **Content** from the dropdown:

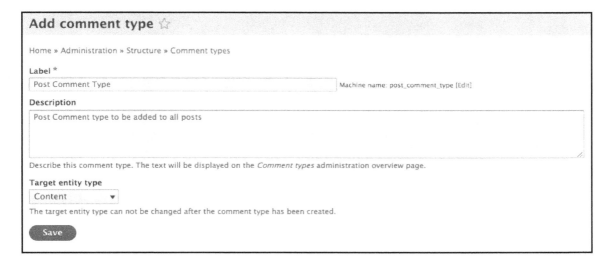

We can now click on the **Save** button to successfully create our new Comment type. We will not add any additional fields now, as the process is identical in nature to content types.

Adding Comment type field

Next, we need to add our new comment type as a field to our Post content type. Begin by navigating back to /admin/structure/types/manage/post/fields, or use the Admin toolbar and click on **Manage - Structure - Content types** then select the **Manage fields** button next to the Post content type.

We can now add our new Post Comment type by performing the following steps:

1. Click on the **Add field** button.
2. Choose **Comments** from the **Add a new field** dropdown.

3. **Label**: Post Comments.
4. Click on the **Save and continue** button.
5. Choose **Post Comment Type** from the **Comment type** dropdown.
6. Click on the **Save field settings** button.

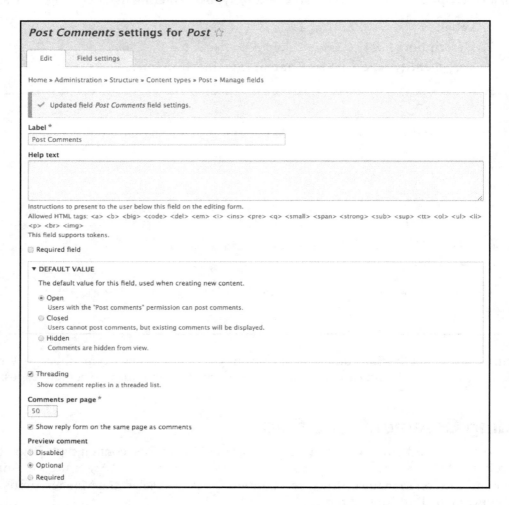

This screen may look somewhat familiar. The comment option that were part of the content type configuration in Drupal 7 are now part of the field settings. While we will leave the default settings, we do have the option to specify whether comments are open, closed, or hidden by default, whether we want to show threaded replies, and the number of comments to show per page.

For demonstration purposes, we can click on the **Save settings** button to complete the addition of our comment field.

Working with form and content display

Content form display is just as important as the content itself, and knowing how to provide our end users with a better authoring experience is simple with Drupal 8.

Start by navigating to `/node/add/post` or by using the Admin toolbar and clicking on **Content** and then selecting **Add content** and then **Post**:

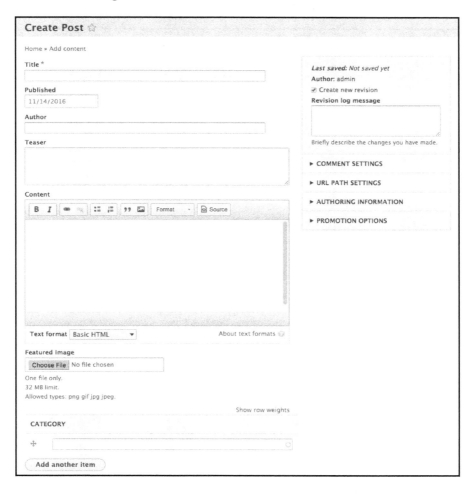

At first glance, we can see that the flow of our form is not very friendly. Our **Featured Image** and **CATEGORY** fields are displayed at the bottom of our form when it would make much more sense to have them displayed after the **Author** field. Also, how to select a Category for a Post may not be very clear to the user. Finally, some fields should not be displayed if we don't expect the user to interact with them.

Drupal 8 provides us with the ability to rearrange fields, change the format of how fields are displayed, and even disable the display of fields using the **Manage form display** for each content type. We can make our Post form more usable by navigating to `/admin/structure/types/manage/post/form-display` or by using the Admin toolbar and selecting **Manage -Structure-Content types**, then choosing **Manage form display** from the drop-down button next to the **Post** content type:

Reordering fields

Next to each field, we will see a navigational arrow that will allow us to reorder the way fields will be displayed to the end user. Taking a moment to review the fields our Post content type has will make much more sense if our fields are in the following order:

- Title
- Published
- Author
- Category
- Featured Image
- Teaser
- Content
- Post Comments

Let's place the fields in the correct order by dragging them into positions based on the mentioned order and then click on the **Save** button to complete our changes. If we navigate back to our **Create Post** form and review the changes we made, we should notice that our fields are now appearing in the order we specified.

Modifying Field Widgets

Another handy feature is being able to modify the settings or widgets that a field is currently using to help improve the overall user experience. One such field is our Taxonomy Category field, which allows for multiple values. Looking at our **Create Post** form, we can see that the user is prompted to enter a term, but it's not quite clear how they are supposed to input it:

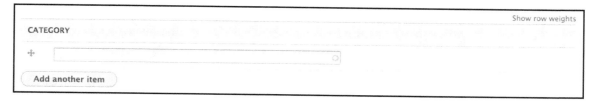

We can change the input to display a checkbox for each term instead of the current input, by simply modifying the **WIDGET** type from the **Manage form display** page. Begin by navigating back to `/admin/structure/types/manage/post/form-display` and change the Widget from **Autocomplete** to **Check boxes/radio buttons**, then **Save** the changes.

Now that we have changed the display, if we navigate back to our **Create Post** form, we will see that our **Category** field is looking much cleaner:

Disabling fields

Hiding unneeded fields will also improve the user experience when entering Post content. We can take advantage of the **Disabled** section located under the **Manage** form display page to remove fields by simply dragging them into the **Disabled** area.

Begin by navigating back to `/admin/structure/types/manage/post/form-display` and then drag the following fields into the **Disabled** section:

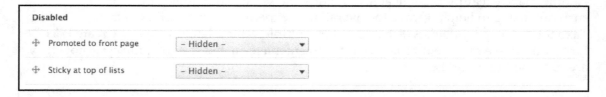

Now that we have prevented any unnecessary fields from being displayed, we can navigate back to our **Create Post** form and verify that the two fields are no longer displayed.

Let's create our first Post by completing the fields on our form. Feel free to enter whatever values are needed to complete the form, ensuring that you include an image and tag the post with a category:

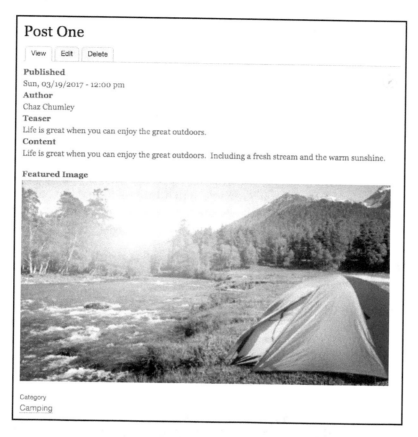

Now that we have created a Post, we can view our content as an end user would. There are a couple of items that may seem strange at first. We are displaying labels above each field, and also, we are displaying both the **Teaser** and **Content** fields on the **Default** display. We will address all of this in Chapter 6, *Content Authoring, HTML5, and Media*.

Before we move on to the next chapter, there is one last thing to cover.

Using Drupal console to generate dummy content

Sometimes when first developing a Drupal site, we may have the need to utilize dummy content to assist with testing form, functionality, and display. While it is nice to have real content, it can be difficult to have clients begin entering data while development is still taking place.

To help us with the tedious task of entering dummy content, we have a few choices. The first choice is to use a contribute module such as **Devel** (`https://www.drupal.org/project/devel`), which will generate content for us using the Drupal Admin UI. While this is a great module for development, it requires installing it, configuring it, and then using it.

A better solution is to use the Drupal Console, which we installed and configured in `Chapter 1`, *Developer Workflow*. Drupal Console will allow us to use the command-line to perform the same tasks the Devel module or manual content creation would require.

Creating vocabularies

If we open a Terminal window, we can use Drupal console to generate vocabularies for us with dummy content simply by entering the following command and then following the prompts:

```
drupal create:vocabularies
```

The preceding code is illustrated in the following screenshot:

```
⇒ drupal create:vocabularies

// Welcome to the Drupal vocabularies creator

Enter how many vocabularies would you like to create [25]:
> 1

Enter the maximum number of words in vocabulary names [5]:
> 5

 --------------- -------------------------------------------
  Vocabulary Id   Name
 --------------- -------------------------------------------
  m9510fna        Blandit Ideo Jumentum Rusticus Virtus
 --------------- -------------------------------------------

[OK] Created "1" vocabularies successfully
```

Now, if we were to navigate to /admin/structure/taxonomy, we would see that we have a new Taxonomy vocabulary generated for us. It is handy and time saving to use a single command in Drupal console.

Creating comments

If we open a Terminal window, we can use Drupal console to generate dummy comments for us simply by entering the following command and then following the prompts:

```
drupal create:comments
```

The preceding code is illustrated in the following screenshot:

To attach the comments to a node, we need to know the node ID for the content. Now, if we were to navigate to /admin/content/comment, we would see a list of dummy comments and the content they are associated with.

Creating nodes

Finally, if we open a Terminal window, we can use Drupal console to generate nodes with dummy content simply by entering the following command and then following the prompts:

```
drupal create:nodes
```

The preceding code is illustrated in the following image:

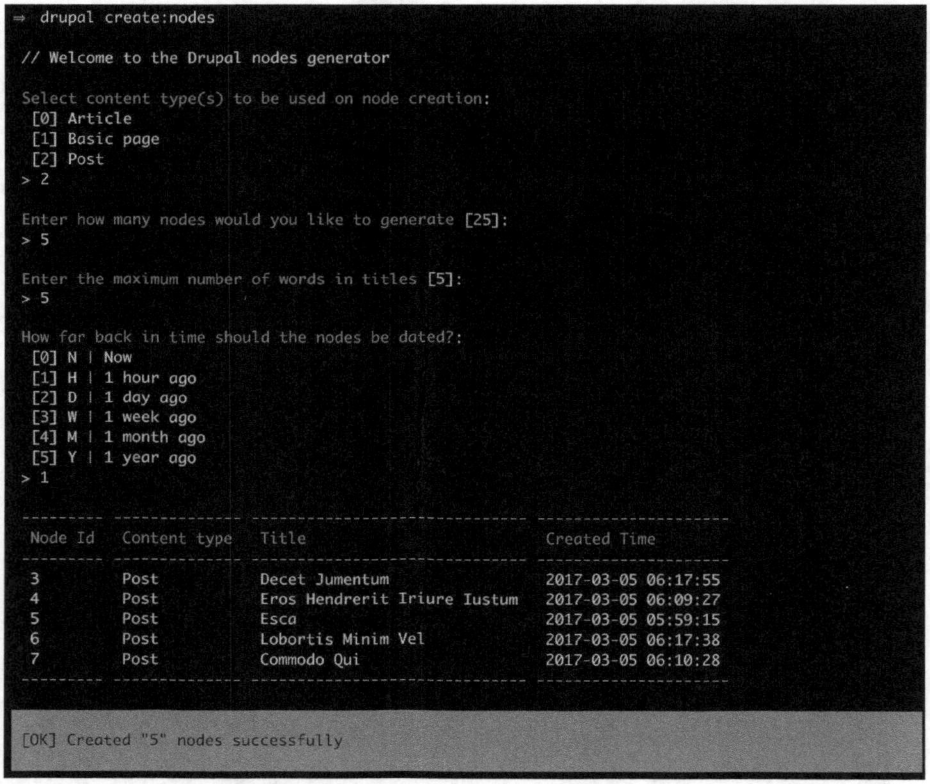

Now, if we were to navigate to /admin/content, we would see a list of dummy nodes for the selected content type.

Knowing how to master using Drupal console will speed up development time when building Drupal 8 websites. Ensure that you always refer to the list of functions that Drupal console provides.

Summary

We covered a lot of information in this chapter by learning how to master content types, Taxonomy, and Comment types. Starting with exploring content types, we got first-hand knowledge of just how flexible Drupal 8 is in allowing us to configure how content can be captured and displayed. Including managing fields using the Field UI provides for a consistent site-building experience.

Next, we looked at how to categorize content using Taxonomy, Vocabularies, and terms. We then added term reference to custom content types, allowing for site admins to tag content, which in turn allows users to filter content easily.

We also dove into the new comment types and how Drupal has moved this functionality into core to be managed like content types with its fieldable displays. We then added our comment type as a field, which enables users to comment on content.

Finally, we took another look at Drupal console to assist us with generating dummy content, including vocabularies, terms, comments, and nodes.

In the next chapter, we will explore working with blocks and discuss how everything in Drupal 8 is now a block. We will also look at a new way to place blocks using experimental core modules.

5
Working with Blocks

As we dive deeper into Mastering Drupal 8, we will begin to understand that almost all content is now contained within blocks . We can think of blocks as small sections of content that can be placed into regions, either defined by Drupal or defined by custom regions added to a theme. Drupal provides us with several types of block that contain the main navigation, site branding, Breadcrumbs, main page content, and more.

If you are familiar with blocks in Drupal 7, you will be happily surprised to find that blocks can now be reused. This gives us the flexibility of placing the same block into multiple regions based on the needs of our website. Another great feature of blocks in Drupal 8 is the ability to create custom blocks that have all the same features as content types. This includes the ability to add fields and view modes.

To give us a better understanding of how best to work with blocks, we will look at mastering the following:

- Block layout and Regions
- Block configuration, settings and visibility
- Custom blocks
- Managing fields, form display, and content display
- Using the Place blocks module

Assumptions

Mastering Drupal 8 makes the assumption that you are already running a local AMP stack and have a familiarity with installing Drupal using the standard means of downloading, setting up a database, configuring a local host, and completing the browser-based install. In Chapter 1, *Developer Workflow* we walked through quickly installing Drupal using Composer, Drush, and Drupal Console. Please ensure you have a working AMP stack and are comfortable working within the command line interface using a terminal window before continuing.

Block layout and Regions

Before we can begin working with blocks, we need to be familiar with Block layout and Regions. We need to know where things are located, what blocks Drupal 8 provides us with, and the concept of Regions.

We can navigate to the **Block layout** page by directly entering /admin/structure/block, or by using the Admin toolbar and clicking on **Structure | Block layout**:

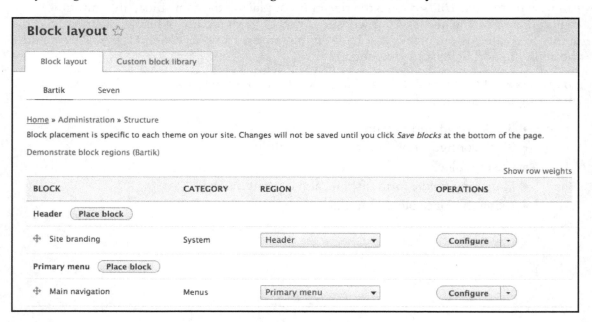

The Block layout page provides the interface that allows us to manage block content by placing blocks into regions. Blocks can be categorized based on their functionality, with the most common types including the following:

- **Core**: Blocks contained within the core installation consisting of items such as page title, primary admin actions, and tabs
- **System**: Blocks that provide system functionality consisting of breadcrumbs, main-page content, messages, site branding, and a few others
- **Forms**: Blocks that contain embedded forms such as the search form and user login
- **Menus**: Blocks that contain menus and menu items, such as Administration, Footer, Main navigation, and Tools
- **Lists** (**Views**): Blocks consisting of Views generated for block content. Generally, these types of block will be created during configuration or site building
- **Custom**: Blocks created from the Custom block library consisting of fieldable blocks with one or more display modes

If blocks consist of content, then we can think of regions as the containers that hold blocks and make up a theme's layout.

Drupal 8 provides the following regions:

- Header
- Primary menu
- Secondary menu
- Highlighted
- Help
- Content
- Sidebar first
- Sidebar second
- Footer
- Breadcrumb

In some cases, we may see additional regions available for use. However, keep in mind that anything outside of the default regions described above have been added to the active theme and are defined within the theme's configuration.

Demonstrating block regions

To view regions defined by the active theme, we can click on the **Demonstrate block regions** link located at the top of the Block layout page. Clicking on this link will take us to the homepage with the regions highlighted.

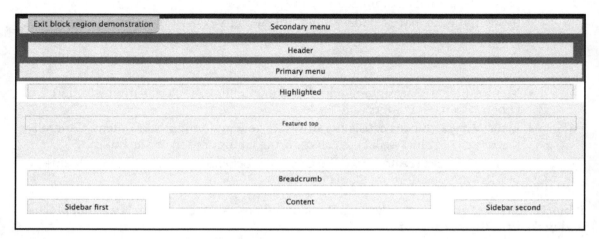

Each Region is simply a container defined by a theme's layout and can contain one or multiple blocks. As we work with blocks and place them into a respective region, we should expect to see the content of the block displayed within the region demonstrated.

To return to the Block layout page, simply click on the **Exit block region demonstration** link located at the top of the page.

Placing blocks into regions

One common task we will find ourselves performing quite frequently is placing blocks into regions. This task is very simple and can be performed by scrolling down the Block layout page, locating the region where we want to place our block, and clicking on the **Place block** button.

Let's try it now by following these steps:

1. Click on the **Place block** button next to the **Sidebar second** region.
2. Locate the **Powered by Drupal** block and click on the **Place block** button.
3. Leave the default settings within the Configure block dialog.

4. Click on the **Save block** button.

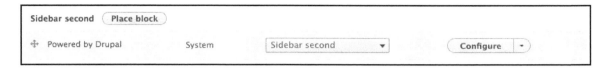

If we click on the Back to Site button within the Admin toolbar, we will be returned to the homepage where we will see the Powered by Drupal block appear in the right-hand column of the page.

Placing a block is straightforward. However, we did not bother with configuring the block and left the defaults when saving it. More often than not, we will want to configure a block based on various contexts.

Block configuration, settings, and visibility

All blocks contain three common areas of configuration: Title, Visibility, and Region. Keep in mind that additional configuration options may be available based on the type of block. For demonstration purposes, we will first look at managing the block title.

Begin by navigating to the Block layout page by directly entering `/admin/structure/block`, or by using the Admin toolbar and clicking on **Structure | Block layout**.

Managing the block title

Block content, whether system generated or custom, can have its display title changed, displayed, and even suppressed. In the case of our **Powered by Drupal** block, we can change the title by simply inputting a different value in the **Title** field and enabling it to display.

If we scroll down the page to the **Sidebar second** region, we can modify our block by clicking on the **Configure** button.

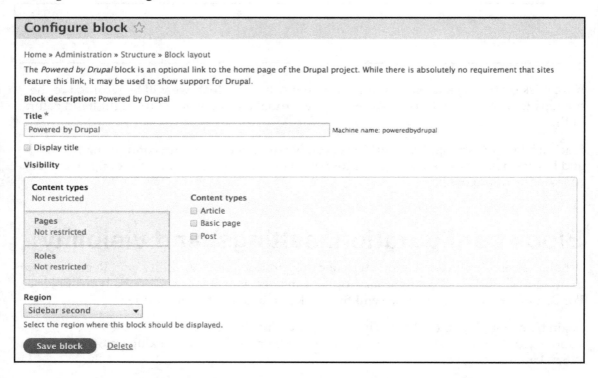

From the **Configure block** page, locate the **Title** field and perform the following actions:

- Change the value to `Powered by Drupal 8`
- Click on the **Display title** checkbox
- Click on the **Save block** button

With our block modified, we can return to the homepage to verify that our block title is now displaying the value we configured.

Using the Contextual menu

Although we can navigate back and forth between the Block layout screen to configure a block, it is much easier to use the contextual menu provided by each block. If we hover over our block, we will see a **Configure block** link.

Clicking on the **Configure block** link will return us directly to the configuration settings for that block. Navigating this way will speed up our development time. As we work to add further blocks, the context menu may contain additional links for editing, deleting, and configuring the block.

Managing visibility settings

Sometimes, we may want to control the visibility of a block based on various contexts. From the **Configure block** screen, if we scroll down to the **Visibility** section, we will see three different contexts to restrict visibility--based on **Content types**, **Pages**, and **Roles**.

Content types restriction

The visibility of content types allows us to determine whether a block is displayed based on the content type of the node or page that the block is placed on. This restriction ensures that a block meant to be displayed on all Article content does not accidentally show on Basic pages.

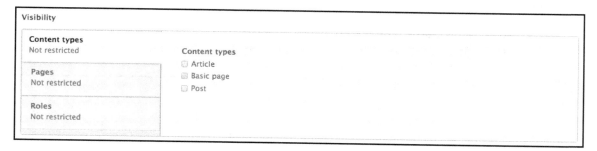

To demonstrate this functionality, we can view the **About Us** page that we created in Chapter 4, *Content Types, Taxonomy, and Comment Types*. There, we will see that our **Powered by Drupal** block is currently displaying in the right sidebar:

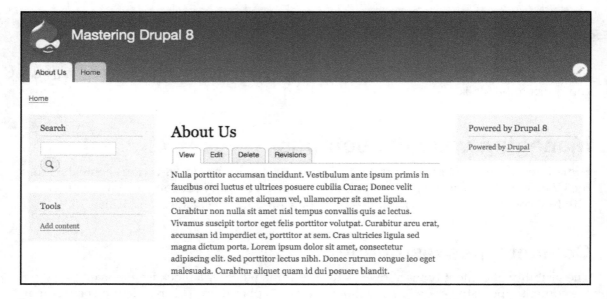

We can prevent the block from displaying on the **About Us** page by using the contextual menu to click on the **Configure block** link and, from the **Configure block** page, following these steps:

- Select the **Content types** tab from the **Visibility** section
- Check both **Article** and **Post** from **Content types**

- Click on the **Save block** button

We will now be back on the About Us page and the Powered by Drupal block is no longer present. This should give us a better understanding of how Content types visibility works with blocks. Go ahead and restrict the visibility for Post content types as well, as we will be referring to our Post content type later in the book. Make sure to verify once again that there is no sidebar present on Post content.

Now that we are getting the hang of this, lets navigate back to the Block layout page and configure the Powered by Drupal block to look at the visibility settings for Pages.

Page restriction

Page restriction allows us to either show or hide blocks of content based on the path to a specific page or set of pages. The path to the page needs to be entered one line at a time and can utilize a wildcard (*) character to specify all children pages. Once we have entered the path, we can choose to negate the condition by either selecting **Show for the listed pages** or **Hide for the listed pages**.

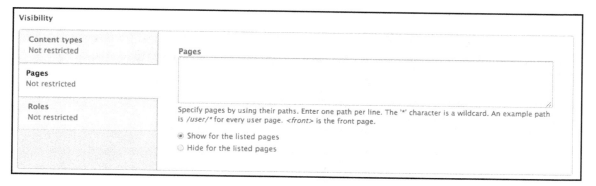

Page restriction visibility is probably the most common visibility setting used for blocks. Especially with Drupal 8 introducing the ability to reuse blocks, is being able to control what page a block displays. This is important to make sure that a block is not duplicated within the same region.

To demonstrate this functionality, we will prevent our block from displaying on the homepage by following these steps:

1. Select the **Pages** tab from the **Visibility** section.
2. Enter `<front>` as the **Pages** path.
3. Select **Hide for the listed pages**.

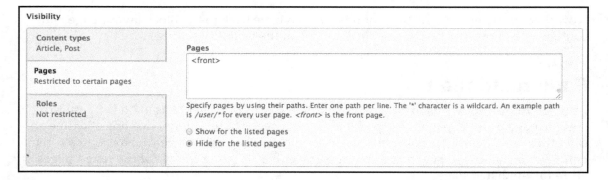

4. Click on the **Save block** button.

If we now navigate back to the homepage, we will see that our Powered by Drupal block is no longer displayed. The only place the block will display is on any Articles we choose to create.

 The only caveat of using this technique to hide or show blocks on pages is that it cannot be combined to use both Show and Hide.

There are modules to extend the functionality of the Block layout page, such as Block Visibility Groups, `https://www.drupal.org/project/block_visibility_groups`, which allows the site admin to easily manage more complex block settings.

Role restriction

The final way to restrict block content is by role. A role is defined by the site administrator and generally consists of an administrator, editor, contributor, an authenticated user, or an anonymous user. Visibility to block content can be restricted by selecting the specific role.

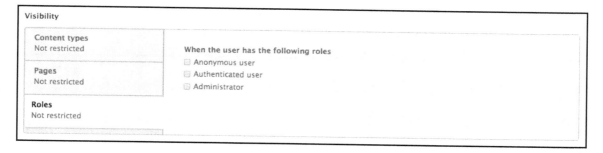

Role-specific visibility can be useful to display admin-only content or membership content to authenticated users without the anonymous user seeing it. Keep in mind that the list of Roles may vary based on what roles our site has defined.

Creating a custom block

So far, we have been working with system-generated blocks. However, with the introduction of fieldable blocks in Drupal 8, we can create custom blocks. Custom blocks are quite powerful and will be used to display content in ways not possible previously without a contributed module.

Begin by navigating to the Block layout page by directly entering /admin/structure/block, or by using the Admin toolbar and clicking on **Structure | Block layout**.

We can create a custom block by following these steps:

1. Locate the **Sidebar second** region.
2. Click on the **Place block** button.
3. Click on the **Add custom block** button.

We are now presented with the **Add custom block** screen that will allow us to create a default custom block that includes a **Block description** and a **Body** field.

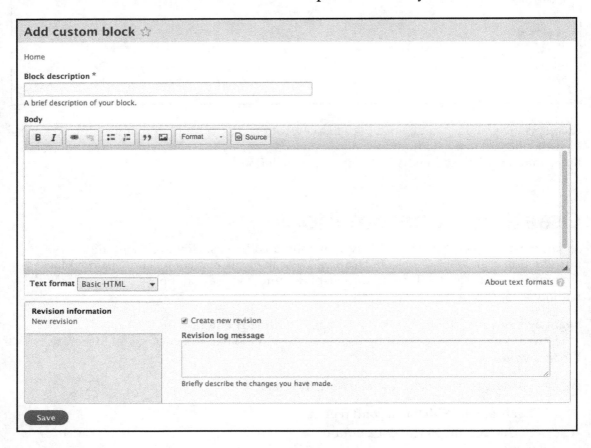

We can continue filling out our custom block by entering the following values:

1. **Block description** is our custom block.
2. **Body** is some basic content.
3. Click on the **Save** button.

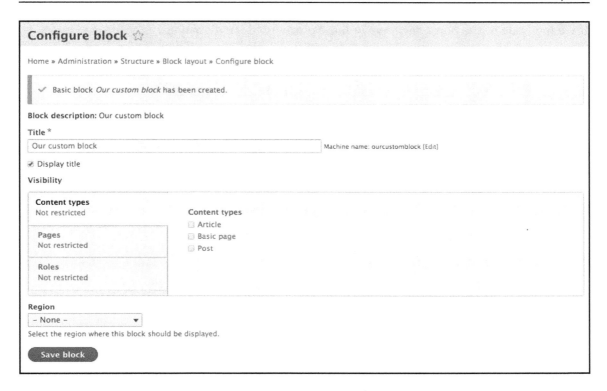

Our custom block has been created, but we still need to configure it just like any other block. Currently we have not assigned our block to a **Region**, which is evident by the **Region** dropdown displaying a value of **Select**.If we try to save the block without defining a region, Drupal will display a HTML5 error specifying that we need to select a Region. We can choose Header Region and then Save the block. We will move the Block to another region using the Block layout in just a moment.

Defining the Region

We can always place a block within any Region by using the Block layout page to select the Region where we want the block to appear. The **Region** drop-down is always visible within each Region and allows us to quickly move blocks around.

To move our new block to the Sidebar second region, we only need to follow these steps:

- Locate the block within the Header Region
- Select the **Sidebar second** region from the drop-down list
- Click on the **Save blocks** button

If we navigate to the homepage, we will see our new block displayed.

Exploring the Custom block library

One difference from Drupal 7 is that block content can no longer be directly edited by selecting an edit link from a context menu or by clicking on an **Edit** button on the Block layout page. Drupal 8 introduced a new section known as the **Custom block library**.

We can navigate to the Custom block library by directly entering `/admin/structure/block/block-content`, or by using the Admin toolbar and clicking on **Structure | Block layout** and then selecting the **Custom block library tab**.

The Custom block library page consists of two sub-sections:

- The **Blocks** tab displays all custom blocks that have been created. Each block is listed by Block description, Block type, and last updated date
- The **Block types** tab displays all block types that have been created. Each block type is listed by the type and description

We will take a closer look at each section beginning with the **Blocks** tab. It is this section where we will be able to **Edit** and **Delete** custom blocks that have been created.

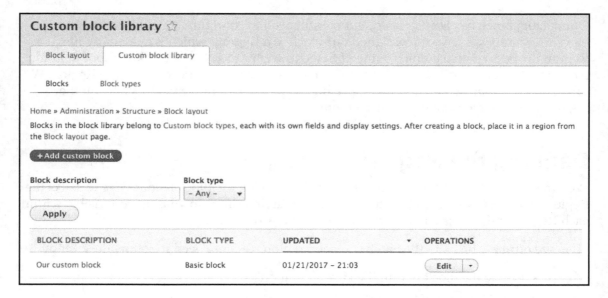

The custom block that we created earlier is displayed in the list of blocks. Located next to each block is the **OPERATIONS** field, which allows us to both **Edit** as well as **Delete** blocks that have been created.

Editing custom blocks

To see an example of how to edit a block, we can click on the **Edit** button next to the block. We will now be taken to the **Edit custom block** page where the **Block description**, **Body**, and any additional fields can be modified.

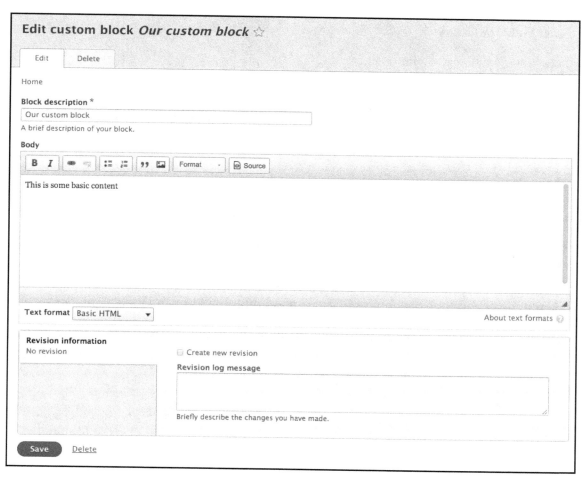

For demonstration purposes, we will not be making any changes to our block. At this point we can navigate back to the **Blocks** section by simply clicking on the **Save** button.

Managing block types

Block types can be equated to Content types, since in Drupal 8, blocks are fieldable and utilize the same Field UI that we have experienced earlier when working with Content types. To get a closer look, begin by selecting the **Block types** tab from the **Custom block library**.

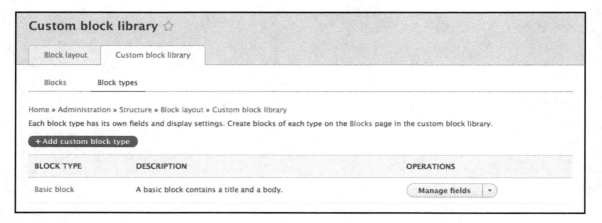

Currently we only have a single block type that Drupal gives us with the standard install, namely a Basic block.

The Basic block type contains a title and a body field and, just like that of a Basic page content type, the block is fieldable and can contain multiple form and display modes for presenting the content. Let's look at how we can manage the Basic block type by adding a new field.

Adding fields to blocks

To add, remove, and configure fields for custom blocks, we need to locate the blocks we want to modify, which in our case is labeled **Basic** block, and then click on the **Manage fields** button.

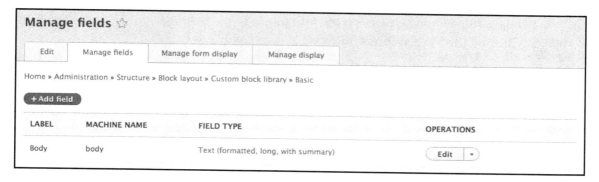

The **Manage fields** UI consists of the following:

- **LABEL**: This is a descriptive name for our field that will be used as a label when inputting content into this field
- **MACHINE NAME**: The machine name is a lowercase field name used by Drupal to distinguish this field from others
- **FIELD TYPE**: This allows us to choose from various field types, such as date, file, text, and more

Currently our block only contains a single **Textfield** that allows us to add content to the **Body** of our block. We can add a new field to our block by following these steps:

1. Click on the **Add field** button.
2. Select **Image** from the **Add a new field** dropdown.
3. Enter a **Label** of **Featured Image**.

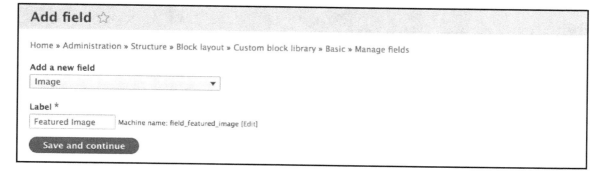

1. Click on the **Save and continue** button.
2. Leave the default settings on the field settings page.
3. Click on the **Save field settings** button.

4. Leave the default settings on the Edit page.
5. Click on the **Save settings** button.

We have successfully added a new field to the **Basic** block type that all future custom blocks can use to add a **Featured Image**.

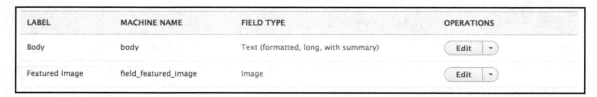

LABEL	MACHINE NAME	FIELD TYPE	OPERATIONS
Body	body	Text (formatted, long, with summary)	Edit ▾
Featured Image	field_featured_image	Image	Edit ▾

Let's try adding one more field. This time we will add a **Textfield** for capturing a Headline:

1. Click on the **Add field** button.
2. Select **Text (plain)** from the **Add a new field** dropdown.
3. Enter a **Label** of **Headline**.
4. Click on the **Save and continue** button.
5. Click on the **Save field settings** button.
6. Click on the **Save settings** button.

We now have a total of three fields that our custom block can capture: a **Body** field, **Featured Image**, and **Headline**. In the current order, our fields may not make logical sense to the end user regarding what information he/she is being asked to input. We can remedy that by managing the form's display of fields.

Manage form display

The Custom block library not only allows us to manage fields using the Fields UI, but we can also manage how form fields will be displayed. This helps to improve the usability of a form.

By clicking on the **Manage form display** tab, we can see which fields will be present on our form, how they will appear, and any configuration options that have been set.

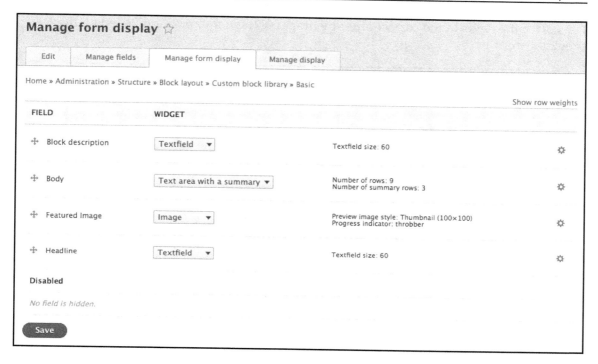

Reordering fields

We can easily reorder the way fields appear by selecting the grab handles located to the left of a field and dragging them up or down on the page. Taking a moment to review the fields in our custom block, it would make much more sense if our fields were in the following order:

- **Block description**
- **Headline**
- **Featured Image**
- **Body**

Let's place the fields in the correct order by dragging them into position, based on the previous order.

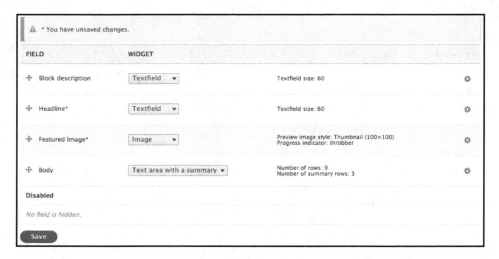

Notice that whenever we reorder fields, Drupal will provide a prompt to remind us that we have unsaved changes. To complete the process, all we need to do is click on the **Save** button.

If we now go to add a new custom block, we will see that our fields are now ordered exactly how we specified on the **Manage form** display page.

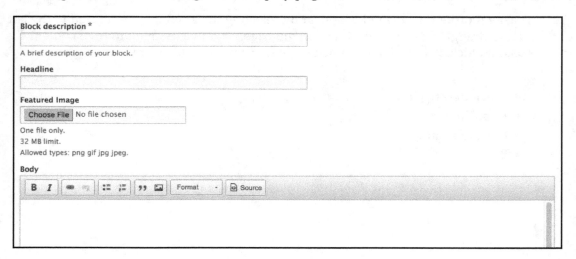

Modifying field formats

Another handy feature is being able to modify the format that a field is currently using. This is often known as a Field Formatter. Field Formatters provide additional configuration per field and allow us to change the length of a **Textfield**, modify the number of rows to display in a text area or, more importantly, add an HTML5 Placeholder to a field.

Let's begin by navigating back to our **Manage form display** page and configure the **Headline** field:

1. Click on the **gear** icon to the right of the **Headline Textfield**.
2. Add this text to the **Placeholder** field: `Please enter a descriptive Headline.`

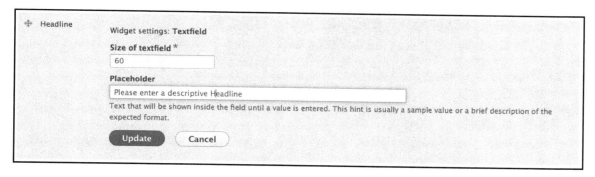

3. Click on the **Update** button.
4. Click the **Save** button.

With our **Placeholder** now added, whenever we create a new custom block, our **Headline** field will prompt users to `Please enter a descriptive Headline`, as shown in the following image:

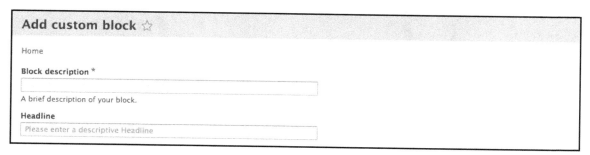

Sometimes it is necessary to clear Drupals cache when adding Placeholders to a form. If this happens to you, then clear the cache and then view the form again.

Managing display

Whenever a new custom block is created, Drupal will generate a single default display that can be used for printing the content. We can manage the display by clicking on the **Manage display** tab.

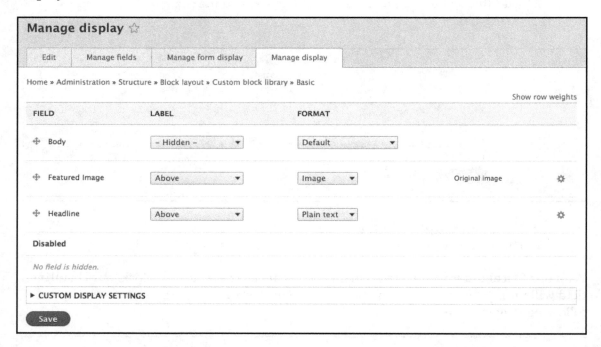

From the **Manage display** page, we can manage several display options ranging from hiding the label to configuring how the label will display. Each field's value can also be formatted using a Field Formatter. The format options vary based on the field type it is referring to. For example, our Body field can be displayed with the Default value, or can also be changed to display the content trimmed to a specific set of characters.

Currently our custom block's fields will print in the order they appear. In the same way that we reordered the form display, we can reorder our fields to print out the **Headline**, **Featured Image**, and **Body** by using the grab handles next to each field.

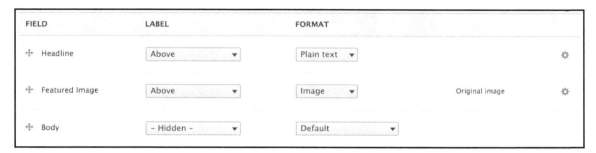

Our fields are now reordered and our changes saved. We can also prevent the labels of each field from being printed by changing the current label from **Above** to **Hidden** for the **Headline** and **Featured Image** fields.

- **Headline**
    - Select**Hidden** from the **LABEL** dropdown
- **Featured Image**
    - Select**Hidden** from the **LABEL** dropdown

Make sure to click the **Save** button these field's labels have been changed. To see our changes, we will need to first edit our custom block and fill in the additional fields, and then preview the changes on the homepage.

We can navigate back to our custom block by directly entering
`/admin/structure/block/block-content`, or by using the Admin toolbar and clicking
on **Structure | Block layout** and then selecting the **Custom block library tab**. Finally, we
can click on the edit link next to our block and add a **Headline**, **Featured Image**, and any
other modifications.

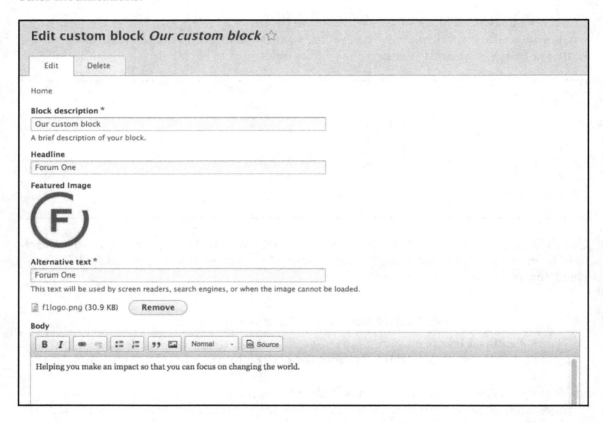

Once we have completed making our modifications, we can click on the **Save** button and then navigate to the homepage where we will see all our changes.

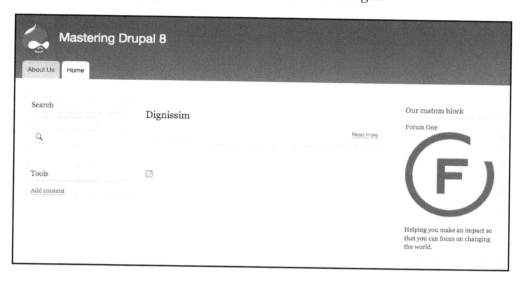

Using the Place block interface

With each iteration of Drupal 8, there is additional functionality being added to the core or added as experimental modules. At the time of writing this, there is a new experimental module that allows the placing of blocks directly on to a page, which reduces some of the need for navigating back and forth to the Block layout page. Interestingly, the new module is titled **Place blocks**. To demonstrate how this new functionality works, we will need to enable the module.

Extending Drupal will be discussed in more detail in Chapter 10, Extending Drupal but for now, just follow along as we walk through how to quickly enable a module.

Begin by navigating to the **Extend** page by directly entering `/admin/modules`, or by using the Admin toolbar and clicking on **Extend**.

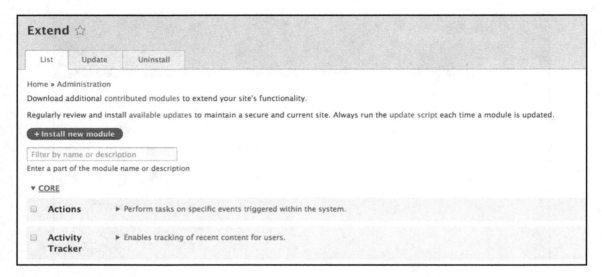

The **Extend** page lists all the modules that Drupal has access to using. Whether it is a core module or a contributed module, we can easily tell which module(s) are being used by the checkbox next to each module's name.

To enable the Place blocks module, we need to scroll down to the **CORE (EXPERIMENTAL)** section and click on the checkbox next to the **Place Blocks** module. Next, we need to click on the **Install** button and then the **Continue** button to complete the process.

We can now navigate back to the homepage by clicking on the **Back to site** link in the Admin toolbar. Once we are back on the homepage or any front-facing page, we will notice a new menu item on the Admin toolbar titled **Place block**.

If we click on the **Place block** menu item, the display of our page will expose all the Regions our theme has specified with the addition of a plus icon indicating that a block can be added to that region. We will choose the Header Region, which we can identify by hovering over the plus symbol in each region.

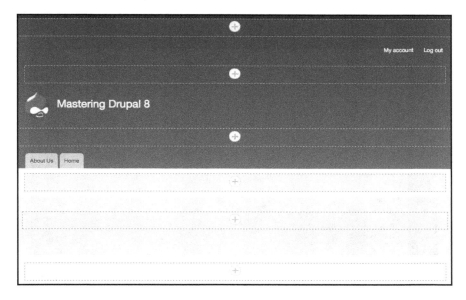

Clicking on the plus icon within any region will open the **Place block** dialog, which will allow us to add a custom block or choose from a list of existing blocks.

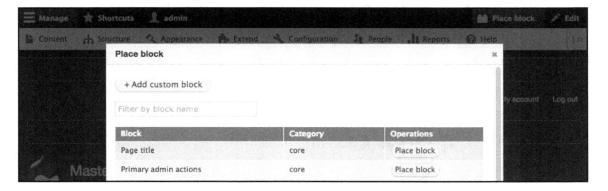

To add a block, simply choose a block from the list and click the **Place block** button. For demonstration purposes, we will select the **Search form** block. Once the block has been chosen, we will be presented with the **Configure block** dialog where we can finish configuring our block.

Finally, we can click on the **Save block** button, which will take us to the Block layout page and display the block added to the region we selected.

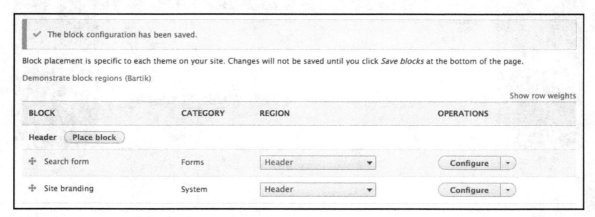

I would have expected that we would have been taken back to the homepage or the page that we initiated the placement from. However, given that the Place blocks module is still experimental, I assume that this workflow will change in the future.

Before closing, let's clean up our page by deleting any of the blocks we added earlier from the Block layout page.

Deleting Blocks from Block layout

This last step is quite simple. We can navigate to the Block layout page by directly entering the URL of `/admin/structure/block` or by using the Admin toolbar and clicking on **Structure** and then **Block layout**.

Deleting a block from the Block layout page does not actually delete the block completely, it only removes the block from displaying within a region. To delete the Search form block, Powered by Drupal 8, and our custom block, we need to click on the drop-down button next to each block and choose the **Delete** link.

We will be prompted to confirm the deletion. Click on the **Delete** button to complete the process.

Summary

Congratulations! You have mastered working with Blocks in Drupal 8. A considerable amount of thought goes into how to best develop a website and the use of blocks is no different. Whether we are using existing blocks or creating custom blocks, the process should now be familiar to that of working with content types.

To recap, we learned how to work with the core functionality of Drupal to perform the tasks included in the following list:

- We explored the Block layout page and demonstrated how Regions can have blocks assigned to them
- We worked with Block configuration, settings, and visibility to control how blocks appear on pages based on multiple configurations

- Not only did we look at system blocks, but we learned how to create custom blocks, add new fields, manage form display, and control which fields are displayed to the end user
- Finally, we used the new Place blocks module to speed up block placement and workflow

Next, we will be taking a closer look at content authoring, HTML5, and media to develop a more robust website while working with Drupal 8.

6
Content Authoring, HTML5, and Media

In this chapter, we will be diving into some of the great improvements that Drupal 8 has implemented, such as the introduction of better HTML5 support, which caused core maintainers to rethink how markup was being output by fields and templates. This resulted in allowing theme developers to control where to use semantic elements, support for ARIA roles to improve accessibility, simplified style and script elements, and the ability for input filters to accept HTML5 elements.

Also, the emphasis on responsive or a mobile first approach to how we use a content management system resulted in a whole rewrite of the theme system and the introduction of Twig. This rewrite included both the Bartik and Seven themes, which are now responsive and allow for content to flow based on the device we happen to be viewing Drupal 8 on.

Finally, the way site builders work with content was rethought to allow for a better content authoring experience with a built-in WYSIWYG editor, better image handling, and even quickly editing content on the fly.

To give us a better understanding of some of these new features, we will look at mastering the following:

- Responsive admin
- CKEditor and text formats
- Working with images
- Managing displays
- Using Better preview
- Custom display settings
- Image styles

Assumptions

Mastering Drupal 8 assumes that you are already running a local AMP stack and have a familiarity with installing Drupal using the standard means of downloading, setting up a database, configuring a localhost, and completing the browser based install. In `Chapter 1`, *Developer Workflow*, we walked through quickly installing Drupal using Composer, Drush, and Drupal Console. Please ensure that you have a working AMP stack and you are comfortable working within the command line interface using a terminal window before continuing.

Responsive admin

First off, Drupal 8 is *responsive* out of the box, meaning that the default Bartik theme, the Seven administration theme, and even the Admin toolbar scale and resize based on the device we are viewing our site on.

We can see this in action by logging in to our Drupal instance and then navigating to our homepage. If we begin to resize the browser window, eventually we will notice the orientation of the Admin toolbar change from a horizontal bar to a vertical bar:

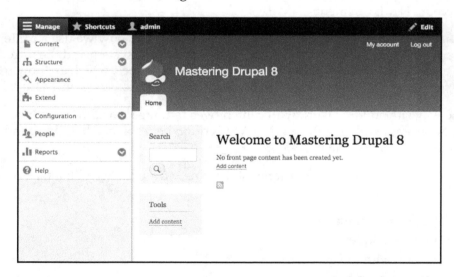

Once the Admin toolbar is at a vertical orientation, we can collapse it into the horizontal bar by clicking on the **Manage** link at the top left-hand side. This allows for more administration space on the screen.

Clicking on the **Manage** link again will re-open the toolbar to allow us to continue navigating to anywhere within Drupal.

By expanding the browser window back to a normal desktop orientation, the Admin toolbar will convert back to a horizontal orientation.

The Admin toolbar is not the only responsive change. If we navigate to `/node/add/page` or use the Admin toolbar and click on **Manage - Content**, and then click on the **Add content** link and then **Create Basic page,** we will be taken to the **Create Basic page** screen:

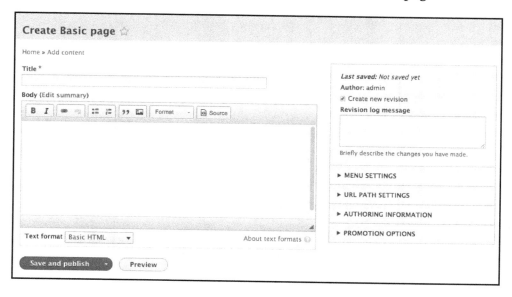

Notice the screen is divided into two columns:

- The first column allows for the entry of a **Title** and **Body**
- The second column contains configuration information such as revisions, menu settings, and more

If we resize the web browser back to a mobile orientation, we will notice that the two-column layout will change to a single column with fields ordered by level of importance. Again, this is providing us with a responsive content editing experience.

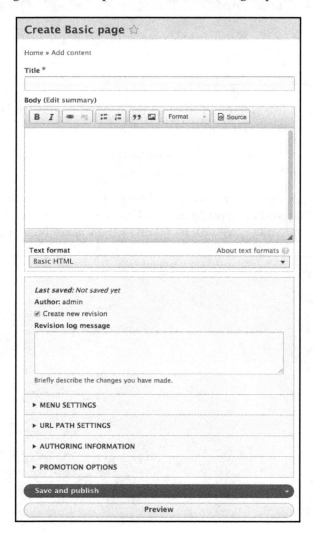

While we may never find ourselves managing Drupal from a mobile device, the fact that it is responsive by nature gives us peace of mind that it is possible to manage a Drupal instance on all mediums.

Something else that makes Drupal's content authoring experience easier to work with is the introduction of a *WYSIWYG* already configured for our use without the need to install and configure contributed modules to add this functionality. While there were a few options in earlier versions of Drupal to choose from, core maintainers finally settled on CKEditor as the default WYSIWYG.

CKEditor and text formats

The moment we begin to work with content types, specifically adding content, we notice that CKEditor is now available.

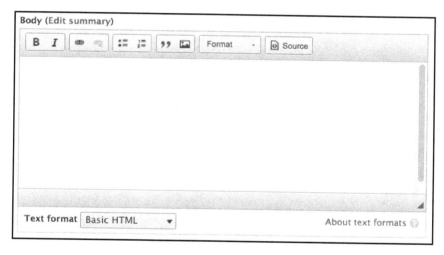

CKEditor comes configured by default with the Standard profile installation, including a few text formats for us to use.

If we navigate to `/admin/config/content/formats` or use the Admin toolbar and click on **Manage - Configuration** and then select **Text formats and editors,** we will be taken to the **Text formats and editors** admin screen:

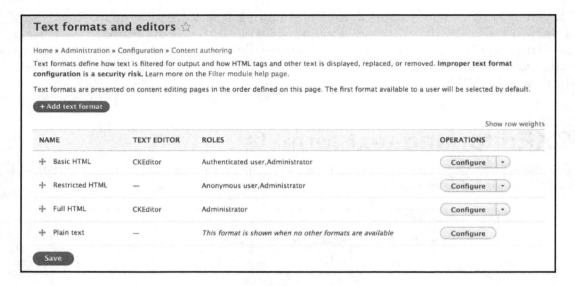

By default, Drupal has created and configured four different text formats for us to use:

- **Basic HTML**
- **Restricted HTML**
- **Full HTML**
- **Plain text**

Each format is configured differently, based on how we expect content to be managed. Based on the configuration, a content editor, site administrator, or authenticated user can perform various actions when adding content.

Based on the needs of our website, we can add additional text formats and configure them accordingly. However, to get a better understanding of how text formats work, let's take a closer look at the **Basic HTML** text format.

Begin by clicking on the **Configure** button next to the **Basic HTML** text format.

Text formats

Text formats are first configured by giving them a display **Name** that can be selected when creating formatted content or when adding text (formatted) fields to content types.

Each text format is also assigned **Roles** that have access to use one or more text formats.

Finally, each text format can choose to use a **Text editor**. By default, we can only choose **CKEditor**.

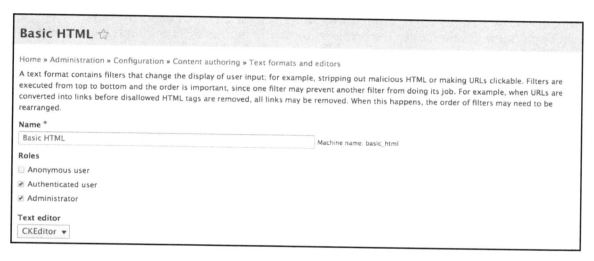

Toolbar configuration

When a text editor is chosen, we are given the option to configure CKEditor. As we can see, there are a multitude of **Available buttons** to select from that can be added to the **Active toolbar**. Buttons can be added by simply dragging them from one location to another.

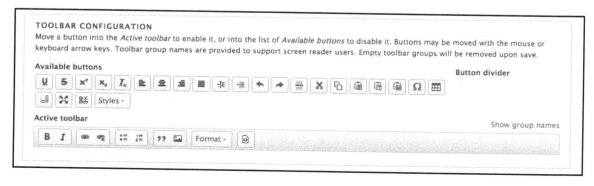

Hovering over each button will display a brief explanation of what action each button performs. It is up to site builders to determine which buttons make sense for users to have access to when creating content.

CKEditor plugin settings and filters

Some buttons provide additional plugin settings. For instance, the **Image** button provides us with additional configuration options that require us to specify an **Upload directory**, the **Maximum file size**, and **Maximum dimensions** for images when they are added. These additional settings allow us to restrict users to ensure images meet certain requirements.

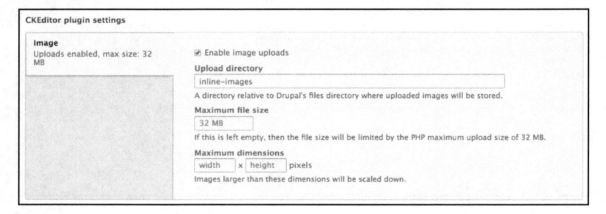

Following to the plugin settings are additional filters that can be enabled.

Enabled filters

Each filter controls how HTML markup will be saved and output when a user begins creating content that uses the text format filter.

Enabled filters

☑ Limit allowed HTML tags and correct faulty HTML

☐ Display any HTML as plain text

☐ Convert line breaks into HTML (i.e. `<br>` and `<p>`)

☐ Convert URLs into links

☑ Align images

    Uses a `data-align` attribute on `<img>` tags to align images.

☑ Caption images

    Uses a `data-caption` attribute on `<img>` tags to caption images.

☑ Restrict images to this site

    Disallows usage of `<img>` tag sources that are not hosted on this site by replacing them with a placeholder image.

☐ Correct faulty and chopped off HTML

☑ Track images uploaded via a Text Editor

    Ensures that the latest versions of images uploaded via a Text Editor are displayed.

Depending on how we choose to configure each text format, we can select different filters to enable. For example, the **Basic HTML - Text format** uses the **Limit allowed HTML tags and correct faulty HTML** filter, while the **Plain text - Text format** only uses the **Display any HTML as plain text** filter.

Depending on how restrictive or how loosely we want to control HTML will determine which filters we enable.

Filter processing order

Whenever multiple filters are enabled, the order in which a filter is called can have different impacts on the content. For this reason, we can reorder filters by dragging each one into the order needed.

Filter processing order

          Show row weights

✛   Limit allowed HTML tags and correct faulty HTML

✛   Align images

✛   Caption images

✛   Restrict images to this site

✛   Track images uploaded via a Text Editor

Also, keep in mind that some contributed modules add additional CKEditor plugins and filters. We may need to specify a specific order that is needed for that module to function properly. It is important to always look at the README file that contributed modules provide to determine if that step is needed.

Filter settings

Some CKEditor plugins provide additional filter settings. In the case of **Limit allowed HTML tags and correct faulty HTML,** we are provided with a list of the **Allowed HTML tags**. Anything that is not present in the list will be stripped out by the WYSIWYG when a user saves their content.

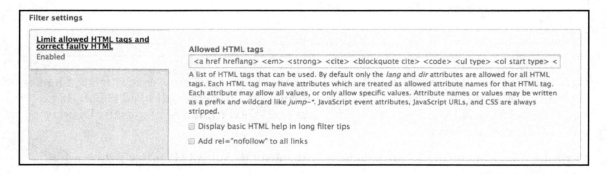

Sometimes we may need to modify this list. A perfect example is an anchor tag that generally needs to have a title attribute or a target attribute added to it. If we do not modify the **Allowed HTML tags** to accept these two attributes, then users may be confused if they choose to add these to a link and they do not work, since the filter would strip the attributes out.

We can easily add additional attributes for a link element by modifying the following:

```
<a href hreflang>
```

to be

```
<a href hreflang title target>
```

Now if we click on the **Save configuration** button, anytime a user needs to add those attributes to an anchor link they will function properly.

Working with images

Images play a vital part of any website build and Drupal 8 provides multiple ways of managing them. The first we will look at involves using CKEditor and the WYSIWYG.

When we looked at how text formats were configured you may have noticed the Image button in the Available toolbar. This Image plugin allows for us to easily add images to content as well as control alignment and captions. To demonstrate this, we will create a Basic page by performing the following steps:

1. Begin by navigating to `/node/add/page` or by using the Admin toolbar and clicking on **Manage - Content**, and then **Add content**, and finally **Basic page.**
2. From the **Create Basic page** form, go ahead and enter a **Title** for `Contact Us`.
3. Next we will add an image to the **Body** field by selecting the **Image** button from the WYSIWYG toolbar.

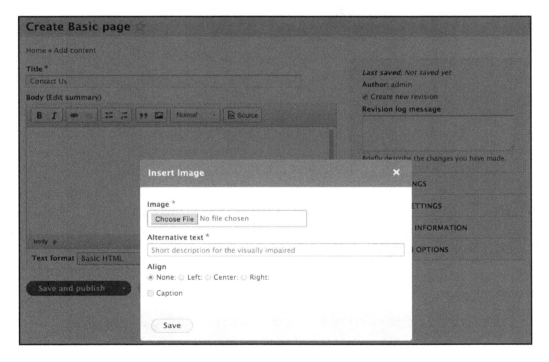

4. From the **Insert Image** dialog, we can select the **Choose File** button to add an image from our computer.
5. Next we can add **Alternative text**. We will skip the **Align** and **Caption** settings for now.

6. Select the **Save** button to complete adding our image.

7. Click on the **Save and publish** button to create the page. While the process of adding an image is simple, we generally have additional content that needs to flow around it.

Image alignment

Since our WYSIWYG is using the Basic HTML filter, the Image button is configured to allow for the **data-align** attribute to be added to `<img>` tags.

This allows us to choose how an image is aligned on the page. We can align images left, right, center, or accept the default location. To demonstrate this, follow these steps:

1. Select the **Edit** tab to take us back to the edit form and then place the cursor within the WYSIWYG directly after the image and add some additional text.

2. Next, open the **Edit Image** dialog by double-clicking on the image.

3. Based on how we want text to flow on our page, we can choose to select the **Left** Align option to have the image float left with text displaying to the right of the image.

4. If we place text before the image and choose to **Right** Align our image, then our image would float to the right with text displaying to the left of the image.

5. Feel free to choose your preferred alignment and then select the **Save** button.

Image captions

Sometimes we may want to provide additional information to complement an image, maybe a photo credit or a lengthier description that provides more context for the image. We can achieve this by enabling the **Caption** option when adding an image. To do that, let's perform the following steps:

1. Open the **Edit Image** dialog again by double-clicking on the image.

2. Select the **Caption** checkbox and then click on the **Save** button.

3. We can now see our image, along with a placeholder for our caption entitled **Enter caption here**. If we place our cursor within the caption field, we can continue adding our caption.
4. Once complete, we can select the **Save and publish** button and **View** our new page.

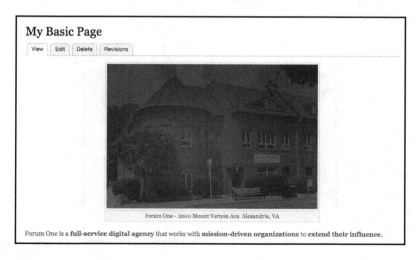

Adding images, aligning images, and adding image captions is a simple task using CKEditor. While we can use the WYSIWYG to add content and format it accordingly, we may find instances where we want to have a little more control over how content is displayed.

Managing displays

In instances where we want to feature an image or we know the same content may be used in multiple ways, it makes sense to have more structured content. The Post content type we added back in `Chapter 4`, *Content Types, Taxonomy, and Comment Types* is a perfect example. Let's perform the following steps to do that:

1. Begin by navigating to `/admin/content` or use the Admin toolbar and click on **Manage - Content** and then select our **Post One** page.

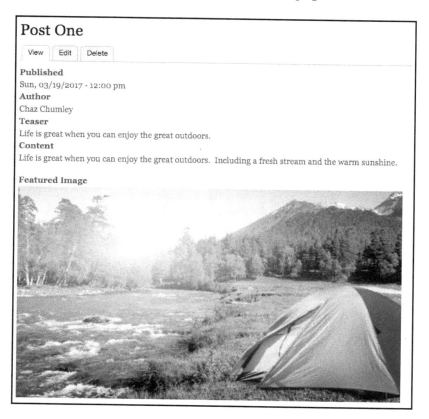

2. Currently the default display of our content is presented, exposing all our fields, including their labels. Being able to manage the display on a per content type basis allows us to suppress what fields are shown, re-order how fields appear, and control how labels are displayed. So how do we manage these different displays and their fields within Drupal?

3. Open a new tab in the browser and navigate to `/admin/structure/types/manage/post/display`, or use the Admin toolbar, select **Manage -Structure-Content types**, and then choose **Manage display** from the drop-down button next to the Post content type.

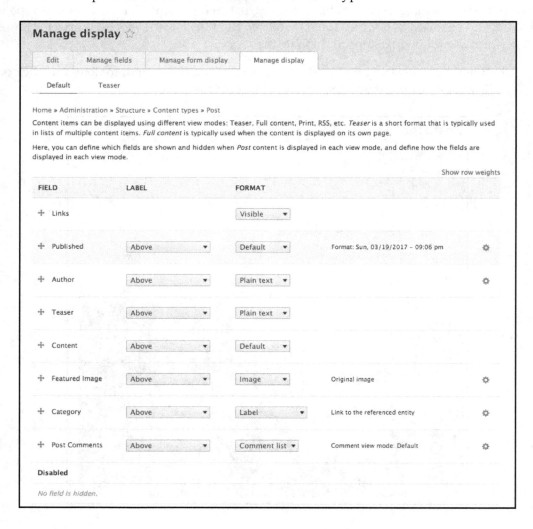

Drupal allows us to control how content is displayed using the **Manage display** page. Sometimes referred to as View modes or Display modes, all content types have two displays enabled for initial use:

- **Default** display
- **Teaser** display

While we can add additional custom display settings, the **Default** display is explicitly set for us. To demonstrate the flexibility of managing fields, we will start with reordering which fields are shown and the order they are shown in.

Reordering fields

Most users when they view a blog post expect to see the title followed by a Featured Image, the Author, any tags, and then the content. We can quickly fix our Post by reordering the fields accordingly:

- Enabled fields in the order they will appear:
    - **Featured Image**
    - **Author**
    - **Published**
    - **Category**
    - **Content**
- **Disabled** fields:
    - **Post Comments**
    - **Teaser**
    - **Links**

The result should look like the following:

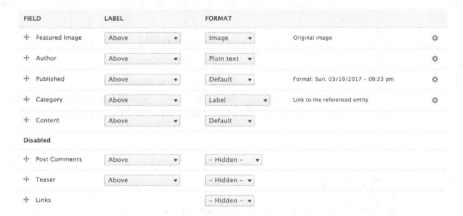

Make sure to click the **Save** button and then switch back to the **Post One** page and refresh the page to see our changes.

It's starting to look a little better. Now it's time for us to control how the labels are being displayed. Tab back over to the **Manage display** page and let's look at the labels.

Controlling labels

When working with labels, we can either hide labels altogether or have them appear **Inline** or **Above** the field they belong to. Let's modify our labels per the following image:

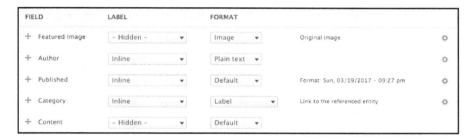

Do not forget to click the **Save** button and then switch back to our **Post One**, refresh the browser, and review the changes.

It's starting to look better. However, it would be nice to have our **Published** date formatted differently. We can easily make this change using Field Formatters. Tab back to the **Manage display** page and let's begin.

Using Field Formatters

Every field has a specific format that is used by Drupal to display the field. Depending on the type of field, the format will differ. Often we can select from one or more formats to use and some formats have additional settings that can be configured. In the case of our **Published** field, we can modify it to display a different date format.

Formatting a date field

To modify the date format of our **Published** field, we have multiple options:

- A custom format that allows for us to specify a PHP date string
- A plain format that displays the year, month, and day
- A time ago format that will display the time in hours and minutes from the current date time
- A default format that will give us the default medium date that we configured on the Regional Date and Time formats page

For demonstration, we will choose to leave the default format but adjust the configuration of the formatter by selecting the gear icon to the right of the field, which will expose more options.

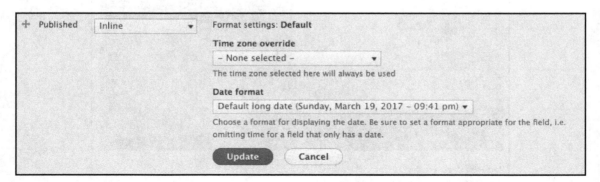

Select the default long date from the **Date format** dropdown and then select the **Update** button to save the change. Feel free to review the changes on the **Post** page.

By now we are getting better at managing the display of fields and we are starting to see just how powerful structured content is for site builders.

Managing the Teaser display

Whenever we want to display a snippet of content, we generally do not want to display all the fields. We can utilize the **Teaser** display to manage the fields by switching displays.

Take a moment and adjust the fields for the **Teaser** display to look like the following:

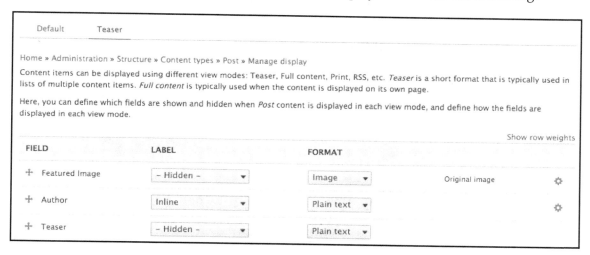

Make sure to click the **Save** button at the bottom of the **Manage display** page.

You may be asking how do I review the changes for the **Teaser** display without creating another page to reference my Post, or by having to create a view that uses the new display? The answer is simple. To preview our changes, we can use the Better preview option.

Using Better preview

Any content type that has been configured to allow previews can use the new Better preview option. We can demonstrate this by performing the following steps:

1. Navigate to our **Post One** page and selecting the **Edit** tab, which will take us to the Edit form page.
2. Next we need to click on the **Preview** button at the bottom of the page.

3. We will now be in Better preview mode and should notice a new navigation bar at the top of our page. The preview bar allows us to switch the **View mode** that is currently being presented.

4. Select the **Teaser** in the **View mode** and we will see our changes.

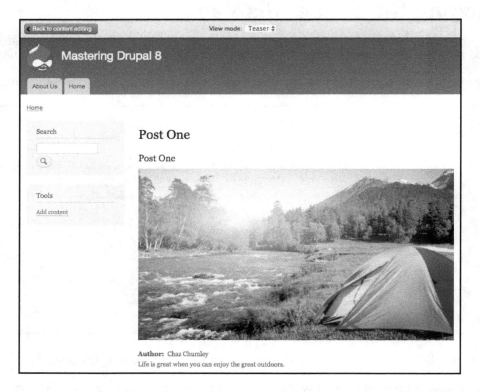

5. Until we begin theming a site or have additional ways to manage content, the Better preview option will come in quite handy. At any time, we can also click on the **Back to content editing** button to switch back to our Edit form.

Custom Display settings

While we have only been working with the **Default** and **Teaser** displays, we are not limited to these two View modes. We have the flexibility to choose additional View modes that best fit our site building needs.

If we tab back to the **Manage display** page and click on the **Default** display link, we can locate the **Custom Display Settings** section at the bottom of the page. Expand the section and we will see additional View modes that can be enabled.

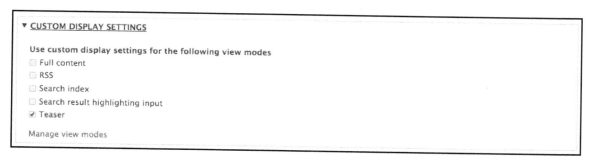

We also have the option of creating new modes that will appear in these options by clicking on the **Manage view modes** link.

If we look at the **View modes** page, we will notice that it is broken into sections based on **Content, Custom block, Comment, Taxonomy term**, and **User**. Since these are all considered entities, they can have **View modes** for presenting their content.

Adding a view mode

To add a new view mode, we only need to have an idea of what we want to call the new display. It is important to be semantic when creating a new view mode so that it makes sense to the site builder when they choose to use it later.

For demonstration purposes, we will create a new view mode for handling a card layout that we will be using in Chapter 9, *Working with Twig*. Let's go through the following steps to create it:

1. Click on the **Add view mode** button.

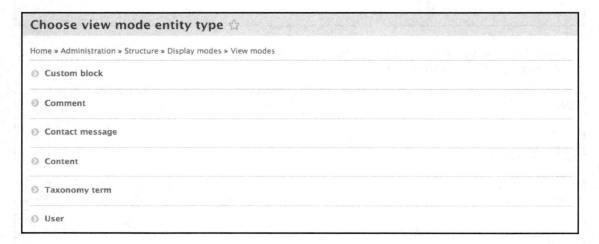

2. Choose **Content** from the **Choose a view mode entity type** page.

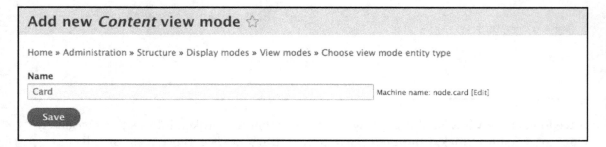

3. Enter the name of Card on the **Add new Content view mode** page.
4. Click on the **Save** button.

5. We now have a new view mode that can be used by all content types and if we tab back to the **Manage display** page and refresh the page, we will see the new view mode available.

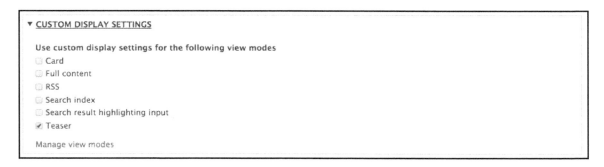

6. Select **Card** from the **Use custom display settings for the following view modes** and then click on the **Save** button to enable the new view mode.

We will return to the new **Card** display later when we explore theming content in Drupal 8.

Image styles

While we were reviewing the Teaser View mode, you probably noticed that the **Featured Image** is quite large. It would be nice if we could change the size of our image to be smaller, but how do we do that?

Drupal provides the ability to create image derivatives or image styles of any image uploaded and used for display. This feature provides us the option of selecting various image styles on the Manage display page. We can also configure additional image styles as needed.

If we tab back to the **Manage display** page, we can see that the Teaser display is currently using the **Original image**.

If we click on the Field Formatter for the **Featured Image**, we can configure our image to use one of the predefined image styles by selecting it from the drop-down list.

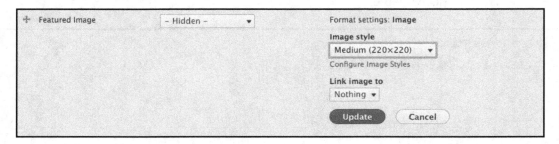

Choose the **Medium (220x220)** from **Image style**, select the **Update** button, and then the **Save** button. Now if we preview the Teaser View mode of our Post, we will see the new Image style being used.

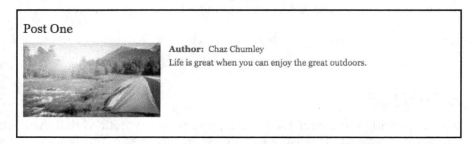

Now that is a much better looking Teaser. Image styles come in handy but where do these predefined image styles come from?

Configuring image styles

We can review the pre-configured image styles installed by Drupal by navigating to `/admin/config/media/image-styles` or by using the Admin toolbar and selecting **Manage - Configuration** and then **Image styles**.

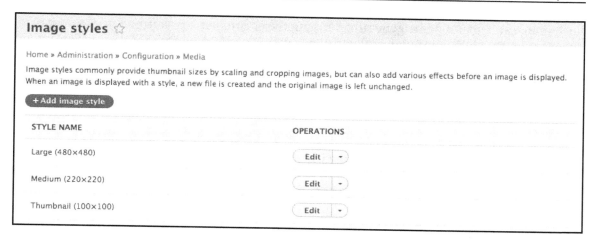

By default, Drupal provides us with **Large**, **Medium**, and **Thumbnail** image styles that will be generated when an image has been uploaded and displayed on a page. If we click on the **Edit** button next to the **Large** image style, we will see how it is configured.

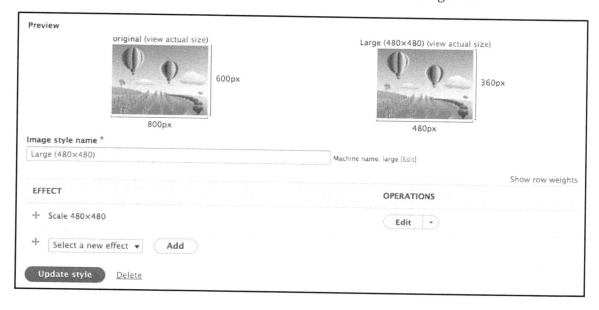

Each image style has a name generally defining the action being performed. In the case of our large image style, it is being scaled to 480 x 480. We can also see what the original image looks like and what the resized image will look like as well. However, there are multiple effects that can be performed on an image:

- **Convert**: Converts an image between extensions (for example, from PNG to JPEG)
- **Crop:** Resizes an image to an exact set of dimensions
- **Desaturate:** Changes an image from color to black and white
- **Resize**: This is the same as **Crop** but without the option to choose the cropping point
- **Rotate**: Rotates an image by selecting the number of degrees
- **Scale**: Resizes an image while maintaining the original aspect ratio
- **Scale and Crop**: Resizes an image, maintaining the original aspect ratio, and then crops based on the width and height

It is worth taking the time to play around with each of the settings to determine how you may want to manage images. Additional effects can be added by using contributed modules.

Adding image styles

New image styles can be added at any time. All that is needed is the name of the new image style and the effect we want to perform. For demonstration purposes, we will create a new image style called `Black and White` and add the **Desaturate** effect to it. Let's do it by preforming the following steps:

1. From the **Image styles** page, click on the **Add image style** button.

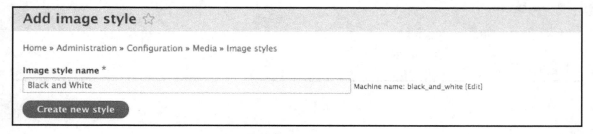

2. Input the **Image style name** as `Black and White`.

3. Choose the **Desaturate** option from the **EFFECT** dropdown and click on the **Add** button:

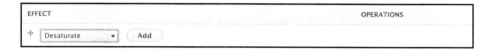

4. Our new image style is now created and can be applied to any image field.

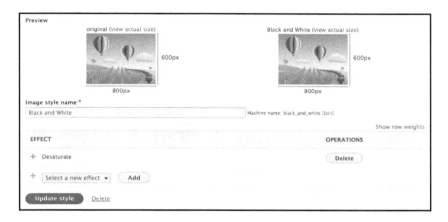

Quick edit

Before we wrap up this lesson, let's talk about the new Quick edit functionality that Drupal 8 introduced. As we have experienced, jumping back and forth between the display and the node add/edit form for content can sometimes be cumbersome and time consuming.

We now have the option of quickly editing a page by using the Quick edit link that is part of the contextual links. In fact, we have already used contextual links when we worked with blocks. The following are the steps to change to the title within the page:

1. If we navigate to our **Post One** page and hover over the content, we will be presented with a pencil icon indicating that we can edit the content directly by selecting the **Quick edit** link:

2. Select the **Quick edit** link and you will notice that each block of content highlighted in blue can be directly edited.

3. Go ahead and try this now by clicking within the title of the page and changing it. For demonstration purposes, I will change the title of **Post One** to `Camping in the Wilderness`.

4. Once the title has been changed, click on the **Save** button to complete the process.

Now that is much quicker to change content when you have a small change and are in a hurry.

Summary

We covered a lot of information in this chapter by looking at the content authoring experience in Drupal 8. Starting with exploring the new responsive admin, we learned that we could easily manage content on mobile devices with responsive themes and the Admin toolbar.

Next we looked at how CKEditor has made working with content in the WYSIWYG a lot more flexible. This includes creating text formats and configuring the available toolbar. Images are easier to add and allow for the addition of alignment and captions.

We also dove into how to manage displays for presenting structured content. From the Default display to the Teaser display, we learned how to reorder fields, control labels, and work with Field Formatters. The addition of custom display settings provides us with a robust mechanism for creating additional displays.

Image styles allow for creating various image derivatives that can have multiple effects applied to them. This allows us to reuse the same image for different displays including the Teaser View mode.

Finally, we looked at the Quick edit functionality to help speed up the editing of content when it comes to simple changes.

In the next chapter, we will explore working with Views and discuss how to easily aggregate content that can be used with multiple displays to list content.

7
Understanding Views

One of the most important contributed modules in previous versions of Drupal was **Views**. It allowed administrators to easily configure lists of content and present them in a variety of different ways. In Drupal 8, Views has been added to the core. Not only does this ensure that this critical functionality is available out of the box, but all core listings of content, including the content administration page, user administration page, and vocabulary and term listing pages, have been converted over to using Views. This allows for a consistent set of tools across all parts of Drupal, as well as a simplified means of changing them to meet your needs. In this chapter, we will be covering:

- Creating a basic list of content.
- Placing your View on either a page or a block
- Adding filtering and sorting to your View
- Changing the formatting of the row
- Adding relationships and contextual filters
- Using query aggregation

Customized lists of contents

When we first install Drupal, it provides us with an initial View for the homepage that lists all content in reverse chronological order. In most cases, this is not sufficient to expose all the content on a site, so we will end up creating several other Views.

Let's begin by creating a basic list of articles.

Start by navigating to `/admin/structure/views/add` or by selecting **Structure-Views** from the Admin toolbar and then clicking the button labeled **Add new view**.

The most common use case is to have a View that outputs content, that is, nodes, of a particular type. However, you can create Views on any type of entity or other table that is exposed to Views. This includes users and taxonomy terms, but also files, comments, blocks, node revisions, and log entries.

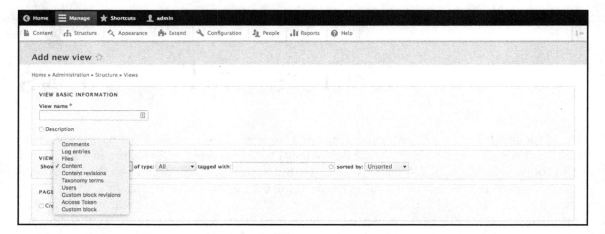

We are going to start with a basic View of contents showing a list of articles. Enter the machine name of articles and select a content type of **Article**, and then click the button labeled **Save and edit**.

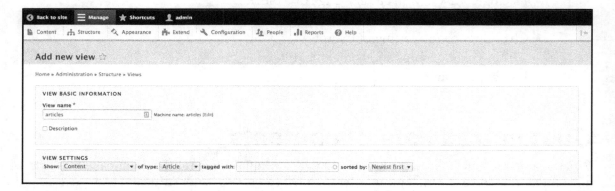

You will then be sent to the View edit page for the new View. This shows the full breadth of options for altering a View:

It also shows a preview showing the results of the View and the timings for the View:

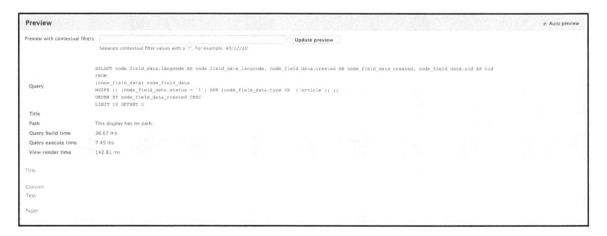

To see the actual SQL generated for the View, you will need to go **Structure | Views** and then click on the **Settings** tab (`admin/structure/views/settings`). From there, select the checkbox labeled **Show the SQL query** and click the **Save Configuration** button.

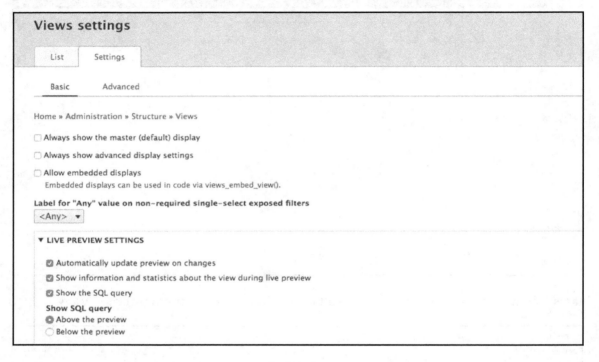

View Settings form

View displays

The initial View we created contains just the Master Display. The **Master Display** provides the initial configuration for the View. Additional displays can be added, which can alter some or all of the View configuration. There are different types of displays that can be placed in different contexts. A number of display types come with Drupal 8 core, including:

- **Attachment**: An **attachment display** is one that can be placed before or after another View. This allows the attached View to use the inputs as the View it is attached, to including pager, arguments, and exposed filters.
- **Block**: A **Block Display** is one that can be placed using the **Drupal block interface**. This means it can be placed in regions based on pages, content types, user roles, and so on.

- **Embed**: An **embedded view** is one that can be displayed from a **Twig template** using the `views_embed_view` function. To allow embedded displays, we would need to enable the setting from the **View settings** page, as shown in the following screenshot:

Views settings

- **Entity reference**: An **entity reference display** allows you to customize the method of selection and display of an entity reference field. You can use this to display fields beyond just the title, restrict the list to a sub-set of entities, change the sort order, and so on.
- **Feed**: A **Feed Display** is one that outputs a View in a format such as RSS or OPML that can be consumed.
- **Page**: A **Page Display** creates a standalone URI that our results can be displayed on. Views adds a **menu router** and optionally a **menu link** so that it can be placed within the menu structure.
- **REST export**: A **REST export display** is one that outputs the content of the View formatted, as either JSON or XML, that can also be consumed by another application.

Creating view pages and blocks

We can create a new page display by selecting the **Add button** from the **Displays** screen and then selecting **Page*** from the list.

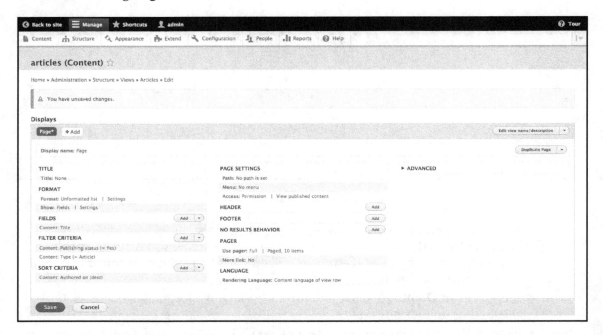

Most settings will be the same as the initial Master Display you initially created. The new configuration is around how a user will be able to get to the View. There will be a new section labeled **PAGE SETTINGS** where we will see options for **Path** and **Menu**.

- **Path** is the URL that a user can place within their browser to navigate to the View page.
- **Menu** is where the new path will be attached to., such as the main menu of our site.

Path is required, so we will need to click on the link that reads **No path is set** and enter a new path in the dialog that opens. The path should be entered without a leading slash, for example it should be like `articles` and not `/articles`.

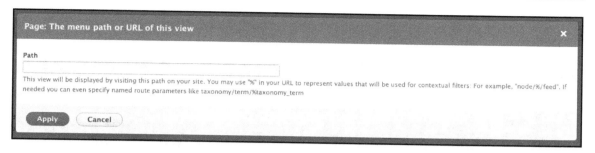

You can optionally add a menu link to our page. Clicking on the link that reads **No menu entry** will bring up a dialog where we can add one of a few different types of menu links:

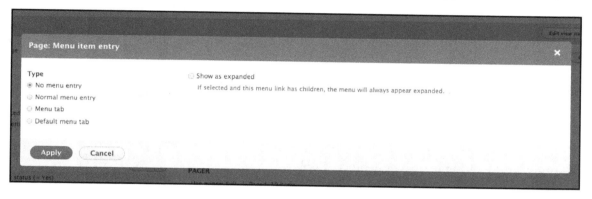

Menu link dialog

- **Normal menu entry**: The most common selection is Normal menu entry which adds a link within the selected menu tree. This allows us to place the View page within a menu structure, have it highlight the menu items that are the ancestors in the tree, as well as provide the correct Breadcrumbs.
- **Menu tab**: This shows as a tab on another page like how the View, Edit, and Delete tabs show on a node detail page.
- **Default menu tab**: If the View is intended to be the initial option selected when the user visits the page, like how the View tab is the default option when the user visits the node page, we would select **Default menu tab**.

For our example, we will select **Normal menu entry** and then give it a **Menu link title** of Articles. Click **Apply** and then **Save** for the View.

If we then navigate to the home page we will see a new link within the primary navigation for **Articles** that will display our View.

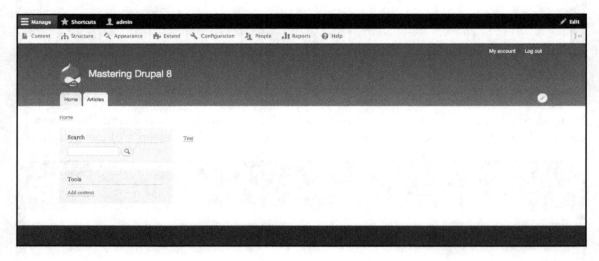

View Page

If you wanted to create a View that can be displayed on an existing page, the home page for example, you would create a new block display.

Block display

Begin by navigating back to our **View** and then selecting the **Add button** and choosing **Block*** from the list.

Block display configuration

Just like the earlier **Page Display**, we will see configurations specific to the block under **Block settings**. These include the **Block name**, **Block category**, and **Allow settings**. If we do not provide a different name for our block, it will use the name of the View within the **Block configuration settings**. We can also allow users who place block displays on a given page to specify the number of items per page to display. Once you have completed this step, click the **Save** button to persist all of your settings.

To place the **View** block on a page, we can navigate to `/admin/structure/block` or use the Admin toolbar and select **Structure - Block layout**. Clicking the **Place block** button next to the **Content** region will open a dialog where we can locate our **Block Display**.

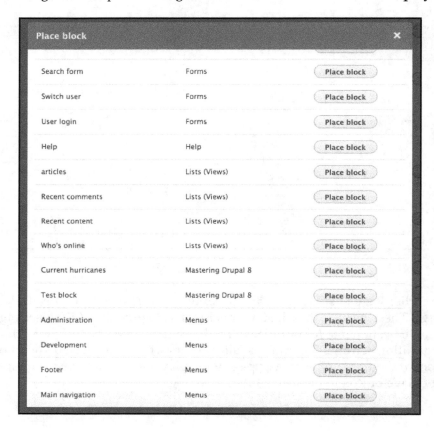

Click the **Place block** button next to articles. On the **Configure block** screen, we can see where we can select the number of **Items per block**.

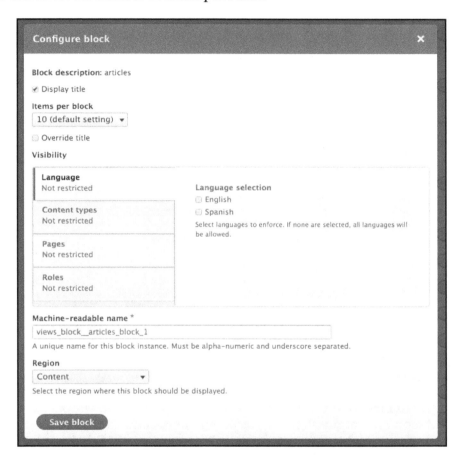

Block configuration dialog

Working with filter criteria and sorting

A View filter restricts the entities displayed by the View to only those matching a specified criterion. When we created our initial View, and selected the type of content to view we started with filters for the **Content type** and **publication status**.

If we navigate back to our **View** and click on the **Add button** next to **Add Filter criteria** we will be presented with a dialog where we can add additional filters.

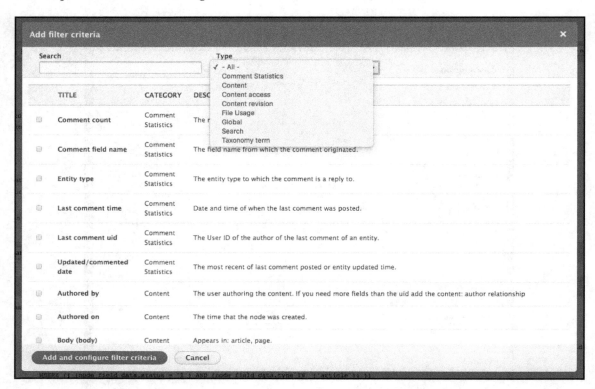

There are a great number of filters that can be applied to content. In Drupal 8 core, we can add filters based on content revisions, access permissions, comments, taxonomies, and any fields or attributes attached to the content itself. Different types of field have different parameters that may be applied to them.

For instance, if we wanted to show a list of Articles that had been created or updated within the last week we would select **Changed** from the list of options and click **Add and configure filter criteria**.

Since that field is a date, we can provide several operators to use, as well as the date or date ranges to compare against. To get only the last seven days, we would select I**s greater than or equal to** as the operator and -7 days for the **Value**.

Clicking **Apply (this display)** adds it to the set of filters for the Display.

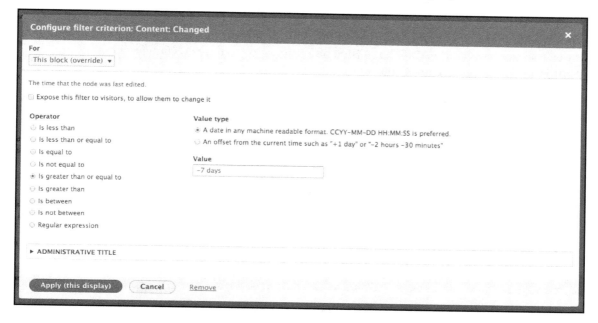

Rearrange filter criteria dialog

If we are on any Display other than the Master Display, we will see a drop-down box labeled **For**. This allows us to specify whether this new filter will apply to all Displays or only for the specific display we are altering. If we select that the filter applies to only the current Display, it will not be added to any other Display.

When editing the Master Display, all changes are applied to all Displays that have not been overridden. If we want to remove Display customizations we can open the drop-down next to Filter criteria and select **And/Or Rearrange**. This will open a dialog where we can alter the order in which the filters are applied, apply the filters in groups, as well as revert the Display to the default values. Selecting **Revert to default** from the **For** drop-down will change the button title to **Revert to default**. Clicking this will discard any customizations specific to the current Display and set it to match the Master Display.

Rearrange filter criteria

In addition to adding new filter criteria, we can create groups of them. By default, all filter criteria added are in a single group with the AND operator. So, the View will find any nodes that are published AND have the content type of **Article** AND were created or modified within the last seven days.

Settings dialog for Sticky at top of lists

If we wanted to change this to allow administrators to also mark nodes as Sticky at the top of lists and have them also show up in the View, regardless of when they were published, we would not be able to simply add that as an additional filter.

Adding that filter is the same process as before: click the **Add** button, find **Sticky at top of lists** and select its checkbox, click **Apply (all displays),** and select **Yes** for **Sticky status**.

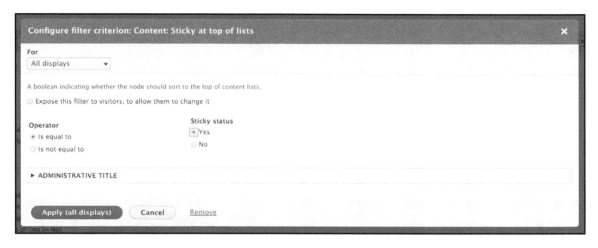

New filter group

Of course, right now this shows no results since we don't have any Articles that were changed recently or marked as Sticky. To get the filter criteria in the correct order we need to open the **And/Or Rearrange** dialog. On that dialog, click the **Create new filter group** link, which will add a new area with the text **No filters have been added. Drag to add filters.**

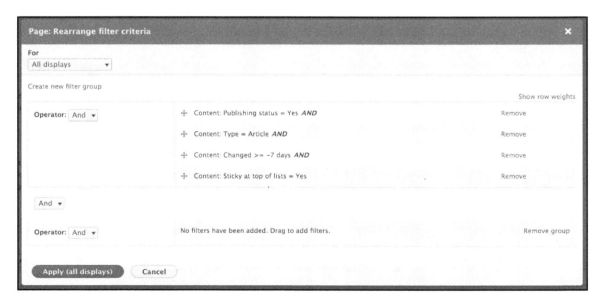

Adjusting filter grouping

From there, we want to drag the **Content: Sticky at top of lists = Yes** and the **Content: Changed >= -7 days** rows down to the new filter group, select **Or** for **Operator** and then click **Apply (all displays)**. Alternatively, you can click the **Show row weights** link and select **Group 2** instead of **Default group**.

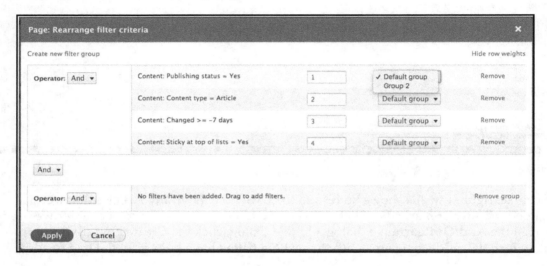

New filter group

Once you've changed the filter criteria, click the **Apply (all displays)** button to save the configuration for the View.

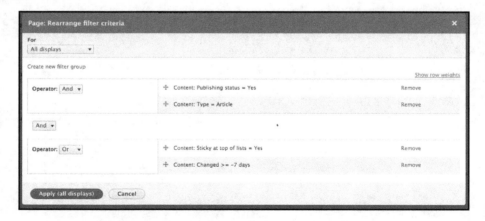

Adjusting filter grouping

Expose filters

Any filter can also be exposed to the user to allow them to select values. If you select the checkbox labeled **Expose this filter to visitors, to allow them to change it**, it adds a form element to the top of the view. The label for the field, whether it accepts multiple values, and the query parameter name are all things that can be configured.

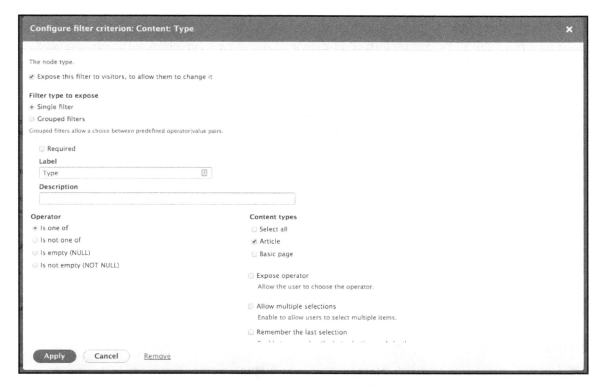

Exposed filter configuration dialog

Formatting rows

Creating your first View through the wizard starts with outputting the title of the node. There are a great number of options available to customize the output of each element loaded by the View.

Row styling

Each row from the View can be output in different ways. You can change the output type by clicking on the link next to the label for **Show**, showing the currently selected row format.

Row styling options dialog

Fields

The initial row styling from the View wizard is to display **fields**. These fields are either fields on the entity or aggregates or meta-fields defined by different modules. A View created by the wizard starts with the field for **Content: Title**. Additional fields can be added by clicking on the link for **Add** next to the section title for **Fields**. Many of the options are the same as shown in the dialog for filtering a View:

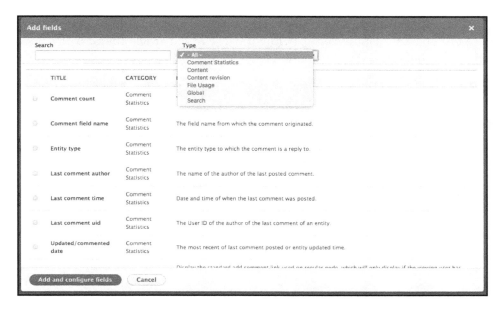

Add new field dialog

Imagine that, for our current list of articles, we want to display the author of the node as well. We can enter the term `author` in the search screen to find appropriate fields. There are a number of fields that show up. In this case we'll select the username of the author of the current node revision.

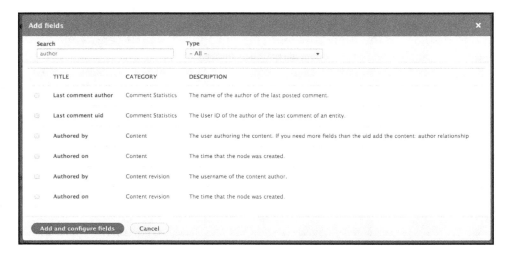

Author fields available

Clicking the button to **Add and configure fields** and then the button for **Apply** will add that field to our current display. Now, below the title of the article found by the view, the name of the user that created or last edited it appears.

The order that the fields are listed in the View configuration determines the order they are output and adding a new field will place it at the end of the list. To change the order, open the drop-down next to the **Fields** and click **Rearrange**. From the dialog that appears we can drag the fields into the desired order. This dialog also allows us to remove fields from the display by clicking the **Remove** link next to the field:

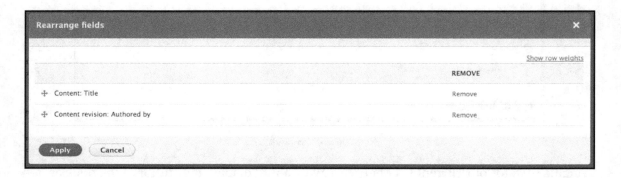

Rearrange field dialog

Content

In addition to displaying the View row by field, you should also use entity view modes. This is useful to ensure consistency between Views and other displays of the entity. In order to enable this, select **Content** from the radio buttons for row style and click **Apply**. From there, you can select the view mode for the node. Select **Teaser** from this list to show each row using the Teaser view mode.

View Mode dialoug

```
Content
Test
Submitted by admin on Sun, 03/20/2016 – 23:24
test
Read more Add new comment
```

Teaser view mode for article

Field formatting

Each field output by the View can be customized in a number of ways. You can also define whether and how a label is shown and whether to display the field at all:

- **Formatter**: Each field in the View can have a formatter selected and customized. These formatters vary depending on the type of field. For instance, a field that references another type of entity can be displayed as the rendered entity, the entity ID, the entity label, or the author of the entity. The options are the same as those available when defining the formatter for a field in the entity display settings.

- **Style settings**: The **STYLE SETTINGS** section allows you customize the label and wrapper around the field value. You can wrap the value in a specified HTML element and add CSS classes to it, as well as add a label and customize the HTML element and add CSS classes. By default, the value and label are wrapped in a `<div>` with a class based on the name of the field. This can be disabled by unselecting the checkbox labeled **Add default classes**. You can add additional classes to the value element based on the name and type of the field by selecting the checkbox labeled **Use field template**.

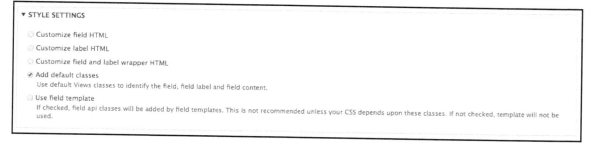

Style settings for field

- **Rewrite results:** The **REWRITE RESULTS** section allows you to set rules on how to alter the content of the field before rendering it. This includes replacing it with static text or HTML, wrapping it in a link, removing whitespace or HTML, and converting new lines to line breaks. When rewriting the value of the field, you can use the value from other fields. You can also use Twig syntax when replacing the field value to completely customize it.

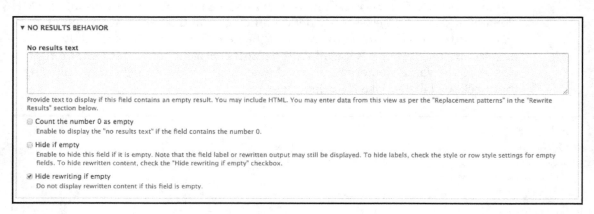

Rewrite results for field

- **No results behavior:** The **NO RESULTS BEHAVIOR** section allows you to configure how the field should be rendered when it is empty. You can provide text or HTML, or simply hide the field in its entirety. By default, an empty field disables field rewriting.

▼ NO RESULTS BEHAVIOR

No results text

Provide text to display if this field contains an empty result. You may include HTML. You may enter data from this view as per the "Replacement patterns" in the "Rewrite Results" section below.

☐ Count the number 0 as empty
Enable to display the "no results text" if the field contains the number 0.

☐ Hide if empty
Enable to hide this field if it is empty. Note that the field label or rewritten output may still be displayed. To hide labels, check the style or row style settings for empty fields. To hide rewritten content, check the "Hide rewriting if empty" checkbox.

☑ Hide rewriting if empty
Do not display rewritten content if this field is empty.

No results behavior for field

View formats

There are a number of options on how to present the rows loaded by the View. Each View format has a different set of options available and provides a very different output. You can change the format for the View by clicking on the link next to the label for **Format** showing the currently selected format:

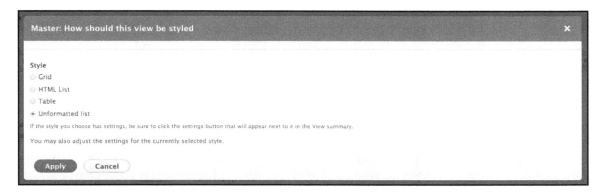

View format options dialog

Unformatted list

The default option is to display them as an **Unformatted list** that is wrapped in a `<div>` element. Clicking on the link for **Settings** next to **Format** shows a dialog with options to set the classes on each `div`, as well as how to group results:

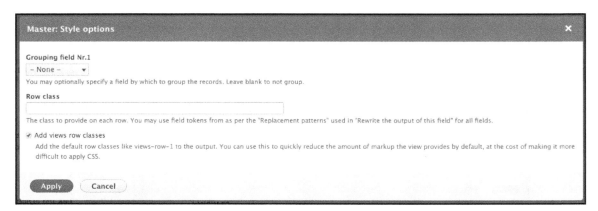

Unformatted row settings dialog

Grouping allows you to organize rows by one of the fields. Using the current View displaying fields, we can enable grouping on the **Content revision: Authored by** field and click **Apply**. Each unique entry in the selected field becomes a header element with the rows with that item listed below it:

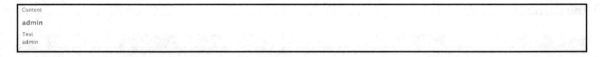

Grouping by Content revision author

Grid

Selecting grid for the View format creates a table to place the results in. You are prompted to enter the number of columns for the table and then the results are placed into a number of rows and columns, with each result forming a cell. You can select whether the results are striped horizontally or vertically, as well as whether each cell should have a percentage width added. For example, the default settings with four columns will add a `style="width: 25%"` attribute to each cell. At present, there is no option to add blank cells to fill out the columns as there has been in previous versions of Views.

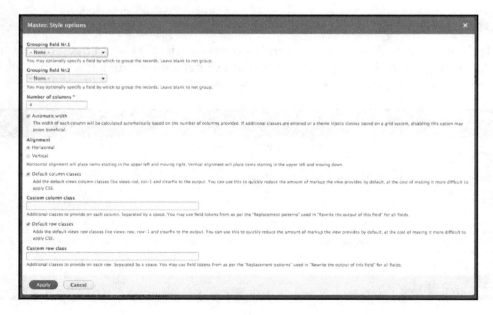

Grid settings dialog

HTML List

Selecting **HTML List** for the View format displays each result as a list item within an ordered or unordered list.

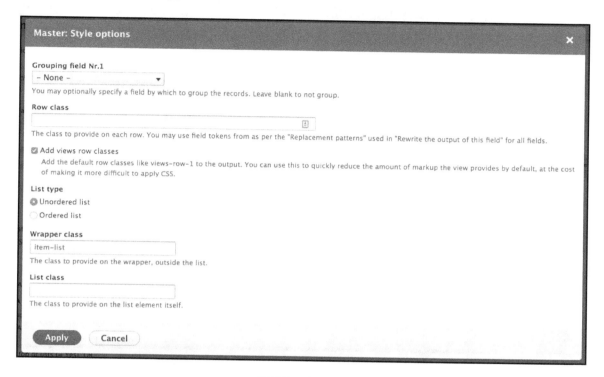

HTML List settings dialog

Table

Selecting **Table** for the View format shows the results in a table with headers. Each field type becomes a column with each value being a cell for the given row. This format is only available for field displays of content. The headers can be made sortable, which allows a user to click on it to change the sorting of the table to that field and then control the direction. Tables from Views, like all tables in Drupal 8, are natively responsive. Selecting **High** for **Responsive** for a column ensures that the column is visible at all breakpoints described in the theme.

Selecting **Medium** means that they will be hidden at the mobile breakpoint and **Low** at the tablet breakpoint.

Table settings dialog

Using advanced features

When you start to edit the View, you see an entire section in the right-hand side of the screen collapsed and labeled **Advanced**. In there are a host of useful settings controlling how the database is queried, what fields can be displayed, how caching is implemented, and how filters and pagers work.

Relationships

A relationship is a way for a View to traverse a connection to another type of entity. For example, in the list of articles with the content revision author, we were able to get the username of the author, but no other information. There are a number of fields like this that allow some small amount of information from each node, but not all of it. In order to get more information about the content revision author, or the taxonomy terms that have been applied to a node, or information about nodes that are referenced from or reference that node, you need to create a relationship.

With the view of articles from earlier let us add some more information about the author. First, we need to add a relationship to the content revision author. Click the **Add** button next to the section title for **Relationships**. Enter `author` in the search field and select **User** for **Content revision** and click the **Add and configure relationships** button.

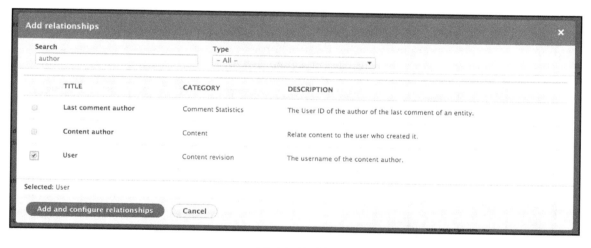

Add relationships dialog

On the following screen, there is a checkbox labeled **Require this relationship**. This filters out all nodes that do not have the relationship so that it functions as an INNER JOIN rather than an OUTER JOIN. Selecting this will generally make the query more performant and, since each content revision always has a user, it is better to require it for this purpose.

Relationship configuration dialog

Now that we have added the relationship to the user we can output, filter, or sort by any field on that user. If you create multiple relationships to the same category of field, a dropdown will appear on the configuration screen to select which relationship it is from.

Add field dialog showing fields from user relationship

Contextual filters

Contextual filters are ones that can be passed in the URI. This allows you to create Views displays that can display information based on a node ID, user ID, term ID, and so on. However, they do not allow the user to change that information on the View itself as they would be able to do with an exposed filter. For instance, if we wanted to show our current View on a user's detail page and have it restricted to that user, we would need to add a Contextual filter. Click the **Add** button next to the section title for **Contextual filters**. Select **User** from the dropdown labeled **Type** and scroll down and select the checkbox for **User ID** , then click the **Add and configure contextual filter** button.

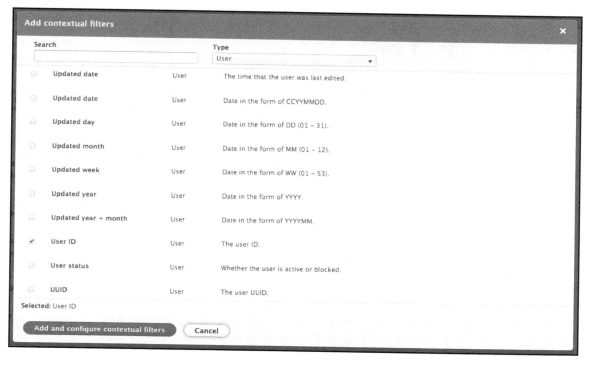

Add contextual filter dialog

On the following settings page there are a number of options. If you have relationships on the current View, you first need to select which one the current contextual filter applies to. If only one supports the current field, that is the only one that will be shown; if multiple ones do, you can choose between them.

The next set of options describe how the View should behave if a value is not provided. The contextual filter value can be provided programmatically, by the `views_embed_view` function for example, or by specifying it in the path for a page display. In cases where it is not the View, it can act in a number of different ways.

Display all results for the specified field

If this option is selected, the View will act as if there were no filter applied when a value is not provided. This means that, instead of filtering the View to only a given user's articles, it will simply display all articles.

Provide a default value

If this option is selected, a default value will be used when no contextual filter value is provided. There are a number of methods to determine what this default value will be:

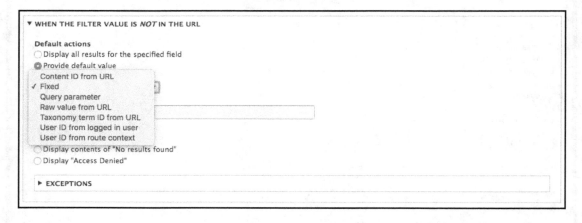

Default value options

- **Fixed**: If selected, the default value will always be the same regardless of the circumstances. You are prompted to enter a value, which will be substituted for the contextual filter value if none is provided.

- **Content ID from URL**: If selected, the View will use the node ID from the current URL. This can be from a URL, such as /node/1, or from a URL alias.
- **Query parameter**: If selected, you are prompted to enter the name of a query parameter to check for a value and then a fallback value in case that query parameter is not provided. For example, setting the parameter name to **id** and having a URL of /articles?id=1 would give a default value of 1.
- **Raw value from URL**: If selected, you are prompted to enter the path component as a number from 1 to 10. This retrieves the value, treating the URI as a slash-separated array starting from 1. For example, with the URL /articles/1, setting the path component to 2 would give a default value of 1.
- **Taxonomy term ID from URL**: If selected, the View will use the taxonomy term ID from the current URL. This can be from a URL such as /taxonomy/term/1 or from a URL alias.
- **User ID from logged in user**: If selected, the View will use the user ID from the current session.
- **User ID from route context**: If selected, the View will use the user ID from the current URL. This can be from a URL such as /user/1 or URL alias. It will also provide the user ID on menu routers that contain a {user} parameter. There is also a checkbox to allow the user ID to be provided from the author of a node. In that case, being on a URL such as /node/1 would provide the user ID corresponding to the author of the node with an ID of 1.

Hide view

If this option is selected, the View will not be present on the page if no contextual filter value is provided. This includes any header, footer, or attachment Views as well.

Display a summary

If this option is selected, the View will display a list of possible contextual filters that could be used, along with a count of the number of items that would be returned if you were to use that filter. If we wanted to provide a list of users that had edited articles and then allow someone to click on a particular user to see their Articles, this is what we would do. For example, select the following:

Display a summary default value

This then shows the list of users along with a link that would then provide the contextual filter.

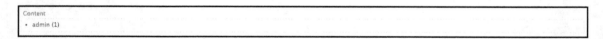

Display a summary content

Display contents of "No results found"

If this option is selected, the View will display the content of the "No results behavior" set. This includes any custom text, rendered entities, and so on that you had configured in that section.

Display "Access Denied"

If this option is selected, the View will return a 503 error when no value is provided.

Query aggregation

Views can be used to not only provide lists of contents, but also to provide aggregate functions on that content as well. You can enable aggregation by clicking on the **No** link next to the **Use aggregation** label, selecting the checkbox labeled **Aggregate**, and then saving either all displays or only the current display. Once you enable aggregation, all fields, filters, and sorting criteria gain a link next to them to set **Aggregation settings**.

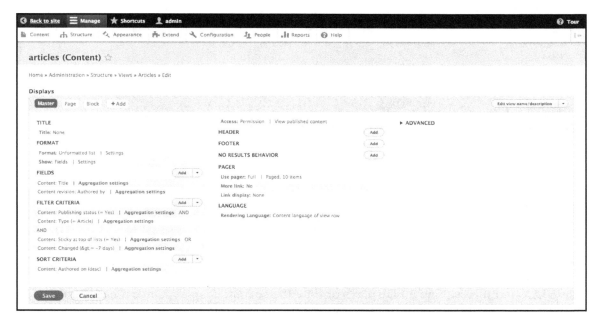

Aggregation settings for fields

Views allows you to perform grouping, counts, sums, minimum, maximum, standard deviation, and so on on any of these fields. Views leverages the database's ability to perform these functions and treat the output as the result of the query to be displayed, filtered, or sorted by.

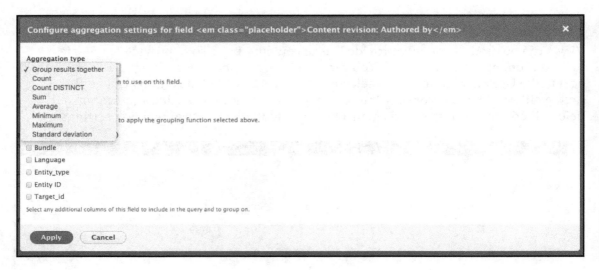

Aggregation settings options

AJAX

On some pages, you may wish to have pagination, exposed filters, or table sorting refresh the View using AJAX, rather than refresh the entire page. This is particularly helpful on block displays, especially when there may be multiple filters or pagers on the same page. All that is necessary is to click **No** next to the label **Use AJAX**, selecting the checkbox for **Use AJAX** and then saving all Displays or only the current Display. Once it has been enabled using those functions, it causes a small animated GIF to be displayed to indicate progress and then have the content of the View replaced when the site responds.

Using AJAX to perform these operations means that the current URL is not updated to reflect the page, filter, or sorting criteria used, which means navigating to a bookmark or refreshing your page will reset these values.

Summary

At its heart, Drupal is a **content management system (CMS)**. A major draw for the platform is being able to quickly and easily create lists of this content. We have touched on the major features of Views that will allow us to use this content throughout the site.

8
Theming Essentials

Before we can get started with creating or managing themes in Drupal 8, we need to have a better understanding of exactly what a theme is. From there, we will have the basis for how we work with themes in Drupal and the various configurations and components that are part of the theming ecosystem.

Let's get started by exploring what we will cover along the way:

- We will explore the Appearance interface and the core default themes while learning how themes are administered, how to install and uninstall themes, how they are configured, and the different settings a theme can have
- Then, we will take a closer look at the `themes` folder structure and the different files that make up a theme
- Finally, we will work with the various files that make up a theme, along with creating the structure that will allow us to build our first custom theme

Assumptions

Mastering Drupal 8 assumes that you are already running a local AMP stack and have a familiarity with installing Drupal using the standard means of downloading, setting up a database, configuring a localhost, and completing the browser-based install. In Chapter 1, *Developer Workflow*, we walked through installing Drupal using Composer, Drush, and Drupal Console. Ensure that you have a working AMP stack and are comfortable working within the command-line interface using a terminal window before continuing.

What is a theme?

In simple terms, a theme is the presentational layer. Regardless of the **content management system** (**CMS**), without a theme, all you have is content that looks very much like a Word document.

A theme generally consists of HTML markup, CSS, JavaScript, and media (images, video, and audio). It is this combination of technologies that allows the graphic designer to build something visually rich that can then be applied on top of the logic a web developer is building in Drupal. Sometimes, a web developer may be the person who implements the theme, but in most cases, you will hear the term themer or a frontend developer, which describes the person who fills that role.

However, before we dive right into creating a theme, it helps to have a better understanding of how to work with themes within the Appearance admin.

Exploring the Appearance interface

The Appearance interface in Drupal 8 can be located by navigating to `/admin/appearance` or using the Admin toolbar and clicking on **Manage - Appearance**.

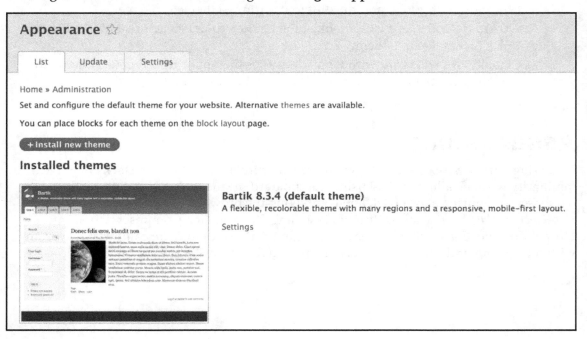

The **Appearance** page allows us to work with themes in Drupal, that is, anything from installing, uninstalling, and configuring the default theme for our website. We will explore the various functions within this section, starting with the default themes that Drupal 8 ships with.

Drupal's core themes

By default, Drupal 8 ships with four themes. As part of the standard installation profile, Drupal will install and configure the Bartik and Seven themes. Each of these themes serves a specific function in the workflow. Let's take a look at them in more detail.

Bartik

Bartik is considered the default theme in Drupal and is familiar to most, as it has been part of the Drupal ecosystem for quite a while now. We can think of Bartik as the frontend theme or what we see when we first install Drupal. The Bartik theme is what you will visually see when you are not navigating within the Drupal administrative screens.

Seven

Seven is the default admin theme, and it provides a clean separation between the frontend and backend of Drupal. This is great, as it will always allow us to navigate through the administrative areas if our default theme generates any errors that may cause a blank white screen while theming.

Stark

Stark is an intentionally plain theme with no styling at all to help demonstrate the default HTML and CSS that Drupal will output and is great to learn how to build a custom theme.

Classy

This is the fourth theme. **Classy** is a base theme, which both Bartik and Seven use, that provides both with clean well-documented markup and CSS classes. Classy is hidden from the Appearance page by default, but having a clear understanding of how it is constructed is important.

Theme states

One of the advantages of Drupal is the ability to have multiple themes available to use at any time. However, it is important to differentiate among installed, uninstalled, and default. We can consider these as the theme's states.

Installed themes

Installed themes are always located in the **Installed themes** section of the Appearance admin and are available for Drupal to use for either the frontend or backend of the CMS. However, there can only be one theme set as the default at any given time. We can see a list of installed themes, as shown in the following screenshot:

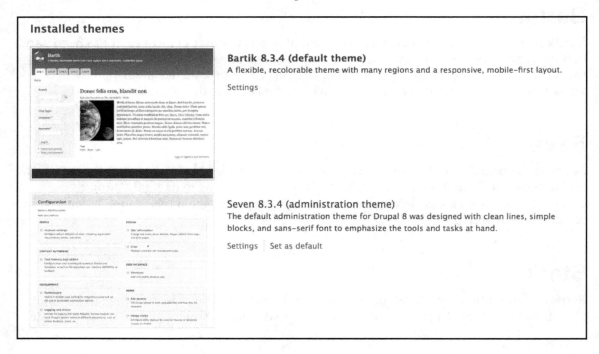

Uninstalled themes

Uninstalled themes are themes that Drupal is aware of within the `core themes` folder or the `custom themes` folder, but have not been placed into an installed state. One or multiple themes can be present at any time within the **Uninstalled theme** section, as shown in the following screenshot:

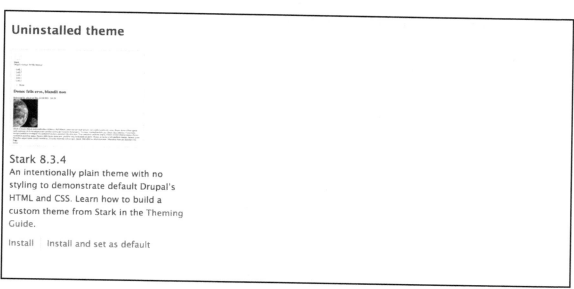

Default theme

It's important to remember that the default theme is always the current theme being displayed to users when viewing our website. The default theme is also displayed when logged in, but not within an Administrative section of Drupal. Anytime a theme is set as default, it will always be considered installed as well.

Installing and uninstalling themes

The act of installing or uninstalling a theme is a common practice when administering a Drupal website. Let's try installing Stark and making it our default theme in place of Bartik.

Step one - installing a theme

Currently, the only uninstalled theme is Stark, and we can easily move this into the installed state by following these two steps:

1. Click on the **Install and set as default** link.
2. Scroll back to the top of the Appearance admin.
3. If we now look at the **Installed themes** section, we should see that we now have three themes installed: Stark, Bartik, and Seven. We can also tell that Stark is now our default theme by looking at the right of the theme, which will be marked as (**default theme**).

We can also see what the Stark theme looks like by clicking on the **Back to site** link in the Admin menu. We are now presented with an un-styled page, which helps to demonstrate the clean markup of Drupal.

Step two - uninstalling a theme

Let's navigate back to the Appearance admin located at `/admin/appearance` and uninstall the Stark theme by following these two steps:

1. Locate the Bartik theme and click on **Set as default**.
2. Locate the Stark theme and click on **Uninstall**.

We saw how simple it is to install and uninstall themes within Drupal 8. Another common task we will find ourselves completing within the Appearance admin is adjusting the settings of a theme.

Theme settings

Theme settings range from toggling the display of certain page elements or updating the default logo supplied by the theme, to providing a shortcut icon or favicon that is displayed in the address bar of most browsers.

Let's explore these in more detail by clicking on the **Settings** link for the Bartik theme and then on the **Global settings** tab:

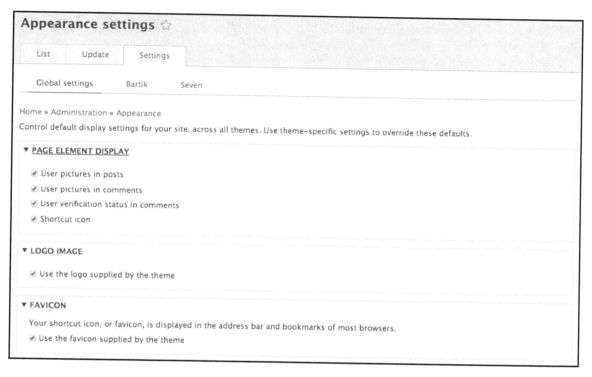

Toggling the display of page elements

Having control over certain page elements of a theme can come in handy when we want to hide or show specific items. Most of the items listed pertain to user settings, such as user pictures in posts or comments, user verification status in comments, and the Shortcut icon.

Simply checking or unchecking an item will toggle the display of that item on or off. Also, keep in mind that toggling the Shortcut icon will disable the ability to add a shortcut icon as the visibility of that section is also disabled.

Gone are Logo, Site name, Site slogan, Main menu, and Secondary menu from the theme settings. These were present in Drupal 7, but have now been moved into blocks and block configuration.

Logo image settings

Another nice option within the Appearance settings admin is the ability to manage the themes logo. By default, Drupal displays the infamous Drop logo, but we can replace that logo with our own.

Let's begin by following these steps:

1. Locate the **LOGO IMAGE** section.
2. Uncheck **Use the logo supplied by the theme**.
3. Click on the **Choose file** button under the **Upload logo image** field.
4. Locate and select a logo you want to use.
5. Click on the **Save configuration** button.

Our new logo has now been placed in the `/sites/default/files` folder of our Drupal installation, and is available for display on the homepage.

Favicon settings

If you are wondering what a favicon icon is, don't worry. It is the small image located in the browser window next to the URL address--if you are using Google Chrome, next to the page title of the website you are visiting.

Often, this step is overlooked when creating or working with themes in Drupal, but the steps involved in adding a shortcut icon is exactly like adding a logo.

Start by navigating to `/admin/appearance/settings` and following these steps:

1. Locate the **FAVICON** section.
2. Uncheck **Use the favicon supplied by the theme**.
3. Click on the **Choose file** button under the **Upload favicon image** field.
4. Locate and select a favicon you want to use.
5. Click on the **Save configuration** button.

Our new favicon has now been placed in the `/sites/default/files` folder of our Drupal installation, and is available for display in the browser.

So far, we have been working with global settings. However, individual theme settings can be applied as well. In fact, if we navigate back to the Appearance settings located at `/admin/appearance/settings`, we will see that Bartik and Seven can each have their own settings configured.

Theme-specific settings

Drupal 8 allows for the configuration of theme-specific settings. These can vary based on the theme and the amount of extensibility that a theme provides. For example, if we click on the Bartik theme, we will note that it provides us with an ability to change the **COLOR SCHEME** through a series of presets, whereas the Seven theme does not.

Keep in mind that contributed themes installed in Drupal may provide additional configuration options, so it is important to both look at the README file that comes with the theme and check the settings for that theme to ensure that it's configured properly.

Using prebuilt themes

Additional themes for Drupal 8 can be found in several places. Some of these themes must be purchased, whereas others are free to use. We can browse `Drupal.org` to find prebuilt themes and look at how to install them using the Drupal admin.

You can begin by navigating to `https://drupal.org/project/project_theme`.

The **Download & Extend** section of `Drupal.org` allows us to filter results based on various options. We can find Drupal 8--specific themes by performing the following steps:

1. Select **8.x** from the **Core compatibility** drop-down.
2. Click on the **Search** button.

3. With a selection of themes compatible with Drupal 8 to choose from, one result looks promising and that is the **Bootstrap 3** theme, shown in the following screenshot:

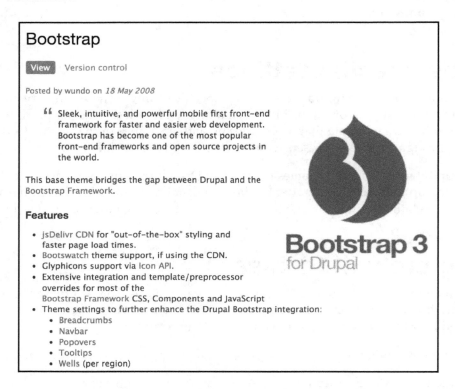

If we scroll down to the **Downloads** section of the page, we will be presented with several versions of the Bootstrap theme. We will click on either the `tar.gz` or `.zip` version that corresponds to Drupal 8. Once the file is downloaded, we will extract the contents of the file and place it within our `/themes` folder, as follows:

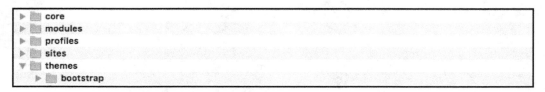

We can now navigate back to the Appearance admin located at
`/admin/appearance/settings`, scroll down to **Uninstalled themes**, and as we did
earlier, click on the **Install and set as default** link for Bootstrap 3 theme.

If we now navigate to our homepage, we will see that the new theme has been installed:

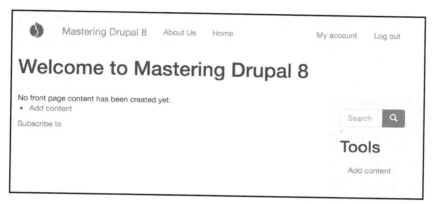

Keep in mind that our website may reflect different content depending on what content was
present prior to installing and enabling our new theme.

When using prebuilt themes, depending on the theme's author, there may be additional
theme settings available. Bootstrap 3 comes with quite a few additional settings to control
general settings, such as responsive images, and components such as Breadcrumbs, Navbar,
and more. Anytime we choose to use a prebuilt theme, make sure that you visit the theme's
settings to configure anything else that may be needed.

So far, everything has been very visual, and we have not yet touched the surface of what is
involved in working with themes in Drupal 8. To understand how a theme is rendered, we
need to explore some key concepts:

- Folder structure and naming conventions
- Managing configuration in Drupal 8
- The role of templates in Drupal

Folder structure and naming conventions

In Drupal 8, the folder structure is changed to make it more logical. Everything that ships with Drupal now resides in a `core` folder, including the default themes, which are now contained within the `core/themes` folder. However, any themes that we download or develop ourselves now reside within the `/themes` folder, which we saw when we installed the Bootstrap 3 theme.

Just to iterate, the folder structure comprises the following:

- **Default themes**: These themes reside in the `/core/themes` directory, and include Bartik, Classy, Seven, Stable, and Stark
- **Custom themes**: These themes reside in the `/themes` directory at the root level of our Drupal installation and will contain any contributed themes or custom themes

Before we can begin creating our own custom themes, we need to have a better understanding of how themes are configured and exactly how they let Drupal know where to display content and how the content should look.

Managing configuration in Drupal 8

Theme configuration in Drupal 8 has now adopted YAML. YAML is a human-friendly data serialization standard used by many programming languages, including Symfony, which Drupal 8 is now built on. With this adoption, the syntax to create an `information` file has now changed as well. One important concept when creating or editing any `*.yml` file is that proper indentation is required. Failure to properly indent configuration can lead to errors or to the configuration not loading at all. We can dive deeper into the specifics of YAML and find out more detailed information at the Symfony website (`https://symfony.com/doc/current/components/yaml/yaml_format.html`).

Reviewing the new info.yml file

The `*.info.yml` file is required to create any theme. It helps us to notify Drupal that a theme exists and provides information to the Appearance interface that a theme is available to be installed. We will be working with `*.info.yml` files when creating any theme, so let's look at the makeup of a basic `example.info.yml` file:

```
name: Example
description: 'An Example theme.'
type: theme
package: Custom
base theme: classy
core: 8.x

libraries:
  - example/global-styling

regions:
  header: Header
  primary_menu: 'Primary menu'
  secondary_menu: 'Secondary menu'
  breadcrumb: Breadcrumb
  help: Help
  highlighted: Highlighted
  content: Content
  sidebar_first: 'Left sidebar'
  sidebar_second: 'Right sidebar'
  footer: Footer
  page_top: 'Page top'
  page_bottom: 'Page bottom'
```

At first glance, the `example.info.yml` file is logical in structure and syntax. Starting from the top and moving our way down, the file is broken down by different sections of metadata containing **general information**, **libraries**, and **regions**. This information is described using a `key:value` format. We will begin with understanding how basic metadata works.

Metadata

The metadata contained within a theme's `*.info.yml` file helps to describe what type of document it is. In our case, it begins to describe a theme, including the name, description, and the version of Drupal the theme works with. Some metadata is required for the theme to function properly, so let's explore the keys in more detail as follows:

- **name** (required): This is the name of our theme.
- **type** (required): This is the type of extension (theme, module, or profile).
- **base theme** (required): This is the theme that the current theme is inheriting. In most cases, it is recommended that we reference either classy or stable as our base theme. If we choose not to reference a base theme, then we will need to set the value to false (`base theme: false`).
- **description** (required): This is the description of our theme.
- **package** (optional): This is used to group similar files when creating modules.
- **version** (optional): This is created by a packaging script.
- **core** (required): This specifies the version of Drupal that a theme is compatible with.

One of the most common mistakes when creating a `*.info.yml` file is forgetting to change the core value to 8.x. Failure to set this value will result in the theme not being displayed within the Appearance interface in the admin. The next section of a `*.info.yml` file allows us to manage assets (CSS or JS) using the new concept of libraries.

Libraries

Drupal 8 introduced a new, high-level principle of managing assets using a libraries configuration file that can be loaded globally or on a per page basis. This concept helps to improve frontend performance as well as ensure that any dependencies that an asset needs is loaded properly. One advantage of this is that jQuery no longer loads on every page as it did in the previous versions of Drupal.

The concept of a `*.libraries.yml` configuration file also means that the style sheets and scripts properties that we may have been familiar with in Drupal 7 no longer exist. Instead, the process to manage assets includes saving any CSS or JS files to our theme's CSS or JS folder and then defining a library file that references the less we want to use in our theme.

Defining a library

When defining a `*.libraries.yml` for a theme, each library will reference the location of individual CSS or JS files and be organized using the SMACSS (`https://smacss.com/`) style categorization:

- **Base**: This defines CSS reset/normalize plus HTML element styling
- **Layout**: This defines the macro arrangement of a web page, including any grid system
- **Component**: This defines the discrete, reusable UI elements
- **State**: This defines the styles that deal with client-side changes to components
- **Theme**: This is purely visual styling for a component

In most cases, a simple library reference will follow the theme categorization. For example, if we want to create an `example.libraries.yml` file that included assets for CSS and JS, we would create a library that pointed to our assets, as shown here:

```
libraryname:
  css:
   theme:
      css/style.css: {}
  js:
    js/scripts.js: {}
```

We would then reference the library within our `example.info.yml` configuration simply by adding the following:

```
libraries:
  - example/libraryname
```

This would result in Drupal adding both CSS and JS files to every page contained in our library. Where this becomes powerful is in the management of assets, as we will need to make modifications to our `example.libraries.yml` file only if we ever need to add or remove assets.

Overriding libraries

Libraries can also be overridden to modify assets declared by other libraries, possibly added by a base theme, a module, or even the Drupal core. The ability to override libraries includes removing as well as replacing assets altogether. The same way we reference a library from our `*.info.yml` file, we can override libraries by adding the following:

```
libraries-override:

  # Replace an entire library.
  core/drupal.vertical-tabs: example/vertical-tabs
  # Replace an asset with another.
  core/drupal.vertical-tabs:
    css:
      component:
        misc/vertical-tabs.css: css/vertical-tabs.css
  # Remove an asset.
  core/drupal.vertical-tabs:
    css:
      component:
        misc/vertical-tabs.css: false
  # Remove an entire library.
  core/modernizr: false
```

In this case, the `libraries-override` configuration achieves something different for each line. Whether it is replacing an entire library or removing an asset, we now have the flexibility to control assets.

Extending libraries

Libraries can also be extended to allow overriding `CSS` added by another library without modifying the original files. This can be done by adding the following to our `*.info.yml` configuration:

```
libraries-extend:
  core/drupal.vertical-tabs:
    - example/tabs
```

In this case, the `libraries-extend` configuration is extending Drupal's own `core.libraries.yml` file and the `drupal.vertical-tabs` library with additional styling.

While we now have a general understanding of how libraries are defined, overridden, and extended, we have only dealt with libraries globally loaded into our Drupal instance using our configuration. However, there are two more methods to include assets within a page directly, without the need to add it to every page.

Attaching a library

In many cases, we may be developing some of the CSS or JS functionality that is specific to an individual page. When we are presented with this requirement, we can attach a library to a page using two different methods.

Using Twig to attach a library

While we will cover Twig a little later, we need to pause for a moment to explain a Twig function used with referencing a library named {{ attach_library() }}. This function allows us to add a library that may include CSS or JS that will load on that page only to any Twig template.

For example, if we wanted to add the **Slick Carousel** (http://kenwheeler.github.io/slick/) to our page, we may define the library within our example.libraries.yml file, as follows:

```
# Slick
slick:
  version: VERSION
  css:
    theme:
      vendor/slick/slick.css: {}
  js:
    vendor/slick/slick.min.js: {}
  dependencies:
    - core/jquery
```

We could then turn around and add the following to our Twig template:

```
{{ attach_library('example/slick') }}
```

This provides us with a nice functionality to define individual libraries for various user functions and to have those assets used wherever we choose to attach them.

Using the preprocess functions to attach a library

Another method to attach a library to an individual page depends on creating a *.theme file, which allows us to use preprocess functions to manipulate page variables. We will focus a lot more on creating a *.theme file a little later, but it's important to note that we could attach the same Slick Carousel to our homepage without globally calling it using a preprocess function:

```
function example_preprocess_page(&$variables)
{
        if ($variables['is_front'])
        {
                $variables['#attached']['library'][] = 'example/slick';
        }
}
```

Here, we are checking to see whether we are on the homepage of our website, and attach the Slick library using the #attached library array. Again, this may seem a little bit advanced at this point, but does merit mentioning.

The last section we will want to cover when working with any *.info.yml file is about Regions that can be defined for the layout of our theme.

Regions

Regions play a critical part in theming, as Drupal needs to know exactly where content can be displayed. This has an impact on what regions are visible to the Block layout for both system blocks and custom blocks that we may want to use. If we do not specify any regions within our *.info.yml file, then Drupal will provide us with regions by default.

Note that if we decide to add additional regions to our theme, we must also add the defaults or else we will not have access to them. Also, any regions that already have content assigned to them that have been removed by our theme will have the content disabled on the Block layout page.

Default Regions:

```
regions:
  header: Header
  primary_menu: 'Primary menu'
  secondary_menu: 'Secondary menu'
  breadcrumb: Breadcrumb
  help: Help
```

```
highlighted: Highlighted
content: Content
sidebar_first: 'Left sidebar'
sidebar_second: 'Right sidebar'
footer: Footer
page_top: 'Page top'
page_bottom: 'Page bottom'
```

The value for each key is what is displayed in the Block layout within the Drupal UI and can be named whatever we want to name it.

If we choose to add additional regions to our theme, we will need to ensure that we also print them out within our `page.html.twig` template.

Adding assets to CKEditor

Something new to Drupal 8 was the addition of a WYSIWYG. The preferred choice was CKEditor, which means that we no longer must install additional modules to provide our users with a better content editing experience.

The one drawback of using a WYSIWYG is that the styles in the editor and what the end user sees are sometime quite different. The reasoning is that the themes styling is not inherited by the WYSIWYG. We can now remedy this by adding additional metadata to our `information` file by adding the following:

- `ckeditor_stylesheets`
- `css/styles.css`

`https://fonts.googleapis.com/css?family=Open+Sans`

The above metadata adds a reference to the theme's style sheet and also adds Google fonts to the editor. This helps to bridge the gap between the backend and frontend.

The role of templates in Drupal

We may have heard the term *template* before when talking to someone about theming, but what exactly is a template? We can think of a template as a text file no different from any `HTML` document that provides a method for separating the presentation layer from the business logic.

In traditional PHP websites, we can mix PHP with HTML and CSS, which makes managing web pages both difficult and dangerous. Drupal provides us with the ability to use templating engines to enforce the separation of the two, so we can begin to focus more on the HTML and CSS and worry less about the PHP.

How templates work

In general, templates can contain HTML markup and PHP variables that output content contained within a Drupal database. Templates can be as small as a few lines of HTML that hold the presentational layer for a block that is displayed in a region on the page, or the actual page itself, with containers defined for header, content, and so on:

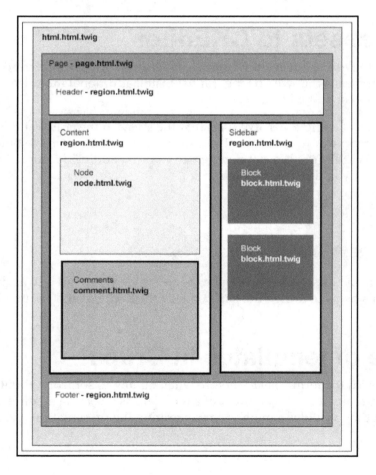

If we break down the image into logical sections of a website, we can begin to get an idea of what constitutes a template. A template can be any of the following:

- **HTML wrapper**: This contains the top-level HTML markup, including title, metadata, style sheets, and scripts, and it is commonly referred to as `html.html.twig`.

- **Page wrapper**: This contains the content generally found between the body tags of an HTML document, and it is commonly referred to as `page.html.twig`.

- **Header**: This is also known as a region, generally containing the header content of our web page. This can be part of the `page.html.twig` template or may reside in a region specified within our configuration file. This is commonly referred to as `region.html.twig`.

- **Content**: This is also considered a region, generally containing our main content. This can consist of multiple subcontent regions, such as nodes and comments. Nodes and comments each have their own respective templates referred to as `node.html.twig` and `comment.html.twig`.

- **Sidebar**: This is also considered a region. This can contain blocks of content. Blocks are either created by the end user or by Drupal itself. The content within these blocks generally resides within `block.html.twig`.

- **Footer**: This is another region containing HTML content as well as blocks of content.

Drupal and the theme engine it uses to convert the markup and variables into HTML interpret each individual template or series of templates. We have full control over what is the output of using the new Twig templating engine.

Once we begin theming, we will start to see a pattern of how templates are used, and as we gain more experience, we will find ourselves using fewer and fewer templates. However, to begin with, we will build examples of each to help clarify their functionality within Drupal.

Where to find templates

The nice thing about Drupal is that, by default, the core system provides us with all the templates we need to use. So, knowing where to find the core templates is important because it will allow us to copy them into our own theme folder to override with our own markup.

Let's begin by browsing the `/core/modules` folder. Contained within this folder are the core modules that make up Drupal, along with their respective templates. Most of the core templates will be in the `/core/modules/system/templates` folder.

If we browse the contents of the `templates` folder, we will note that some of the most common templates we will be using includes the following:

- `html.html.twig`: HTML wrapper
- `page.html.twig`: Page wrapper
- `region.html.twig`: Region wrapper

Three more template folders that we need to be aware of are as follows:

- `/core/modules/node/templates`: This contains the templates for nodes
- `/core/modules/comment/templates`: This contains the comment templates
- `/core/modules/block/templates`: This contains the templates for blocks

We will find ourselves frequently overriding templates, so we need to make sure that we know where to find any Twig template that we will be theming.

Most of us have done some PHP development or are at least familiar enough with it to work with the variables that Drupal outputs. So, as we observe templates, we should be noticing that the files don't end with a file extension of `.php`, but instead end with a file extension of `.twig`. In fact, if we were to look at the `html.html.twig` template located in the `/core/modules/system/templates` folder, we won't even find PHP syntax inside it:

```
<!DOCTYPE html>
  <html{{ html_attributes }}>
    <head>
      <head-placeholder token="{{ placeholder_token|raw }}">
      <title>{{ head_title|safe_join(' | ') }}</title>
      <css-placeholder token="{{ placeholder_token|raw }}">
      <js-placeholder token="{{ placeholder_token|raw }}">
    </head>
    <body{{ attributes }}>
      <a href="#main-content" class="visually-hidden focusable">
        {{ 'Skip to main content'|t }}
      </a>
      {{ page_top }}
      {{ page }}
    {{ page_bottom }}
    <js-bottom-placeholder token="{{ placeholder_token|raw }}">
  </body>
</html>
```

Instead, we will see a general HTML markup along with the Twig syntax that will output content within its place. We will take a closer look at Twig a little later.

Creating a simple theme

Now that we have reviewed the basics of how a theme is installed and configured, there is no better time than the present to create our own simple theme. We will begin by creating a theme named **Twiggy** that we will use to work with exploring how Twig and the theme system works in Drupal 8.

Step one - creating a new folder

Create a new folder under our themes folder called twiggy.

Step two - create an info file

Create a new file named twiggy.info.yml within our new theme folder, and add the following configuration information to the file:

```
name: Twiggy
type: theme
description: 'A simple theme'
core: 8.x
base theme: classy

libraries:
   - twiggy/global

regions:
  header: Header
  primary_menu: 'Primary menu'
  secondary_menu: 'Secondary menu'
  breadcrumb: Breadcrumb
  help: Help
  highlighted: Highlighted
  content: Content
  sidebar_first: 'Left sidebar'
  sidebar_second: 'Right sidebar'
  footer: Footer
  page_top: 'Page top'
  page_bottom: 'Page bottom'
```

Step three - create a libraries file

Create a new file named `twiggy.libraries.yml` within our new `theme` folder, and add the following configuration information to the file:

```
global:
  css:
    theme:
      css/styles.css: {}
  js:
    js/scripts/js: {}
```

Make sure that you also create a CSS folder with an empty `styles.css` file within it and a JS folder with an empty `scripts.js` file within it. We will use these two files to manage any visual or interactive theming.

Step four - copy core templates

Copy the `html.html.twig` and `page.html.twig` templates from the `/core/modules/system/templates` folder and paste it into a `/themes/twiggy/templates` folder. Having these two Twig files will give us a starting point to where we can modify the markup and begin learning Twig.

Step five - include a screenshot

Not always a required step, but one that will help is including a screenshot that represents our theme within the Appearance admin. In general, we can generate a screenshot based on the finished theme, but because we are just starting out, we can copy and include any `.png` file named `screenshot.png`.

Step six - installing our theme

Next, we will need to install our new theme by navigating to `/admin/appearance` and locating our new theme named **Twiggy** under the **Uninstalled themes** section. Click on the **Install** and set as default link to install our new theme.

Our new `theme` folder structure should look like the following:

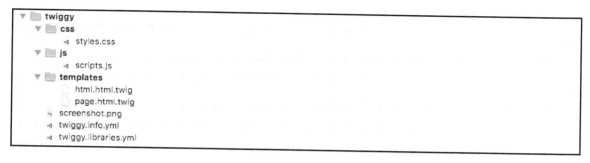

Based on the content that we may have added to our Drupal 8 instance, we should at least have an unstyled blank slate from which to work with once we begin learning Twig.

Summary

Having a greater appreciation for how Drupal 8 has reengineered their theming layer with the introduction of YAML to manage metadata makes working with themes much more enjoyable. Whether we are working with the default themes that are shipped with Drupal 8, installing prebuilt themes, or creating new themes from scratch, understanding what makes up a theme helps to ensure that we know how to best work with assets.

In this chapter, we explored the Appearance interface and installed, uninstalled, and configured themes and their many theme settings. We got a better understanding of how `*.info.yml` and `*.libraries.yml` work to manage a theme and its respective assets.

With our new theme in place, we can begin exploring Twig and all the great features that Drupal 8 introduces to us with this new templating engine in the next chapter.

9
Working with Twig

Before we begin working with Twig, we will need to ensure that our local development environment is set up and configured to allow us to debug Twig. From there, we will have the basis for discovering which templates Drupal uses to output content, how to override Twig templates, and how to work with some of the most common Blocks, Menus, Regions, and Nodes.

Let's get started by exploring what we will be covering along the way:

- We will begin with enabling Twig debugging
- Then we will take a closer look at the Twig syntax that allows us to set variables, print variables, and inspect content
- Next, we will look at Twig filters, control structures, and how to best use Twig to check for the existence of content
- Finally, we will work with Template variables and build a simple page layout using HTML, Twig, and CSS

Assumptions

Mastering Drupal 8 assumes that you are already running a local AMP stack and have a familiarity with installing Drupal using the standard means of downloading, setting up a database, configuring a localhost, and completing the browser-based installation. In `Chapter 1`, *Developer Workflow*, we walked through quickly installing Drupal using Composer, Drush, and Drupal Console. Please ensure you have a working AMP stack and are comfortable working within the command-line interface using a terminal window before continuing.

Configuring settings.local.php

We are all familiar with Drupal's `settings.php` file. However, in Drupal 8, we can now have different configurations per environment by creating a `settings.local.php` file that the default `settings.php` file can reference. This is the first step in allowing us to enable Twig debugging:

1. First, we will need to copy `example.settings.local.php`, located in the `/sites` folder, to the `/sites/default` folder and rename the file to `settings.local.php`.
2. Next, we need to open `settings.php`, located in the `/sites/default` folder, and uncomment the following lines:

   ```
   if (file_exists(__DIR__ . '/settings.local.php'))
   { include __DIR__ . '/settings.local.php'; }
   ```

3. Save the changes to our `settings.php` file.;

With our change in place, we will need to make sure to clear Drupal's cache before our changes will take effect. Now that we have a local settings file in place, we can make a few more configuration changes that will allow us to not worry about always clearing the cache and disabling aggregated files while developing.

Enabling local development services

The first configuration option we will address is modifying the path to our local development services. We will create this new file in just a moment but to ensure we are pointing to the correct file, locate and modify the following line to reflect the new path:

```
/** * Enable local development services. */ $settings['container_yamls'][]
= DRUPAL_ROOT . '/sites/default/local.services.yml';
```

Disabling render and page cache

Another configuration option we can address while having the `settings.local.php` file open is render and page cache. This setting allows us to avoid having to clear Drupal's cache constantly when we make any change.

Locate and uncomment the following lines:

```
/** * Disable the render cache (this includes the page cache). */
$settings['cache']['bins']['render'] = 'cache.backend.null'; /** * Disable
Dynamic Page Cache. */ $settings['cache']['bins']['dynamic_page_cache'] =
'cache.backend. null';
```

Disabling test modules and themes

Another configuration we will want to make to our `settings.local.php` file deals with test modules and themes. By default, our local settings file enables the display of various modules and themes meant for testing purposes only. We can disable them by changing the following TRUE value to FALSE:

```
$settings['extension_discovery_scan_tests'] = FALSE;
```

With these changes made, we will want to make sure that we save our `settings.local.php` file.

Enabling Twig debug

The last piece of configuration requires us to create a `local.services.yml` file that will handle the Null caching we set up earlier, as well as enable Twig debugging:

1. First, we will need to copy `development.services.yml`, located in the `/sites` folder, to the `/sites/default` folder and rename the file to be called `local.services.yml`.

2. Next, remove the following line:

   ```
   parameters: httpd.response.debug_cacheability_headers: true
   ```

3. Add the following lines to the bottom of the file:

   ```
   # Enable Twig debugging # # parameters: twig.config: debug: true
   auto_reload: true cache: false
   ```

4. Save the file.
5. Clear Drupal's cache.

We can validate that Twig debugging is now enabled by navigating back to our Drupal home page and using Google Chrome's Developer Tools to inspect the page. We should now see Twig comments displayed in various sections of the page:

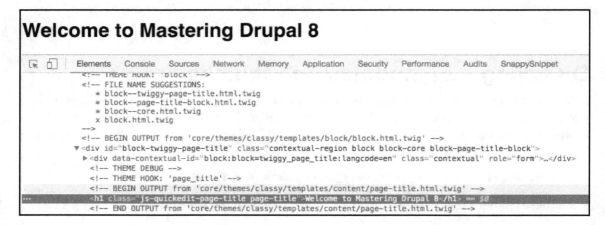

There are a couple of items we should make note of when Twig debugging is enabled:

- **FILE NAME SUGGESTIONS**: This displays suggestions to name Twig HTML templates and displays in the order of precedence in which Drupal folders would look for templates. The default template being used by Drupal also has an X next to the filename.
- **OUTPUT**: This displays the location of the template currently being displayed, which in the previous screenshot is `/core/themes/classy/templates/content/page-title.html.twig`.

Remember that we will only see the debug output when we have Twig debugging enabled as part of our local development environment. It is best to remember to disable debugging before moving a Drupal site to production.

So now that we understand what Twig debug provides us with, let's begin exploring some of the Twig syntax.

Twig fundamentals

Twig (http://twig.sensiolabs.org) is the new template engine introduced to Drupal 8 and is a companion to *Symfony*, the new PHP framework that Drupal 8 is built on. Twig provides us with a fast and secure way to separate content from PHP logic in a manner that makes it easier for non-developers to work with templates. Before we begin working with Twig, let's first dive into the steps involved in enabling Twig debugging.

A Twig template outputs PHP with a template-oriented syntax using opening and closing curly brackets {{ ... }}. This syntax interprets the variable between the brackets and outputs HTML in its place. The following are three kinds of delimiters in Twig that trigger an evaluation to take place:

- The first is Twig commenting, which uses the comment tag {# ... #} to provide comments inline or around a section of HTML.
- Next is the print tag {{ ... }}, which is used to print the result of an expression or variable. The print tag can be used by itself or within a section of HTML.
- The third tag is to execute a statement such as conditional logic, looping structures, or the assignment of values to variables and is expressed by {% ... %}.

Each of the three delimiters will be used when we do any type of theming project in Drupal 8. We will find that they are just as simple as using any regular HTML element, and we will quickly be writing these tags.

Commenting variables

We are familiar with HTML commenting such as <!-- This is a comment -->, which allows us to add descriptive text to our markup. We saw an example of this in the Twig debug output once we enabled it. Twig provides us with the ability to add comments as well using the {# comment #} syntax.

If we open page.html.twig within our editor, we can add a Twig comment by adding the following:

```
{# This is a comment in Twig #} <h1>Welcome to Twig!</h1>
```

Once we save our template, refresh the browser and inspect the heading. We will note that we don't see the comment being displayed. Unlike HTML comments, Twig comments are meant to be hidden from browser output and are meant only for the developer.

Setting variables

Twig can also assign values to variables using a technique named **assignment**. Assignment uses the set tag to place a value into a variable, which can then be used later within a template to output the value.

Open `page.html.twig` and add the following above our heading:

```
{# Setting a variable #} {% set name = 'Drupal' %} {# This is a comment in
Twig #} <h1>Welcome to Twig!</h1>
```

If we save our template and refresh the browser, we will not see any changes to our HTML as we are only setting a variable but not using it anywhere in our document. So how do we then use a variable?

Printing variables

Twig allows us to print variables by simply referencing them within our document using the `{{ variable }}` syntax to trigger the interpreter, in order to replace the variable name with the value stored in it. We can try this by replacing the word `Twig` in our heading with the `name` variable.

Open `page.html.twig` and add the following:

```
{# Setting a variable #} {% set name = 'Drupal' %} {# This is a comment in
Twig #} <h1>Welcome to {{ name }}</h1>
```

If we save our template and refresh the browser, we will see that our heading now says **Welcome to Drupal**. The name variable we set has output the word **Drupal** in its place. This is the same technique that we would use to output variables in Twig templates to display content from Drupal.

In fact, if we sneak a peek at our `html.html.twig` template, we will see a variety of Twig variables being used to output content.

Dumping variables

While theming in Drupal, we will be working with both simple and complex variables consisting of PHP arrays that contain multiple values. Knowing that there can be multiple values, it is sometimes useful to dump the contents of the variable to know exactly what we are working with. The `{{ dump() }}` function allows us to view information about a template variable and is only available to us when Twig debugging is turned on. Let's take our `name` variable for instance and dump the contents to see what it contains.

Open `page.html.twig` and add the following to the bottom of the template:

```
{# Dumping variables #} {{ dump(name) }}
```

If we save our template and refresh the browser, we will now see the `name` variable being dumped to the page, displaying some additional info about our variable.

Using the `dump()` function, we can introspect more than one variable at a time by passing multiple arguments. Let's try this by adding an additional Drupal variable named `is_front`, as shown in the following code sample:

```
{# Dumping variables #} <pre>{{ dump(name, is_front) }}</pre>
```

If we save our template and refresh the browser, we will now see the `is_front` variable being dumped to the page as well as displaying whether we are on the front page of our site.

We can also discover all variables available to us within a Twig template by using a filter with our `dump()` tag. For instance, if we want to see everything available within the `page.html.twig` template for the page variable, we can add the following code:

```
{# Dumping keys #} <pre>{{ dump(page|keys) }}</pre>
```

The result will be a list of all the variables available for us to use to print out content provided to the `page.html.twig` template. This process will become very useful when working with other Twig templates.

By now, we should be comfortable working with a Twig template and variables. However, we can do much more with Twig than just print variables. We can also apply filters to variables to achieve a different functionality.

Filters

Filters provide us with a way to modify variables. Filters are generally separated by a pipe character | and may accept arguments depending on the filter's purpose. Twig currently provides us with 30-plus filters that we can apply to variables.

Let's try out filters now by applying an uppercase filter on our `name` variable.

Open `page.html.twig` and add the following:

```
{# Apply filter to name variable #} <p>{{ name|upper }} Rocks.</p>
```

If we save our template and refresh the browser, we will now see that the `name` variable is converted to uppercase inside our paragraph tag.

We can also use filters to wrap sections of HTML and variables, which apply the filter to more than one item at a time. An example of this would be if we wanted to uppercase a whole paragraph versus just the `name` variable.

Open `page.html.twig` and add the following:

```
<p> {% filter upper %} {{ name }} is the best cms around. {% endfilter %}
</p>
```

If we save our template and refresh the browser, we will now see that the entire paragraph, including the `name` variable, is converted to uppercase.

This is just an example of one of the many filters that can be applied to variables within Twig. For a detailed list of filters, we can refer to
`http://twig.sensiolabs.org/doc/filters/index.html`.

Control structures

There will be situations while theming with Twig where we will need to check whether a variable is `True` or `False`, or to loop through a variable to output multiple values contained in an array.

Control structures in Twig allow us to account for these types of functions using `{% ... %}` blocks to test for expressions and traverse through variables that contain arrays. Each control structure contains an opening and closing tag, like PHP logic. Let's look at a couple of the most commonly used control structures, starting with the `if` tag used to test an expression.

Open `page.html.twig` and add the following:

```
{# Conditional logic #} {% set offline = false %} {% if offline == true %}
<p>Website is in maintenance mode.</p> {% endif %}
```

If we save our template and refresh the browser, we will not see anything displaying yet. The reason is that the `offline` variable is currently set to `false` and we are checking to see whether it is `true`.

Open `page.html.twig` and edit the `offline` variable, changing its value to `true`:

```
{# Conditional logic #} {% set offline = true %} {% if offline == true %}
<p>Website is in maintenance mode.</p> {% endif %}
```

Now resave our template and view the page in the browser. This time, we will see our paragraph displayed.

By now, we are starting to see how control structures within Twig can come in handy to hide or show certain markup within our template based on the value of a variable. This will come in handy when we have certain Drupal regions that we want to display when a block is placed into a region.

The other commonly used control structure in Twig is *looping*. The `for` tag is used to loop over each item in a sequence. For our example, let's try looping based on several items and outputting the count.

Open `page.html.twig` and add the following:

```
{# Looping #} {% for i in 0 ..10 %} {{ i }} {% endfor %}
```

If we save our template and view the page in the browser, we will be presented with the count within our loop displaying on the page, starting at 0 and going to 10.

This is a simple loop, and it only demonstrates the use of the `for` tag. Once we start creating additional Twig templates, we can loop through more complex Drupal variables. More extensive documentation regarding the `for` tag can be found at
`http://twig.sensiolabs.org/doc/tags/for.html`.

Functions

Twig also provides several handy functions that we can use when creating Drupal 8 themes. While the extensive list can be found in the **SensioLabs** documentation, there are a few worth mentioning that are commonly used with Twig.

The first is `url()`, which generates an absolute URL to the Node or path of the current page:

```
<a href="{{ url('front') }}">Home</a>
```

The above use would generate an absolute URL to the home page of our website.

Next is the `path()` function that generates a relative URL path given a route name:

```
<a href="{{ path('entity.node.canonical', {'node': node.id}) }}">View
page</a>
```

The above would generate a relative URL to the current Node.

Again, these are just a few examples. For additional Drupal-specific Twig functions, we can refer to the Drupal 8 API documentation.

Template variables

Drupal 8 uses variables to output data within Twig templates. We know that variables generally consist of anything from a simple string to a complex object containing an array of values. If we look at the `html.html.twig` template, we will see documentation that outlines the variables available to us along with the name of the variable and a description of what the variable contains.

The list of variables is as follows:

- `logged_in`: A flag indicating whether the user is logged in
- `root_path`: The root path of the current page (for example, node, admin, and user)
- `node_type`: The content type for the current node, if the page is a node
- `head_title`: List of text elements that make up the `head_title` variable
- `title`: The title of the page
- `name`: The name of the site
- `slogan`: The slogan of the site
- `page_top`: Initial rendered markup; this should be printed before page
- `page`: The rendered page markup
- `page_bottom`: Closing rendered markup; this variable should be printed after page

- db_offline: A flag indicating whether the database is offline
- placeholder_token: The token for generating head, CSS, JS, and JS-bottom placeholders

Each of the variables that a template has access to can be output using Twig syntax. For example, the head_title variable outputs the title of our page within the <title> element. Drupal also uses {{ attributes }} to print out additional information to our page, for example the <body> element to output CSS classes needed by modules or themes.

Each template we work with uses variables to output database content. What if we want to add additional variables to Drupal? This is where the role of the theme file comes into use.

The role of the theme file in Drupal

Themes can be simple to compose, sometimes containing a single configuration file, a couple of Twig templates, and a few assets. However, there will be times when we need to intercept and override variables and data that Drupal outputs before they reach our Twig templates.

Drupal's API (https://api.drupal.org/api/drupal/8) allows us to create a *.theme file where we can add theme functions that can hook into the API using different types of function calls:

- **Preprocess**: This is a set of function calls specific to different templates that allow us to manipulate variables before they are output to the page
- **Hooks**: This is a set of function calls to hook into the Drupal API that allows us to alter variables and override default implementations

Preprocessors and hooks

The main role of preprocessor functions is to prepare variables to be used within our Twig templates using template_preprocess functions. These functions reference the theme and template we want to intercept. We can write an example of intercepting the html.html.twig template variables used within our Twig theme as follows:

First we need to create a new file called twiggy.theme.

Within our new file, add the following code:

```
<?php /** * Implements hook_preprocess_html(). */ function
twiggy_preprocess_html(&$variables) { // add to classes
$variables['attributes']['class'][] = 'twig'; }
```

Remember to save the file and clear Drupal's cache since we introduced a new file. If we now refresh our home page and inspect the `<body>` element, we will see a new `class` has been added with the value of `twig`. The code block above added to the attributes class the value of twig. This preprocess function allows us to perform numerous functions to assist with theming in Drupal 8.

Currently, our home page is a little boring, so to kick things up a notch, let's look at how to work with our libraries file to add additional assets such as Bootstrap and Google Fonts.

Working with libraries

While Drupal 8 ships with some improvements to its default CSS and JavaScript libraries, we will generally find ourselves wishing to add additional third-party libraries that can enhance the function and feel of our website. In our case, we have decided to add Twitter Bootstrap (`http://getbootstrap.com`), which provides us with a responsive CSS framework and JavaScript library that utilizes a component-based approach to theming.

The process involves three steps:

1. First is downloading or installing the assets that make up the framework or library.
2. Second is adding library entries that point to our assets.
3. Finally, we will need to add a library reference to our `twiggy.info.yml` file.

Adding assets

We can easily add the Twitter Bootstrap framework assets by following these steps:

1. Navigate to `http://getbootstrap.com/getting-started/#download`.
2. Click on the **Download Bootstrap** button.
3. Extract the ZIP file.

4. Copy the contents of the bootstrap folder to our `/themes/twiggy` folder, keeping in mind that we will be overriding both the CSS and JS folders:

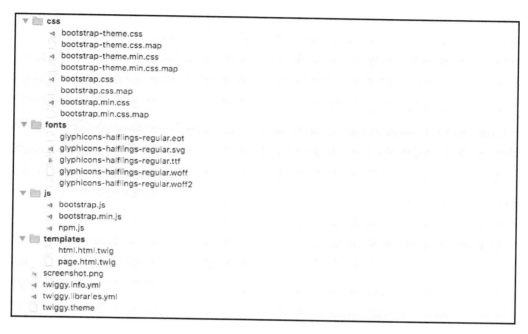

Now that we have the Twitter Bootstrap assets added to our theme, we need to modify our `twiggy.libraries.yml` file to allow us to reference our new assets.

Creating a library reference

Anytime we want to add CSS or JS files to our theme, we will need to either create or modify an existing `*.libraries.yml` file that allows us to organize our assets. Each library entry can include one or more pointers to the file and location within our theme structure. Remember that the filename of our `*.libraries.yml` file should follow the same naming convention as our theme.

We can begin by following these steps:

1. Open `twiggy.libraries.yml`.
2. Delete the `global` library reference.
3. Add a library entry named `bootstrap`.
4. Add a version that reflects the current version of Bootstrap that we are using.

5. Add the CSS entry for `bootstrap.min.css` and `bootstrap-theme.min.css`.

6. Add the JS entry for `bootstrap.min.js`.

7. Add a dependency to `jQuery` located in Drupal's core:

```
bootstrap: version: 3.3.6 css:  theme: css/bootstrap.min.css: {}
css/bootstrap-theme.min.css: {}  js: js/bootstrap.min.js: {}
dependencies: - core/jquery
```

8. Save `twiggy.libraries.yml`.

A quick note about **dependencies**: dependencies allow any JS file that relies on a specific JS library to make sure that the file can include the library as a dependency, which makes sure that the library is loaded before our JS file. In the case of Twitter Bootstrap, it relies on jQuery and since Drupal 8 has it as part of its `core.libraries.yml` file, we can reference it by pointing to that library and its entry.

Including our library

Just because we have added a library to our theme, it does not mean that it will automatically be added to our website. For us to add Bootstrap to our theme, we need to include it in our `twiggy.info.yml` configuration file.

We can add Bootstrap by following these steps:

1. Open `twiggy.info.yml`.

2. Replace the global libraries reference with the one for Bootstrap as follows:

```
libraries: - twiggy/bootstrap
```

3. Save `twiggy.info.yml`.

Make sure to clear Drupal's cache to allow our changes to be added to the Theme registry. Finally, navigate to our home page and refresh the browser so that we can preview our changes:

Welcome to Mastering Drupal 8

No front page content has been created yet.

If we inspect HTML using Chrome's Developer Tools, we should see that the Twitter Bootstrap library is being included along with the rest of our files. Both the CSS and JS files are loaded into the proper row of our document:

```
@import url("/themes/twiggy/css/bootstrap.min.css?oskhp4");
@import url("/themes/twiggy/css/bootstrap-theme.min.css?oskhp4");
```

Introducing web fonts

Web fonts are a common use case when creating any theme and we can take full advantage of **Google Fonts** by adding it to the head of our document. The external reference allows our CSS to render the typography on various pages. The only problem is that currently we are not including the web fonts in our Drupal theme. Because we cannot download Google Fonts and use them locally, they need to be externally hosted. But how do we add externally hosted files to our `twiggy.libraries.yml` file? Let's take look at the following steps:

1. Open `twiggy.libraries.yml`.
2. Add the following entry:

   ```
   google_fonts: version: VERSION css: theme:
   //fonts.googleapis.com/css?family=Open+Sans:300,400:{ type:
   external }
   ```

3. Save `twiggy.libraries.yml`.
4. Open `twiggy.info.yml`.
5. Add the following library reference pointing to the entry of our new Google Fonts:

   ```
   libraries: - twiggy/bootstrap - twiggy/google_fonts
   ```

6. Save `twiggy.info.yml`.

Make sure to clear Drupal's cache and refresh our home page. If we inspect the page, we should see our external reference to Google Fonts being loaded directly after Twitter Bootstrap.

Now that we have Bootstrap and Google Fonts in place, let's look at working with a few Twig templates that will allow us to convert our home page into something that looks a little more like the following:

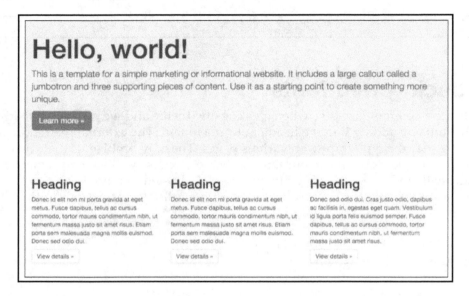

To have our content match the mockup above, we will need to work with various components of Drupal 8, including Pages, Nodes, and Blocks.

Creating our Jumbotron Block

The **Jumbotron** Block consists of three fields: Heading, Summary, and Button. We will take advantage of custom block types to create our new block, which we can then use to create a Twig template that contains the proper markup for Bootstrap to display the content as shown previously.

Step one - Creating a custom block

Navigate to `/admin/structure/block/block-content/types` and perform the following tasks:

1. Select the **Add custom block type** button.
2. Add a **Label**: Jumbotron.

3. Select the **Save** button.
4. Select the **Manage fields** button next to the Jumbotron Block Type.
5. Add the following fields:
   - Headline: Text (plain)
   - Button: Link

6. Select the **Manage form** display tab.
7. Reorder the fields:
   1. **Block description**.
   2. **Headline**.
   3. **Body**.
   4. **Button**.

8. Select the **Manage display** tab.
9. Reorder the fields:
   1. **Headline**.
   2. **Body** button.

Step two - Adding a new Jumbotron block

Navigate to `/admin/structure/block/block-content` and perform the following tasks:

1. Select the **Add custom block** button.
2. Select **Jumbotron.**
3. Add a **Block description**: `My Jumbotron.`
4. Add a **Headline**: `Hello, world!`
5. Add **Body**: This is a template for a simple marketing or informational website. It includes a large callout called a jumbotron and three supporting pieces of content. Use it as a starting point to create something more unique.
6. **Button URL**: `http://getbootstrap.com`
7. **Link text**: `Learn more.`
8. Select the **Save** button.

Step three - Placing the Jumbotron block

Navigate to `/admin/structure/block` and perform the following tasks:

1. Select the **Place block** button next to the **Content** region.
2. Select the **Place block** button next to **My Jumbotron.**
3. Deselect the **Display title** checkbox on the **Configure block** screen.
4. Select the **Save block** button.
5. Select the **Back to site** link in the Admin menu.

Our home page should now look like the following:

Welcome to Mastering Drupal 8

No front page content has been created yet.
- Add content

Headline
Hello, World!
This is a template for a simple marketing or informational website. It includes a large callout called a jumbotron and three supporting piece of content. Use it as a starting point to create something more unique.

Button
Learn more

With our content in place, it's time to start working with Twig templates.

Page template

We already have a `page.html.twig` template in our `theme's template` folder. For demonstration purposes, let's clean it up a bit and only focus on the `page.content` region.

Begin by opening `page.html.twig` and modifying the markup as follows:

```
<div class="layout-container"> <main role="main"> <div class="layout-
content"> {{ page.content }} </div> </main> </div>
```

Make sure to save the template; unlike most times, we do not need to clear the cache this time since the template was already registered with our theme layer.

If we refresh the browser, our page should look a little cleaner. However, one thing to note is that if our site does not contain any content then we will be presented with what Drupal calls the river of news, which is a view of all the latest content. Since we have no content, take a moment to add a Basic page with a title of **Homepage** and some additional content with the value of **Homepage placeholder**. Once this page has been added, our display should look like the following:

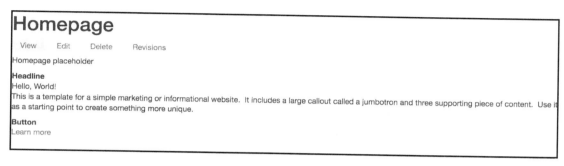

If we were to inspect our page and scroll through the various Twig comments, we would be presented with information telling us that we have a Page title block, a Tabs block, a Content region that contains a Node of content that we just created, and our Jumbotron block. At this point, we could approach theming this page in several ways. For demonstration purposes, we will move on to the Node template.

Node template

Node templates contain all the content and fields that make up a Content type. Each node has a template associated with it and several ways to name Node templates. The easiest way to determine where the template is coming from and what it is named is to inspect the page:

```
<!-- FILE NAME SUGGESTIONS:
   * node--5--full.html.twig
   * node--5.html.twig
   * node--page--full.html.twig
   * node--page.html.twig
   * node--full.html.twig
   x node.html.twig
-->
<!-- BEGIN OUTPUT from 'core/themes/classy/templates/content/node.html.twig'
-->
▶ <article data-history-node-id="5" data-quickedit-entity-id="node/5" role=
"article" class="contextual-region node node--type-page node--view-mode-full"
about="/node/5" typeof="schema:WebPage" data-quickedit-entity-instance-id="0">
…</article> == $0
<!-- END OUTPUT from 'core/themes/classy/templates/content/node.html.twig' -
```

Based on the Twig comments, we know the exact location of the Twig template and that Drupal is using the base `node.html.twig` template. With this information, we can override the template by following these steps:

1. Copy the `node.html.twig` template from `/core/themes/classy/templates/content/node.html.twig`.
2. Paste the copy into `/themes/twiggy/templates`.
3. Rename `node.html.twig` to `node--page--full.html.twig`.

Make sure to clear Drupal's cache and then refresh our page within the browser. Drupal is now using our copy of the template and we can proceed by modifying the markup as needed.

If we open our new node template and review the markup, we can see that there is quite a bit going on. For now, we can simplify the markup quite a bit by replacing everything with a simple `{{ content }}` variable and then save our template.

If we refresh the page, we will notice that visually nothing has changed. The reason is that the content variable will print out all the variables accessible to the Node. If we want to be more specific, then we can output specific fields using a syntax of `{{ content.field_name }}`, so in the case of the **Body** field, we can output it as `{{ content.body }}`.

The challenge with printing out specific field names is that if we add additional fields to our Content type, they will not print, so be careful if you choose to follow this method.

One other thing to point out is that when we printed the Body field specifically, the Page title is still displayed. The Page title is a block that takes the value of the Title field and prints it globally. We can fix this by simply deleting the **Page title** block from the **Block layout** page or by preventing it from displaying on specific content types.

With our **Page title** block removed, we can print the **Title** field within our Node template by adding the following markup:

```
<h1>{{ label }}</h1> {{ content }}
```

Now if we refresh our page, we will see that the **Title** field is being output using the `{{ label }}` variable and wrapped in a Heading 1.

All we have left now is to identify which Block template is being output and modify the template and markup accordingly.

Block template

Each block that Drupal displays also has a `block.html.twig` template that it uses. We can override this template like we did with the Node template. All we need to do is identify the path and the filename suggestion to use.

Begin by inspecting the **Headline** label and identifying which template is being used:

```
<!-- FILE NAME SUGGESTIONS:
   * block--myjumbotron.html.twig
   * block--block-content--8afffa8e-7bf2-40a7-9fd4-b7a86db91049.html.twig
   * block--block-content.html.twig
   * block--block-content.html.twig
   x block.html.twig
-->
<!-- BEGIN OUTPUT from 'core/themes/classy/templates/block/block.html.twig' -->
▶ <div data-quickedit-entity-id="block_content/2" id="block-myjumbotron" class="contextual-region block
block-block-content block-block-content8afffa8e-7bf2-40a7-9fd4-b7a86db91049" data-quickedit-entity-
instance-id="0">…</div> == $0
<!-- END OUTPUT from 'core/themes/classy/templates/block/block.html.twig' -->
```

Based on the Twig comments, we know the exact location of the Twig template and that Drupal is using the base `block.html.twig` template. With this information, we can override the template by following these steps:

1. Copy the `block.html.twig` template from `/core/themes/classy/templates/block/block.html.twig`.
2. Paste the copy into `/themes/twiggy/templates`.
3. Rename `block.html.twig` to `block--myjumbotron.html.twig`.

Make sure to clear Drupal's cache and then refresh our page within the browser. Drupal is now using our copy of the template and we can proceed by modifying the markup as needed.

Open `block--myjumbotron.html.twig` and replace the markup with the following:

```
{{ content.field_headline }} {{ content.body }} {{ content.field_button }}
```

Here we are printing out the three fields that contain the content we want to use. If we refresh the page, we will see that nothing has changed.

Now for us to utilize Twitter Bootstrap's Jumbotron markup to surround our Twig variables with the following:

```
<div class="jumbotron"> <div class="container"> <h1>{{
content.field_headline }}</h1> {{ content.body }} {{ content.field_button
}} </div> </div>
```

Now if we refresh our page, we are starting to look better. However, you may have noticed that we are also printing the labels of the fields we are outputting:

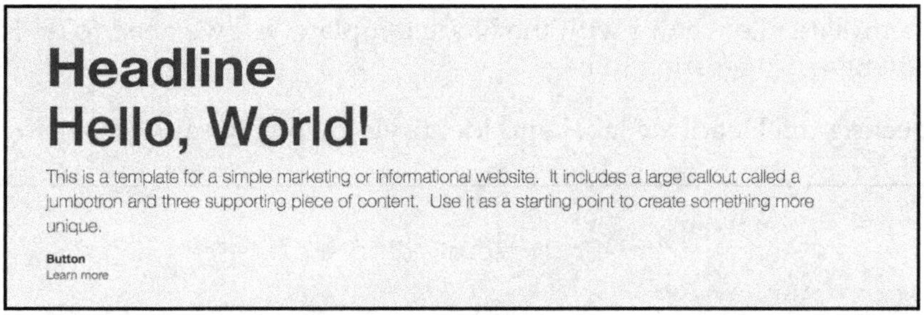

To fix this, make sure to change the **Label** displays on the custom block to **hidden** and then refresh the page:

At this point, the only thing that remains to be themed is our button. Currently, it is displaying as a normal link. There are a couple ways to address this. One is to drill down into the `content.field_button` variable, which is more of an advanced topic. The second is a little easier and involves creating a Field template.

Field templates

Each field that Drupal displays also has a `field.html.twig` template that it uses. We can override this template like we did with both the Node and Block templates. All we need to do is identify the path and the filename suggestion to use.

Begin by inspecting the **Learn more** link and identify which template is being used:

```
<!-- FILE NAME SUGGESTIONS:
   * field--block-content--field-button--jumbotron.html.twig
   * field--block-content--field-button.html.twig
   * field--block-content--jumbotron.html.twig
   * field--field-button.html.twig
   * field--link.html.twig
   x field.html.twig
-->
<!-- BEGIN OUTPUT from 'core/themes/classy/templates/field/field.html.twig' -->
▶<div data-quickedit-field-id="block_content/2/field_button/en/full" class="field field--name-field-
button field--type-link field--label-hidden field__item">...</div>
<!-- END OUTPUT from 'core/themes/classy/templates/field/field.html.twig' -->
```

Based on the Twig comments, we know the exact location of the Twig template and that Drupal is using the base `field.html.twig` template. With this information, we can override the template by following these steps:

1. Copy the `field.html.twig` template from `/core/themes/classy/templates/field/field.html.twig`.
2. Paste the copy into `/themes/twiggy/templates`.
3. Rename `field.html.twig` to `field--field-button.html.twig`.

Make sure to clear Drupal's cache and then refresh our page within the browser. Drupal is now using our copy of the template and we can proceed by modifying the markup as needed.

Open `field--field-button.html.twig` and replace the markup with the following:

```
{% for item in items %} <a class="btn btn-primary btn-lg" href="{{
item.content['#url'] }}" role="button">{{ item.content['#title'] }}</a> {%
endfor %}
```

To explain in a little more detail what is taking place in the markup we just added, we need to understand how fields in Drupal work. First off, since we have the ability when creating fields to limit a field to a specific instance, limit a field to a numbered instance, or set the field to be unlimited instances, Drupal has no idea which one we chose without looping through the fields. Therefore, we use a Twig loop within the field template to determine the number of times the markup should be printed.

Next, since our button contains two different values that we need to access, one for the URL and another for the title, we must traverse the `item.content` variable and grab the array's value for each one. While a little more complex than previous Twig variables, this also has the power of being able to access whatever values we need within Twig templates.

If we take one last look at our Jumbotron, we will see that it now matches the mockup we reviewed earlier:

Congratulations, we are on our way to mastering Twig templates. While this is just a sample of what you can do with Twig, it warrants mentioning that if you want a deeper dive into taking a project from start to finish, make sure to look at *Drupal 8 Theming with Twig*, another great book by Packt.

Summary

In the last two chapters on Mastering Drupal 8 Theming, we covered a lot of material. To state that it is just the beginning of all that you can learn about the theming layer would be an understatement. We have only just touched the surface, but hopefully it is enough to spark your interest in taking a longer look at what can be accomplished with Drupal.

Let's review what we covered in this chapter. We began with setting up our local environment for theming, including enabling Twig debugging. From there, we quickly looked at Twig fundamentals that allowed us to inspect, set, and print Twig variables. Finally, we touched on a handful of Twig templates and worked with library assets to use Twitter Bootstrap to build a Jumbotron.

Next, we will be taking a look at extending Drupal.

10
Extending Drupal

There are a great many things you can do in Drupal by using just the core facilities. However, when you start going beyond those core facilities, you will start to need to write custom code. Many of the site building features of Drupal 8 are similar to previous versions, but with Symfony under the hood, writing new modules in Drupal 8 is very different. In this chapter, we will be covering the following topics:

- Using Drush and Composer in order to aid development
- Creating a new module
- Understanding configuration and plugins
- Working with dependency injection
- Adding new permissions
- Adding menu routes and menu items
- Using events and hooks

Using Drush

One of the indispensible tools for developing in Drupal is Drush. It allows you to interact with modules, users, configuration, caches, and more through the command line, faster than going through the user interface in a web browser. In order to use Drush with Drupal 8, you need to be running the latest stable version of Drush, Drush 8. There are several new features in Drush 8 that make development easier.

The largest is the inclusion of the PsySH REPL to do quick experiments using a bootstrapped version instance of Drupal. Running `drush php` will open up a command shell where you can directly interact with the Drupal API.

```
[vagrant@localhost public]$ drush php
Psy Shell v0.6.1 (PHP 5.6.17 — cli) by Justin Hileman
>>> $query = \Drupal::entityQuery('node');
=> Drupal\Core\Entity\Query\Sql\Query {#10930
    +"conjunction": "AND",
    }
>>> $query->execute();
=> [
    11 => "11",
    ]
>>>
```

Using Composer

Composer is a tool for managing dependencies in PHP. Drupal 8 is based on Symfony and other open source projects. When you download Drupal for the first time, the files for those other projects are not present. They are referenced in the `composer.json` file and will be downloaded when you run `composer install` from the project root. In addition to declaring dependencies on Symfony components, you can also use Composer to download Drupal modules. This is similar to what you could have done with a `drush.make` file, but it automatically handles nested dependencies. For example, if you use Composer to install the Page Manager module, it will ensure that CTools is downloaded without having to explicitly declare it.

To add the Guzzle OAuth Subscriber module to your project, you can add `"guzzlehttp/oauth-subscriber": "^0.3.0"` to the required section of your `composer.json file` and then run the Composer update. You can also run Composer require `guzzlehttp/oauth-subscriber`. Composer will download the module, as well recursively downloading any dependencies that it may have.

In order to have Composer manage Drupal modules and themes, you need to add the following code to your `composer.json` file:

```
"repositories": { "drupal": { "type": "composer", "url":
"https://packages.drupal.org/8" } }
```

This allows you to add items from modules, themes and libraries to your `composer.json` file or install them by running Composer require.

Creating a new module

The simplest way to create a new module is to use the Drupal Console project. Built on top of the Symfony Console, the Drupal Console is a set of tools to scaffold out new Drupal features and run other tasks on a Drupal instance. Some of these commands provide similar functionality to what's already in Drush. For example, if you wanted to download the Chaos Tools module, you could run either `drupal md ctools` or `drush pm-download ctools` and it will pull down the module and place it in your `/modules` directory.

To install the Drupal Console, run the following:

```
# Download and install Drupal Console:
curl https://drupalconsole.com/installer -L -o drupal.phar

# Place it somewhere you can access it:
mv drupal.phar /usr/local/bin/drupal

# Make sure you can execute it:
chmod +x /usr/local/bin/drupal

# Copy configuration files to user home directory:
drupal init --override
```

Where the Drupal Console really shines, is in code generation. This scaffolding allows you to automate some of the tedious file creation necessary to add functionality to a Drupal site. For instance, to create a new module, you can simply run `drupal generate:module` and then answer some simple questions. It will then create the appropriate `.info.yml` file and `optional` `.module` file.

```
[vagrant@localhost modules]$ drupal generate:module

// Welcome to the Drupal module generator

Enter the new module name:
> Mastering Drupal 8

Enter the module machine name [mastering_drupal_8]:
>

Enter the module Path [/modules/custom]:
>

Enter module description [My Awesome Module]:
> Mastering Drupal 8

Enter package name [Custom]:
>

Enter Drupal Core version [8.x]:
>

Do you want to generate a .module file (yes/no) [no]:
>

Define module as feature (yes/no) [no]:
>

Do you want to add a composer.json file to your module (yes/no) [yes]:
>

Would you like to add module dependencies (yes/no) [no]:
>


Do you confirm generation? (yes/no) [yes]:
>

Generated or updated files
 Site path: /vagrant/public
 1 - modules/custom/mastering_drupal_8/mastering_drupal_8.info.yml
 2 - modules/custom/mastering_drupal_8/composer.json
```

Understanding configuration and plugins

In Drupal 7, when you went to extend Drupal core or other contrib modules, you created a new module. This module would contain the .info file that defined information about the module in a custom ini-like syntax. Then there was a .module file, which served as both the manifest of what functionality your module implemented and, of course, the implementation itself. Both of these have undergone substantial changes in Drupal 8. The .info files have been replaced by YAML files and, while the .module file still exists, many things that you would have placed in it have been moved out to separate files that are automatically discovered.

YAML

YAML has taken the place of all other data representation or serialization formats in Drupal 8. All configuration outputs and all module or service definitions are in YAML; basically, if it isn't PHP, JavaScript or CSS, it's YAML. YAML was chosen because it's human-readable and the syntax maps well to normal data types, like lists, associative arrays, and a variety of scalar values. YAML uses white space to define the hierarchy of information instead of enclosures, such as brackets, braces, semi-colons, and so on. Looking at an example, using an .info.yml file for a theme, you'll see a lot of similarities to what you would have had in an .info file in Drupal 7.

```
name: Test
type: theme
description: A test theme.
core: 8.x
libraries:
 - test/global
regions:
 header: Header
 content: Content # the content region is required
 sidebar_first: 'Sidebar first'
 footer: Footer
```

If you were to imagine this as a PHP associative array, it would look like:

```
[
 'name' => 'Test',
 'type' => 'theme',
 'description' => 'A test theme.',
 'core' = '8.x',
 'libraries' => [ 'test/global' ],
 'regions' => [
 'header' => 'Header',
```

```
 'content' => 'Content',
 'sidebar_first' => 'Sidebar first',
 'footer' => 'footer'
 ]
 ]
```

There are some specific rules as to how the values are defined in a YAML file:

- Strings can be surrounded by single or double quotations, but they can also be left unquoted--but unquoted strings are trimmed
- Double quoted strings allow you to embed escape characters such as \n or \t or any Unicode characters
- The values true or false are treated as Boolean values; if you need them as string values, they need to be quoted
- Null values can be entered as either null or ~
- Unquoted values that look like integers, floats, or are in exponential notation (for example, 5e7) will be cast to the appropriate number
- Values that look like ISO-8601 dates and times (for example, 2017-04-23 or 2017-04-23T13:44:19Z) will be converted to Unix timestamps

Plugins

One of the wonderful things about Drupal is how easy it makes it to add new functionality to the platform. In Drupal 7, you would implement an info hook to define your new component and then another one or more hooks to handle the actual functionality. For example, to create a new block you would implement hook_block_info to return an array of blocks defined by your module, and then hook_block_view, hook_block_configure, and so on, to handle the individual interactions with each block. In Drupal 8, these additions are handled as plugins. There are a number of plugin types defined by Drupal 8 core, including:

- **Blocks**: Pieces of content and functionality that are shown around the main page content
- **Entities**: Different types of content, for example nodes, taxonomy terms, and so on
- **Fields**, **widgets**, and **display formatters**: Different ways of capturing information and then displaying it
- **Image effects**: Ways to transform images before they are shown
- **Rules plugins**: Conditionally executed actions and custom events

- **Views plugins**: Adding new ways of displaying content from Drupal
- **Search page plugins**: Alternate methods of searching content

Contributed modules that need a similar ability to discover and use different functionality can define their own plugin types. This is the expected pattern for any modules that expose a similar API. For example, the Salesforce Suite, Search API, and context modules all provide one or more plugin types.

Let's go ahead and create a simple block plugin to test what that looks like. So, the first thing you want to do is scaffold out the block plugin file by running drupal generate:plugin:block. Answer the questions and it will create the necessary file and directory structure:

```
[vagrant@localhost public]$ drupal generate:plugin:block

 // Welcome to the Drupal Plugin Block generator
 Enter the module name [entity_rest_extra]:
 > mastering_drupal_8

 Plugin class name [DefaultBlock]:
 > TestBlock

 Plugin label [Test block]:
 >

 Plugin id [test_block]:
 >

 Theme region to render Plugin Block [ ]:
 >

 Do you want to load services from the container (yes/no) [no]:
 >


You can add input fields to create special configurations in the block.
This is optional, press enter to continue

 Do you want to generate a form structure? (yes/no) [yes]:
 >

 Type [ ]:
 >

 Do you confirm generation? (yes/no) [yes]:
 >

Generated or updated files
 Site path: /vagrant/public
 1 - modules/custom/mastering_drupal_8/src/Plugin/Block/TestBlock.php
 // cache:rebuild

 Rebuilding cache(s), wait a moment please.


 [OK] Done clearing cache(s).
```

This creates the `TestBlock.php` file in the
`/modules/custom/mastering_drupal_8/src/Plugins/Block` directory. This path,
`src/Plugins/{Type}` is where you'll place all plugins for a module. Now you can
navigate to `localhost/admin/structure/block`, click the **Place block** button next to
Content, find your **Test block**, and click the **Place block** button.

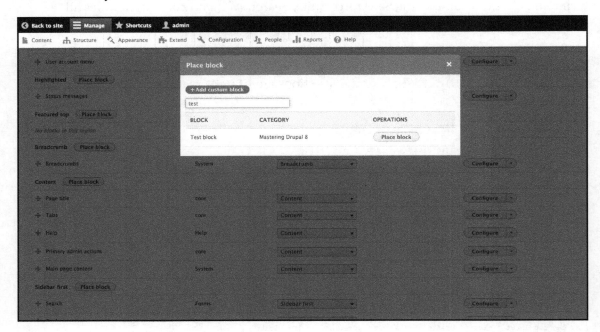

Now click the **Save blocks** button and go back to the home page: you'll see the **Test block** showing the text `Implement TestBlock`.

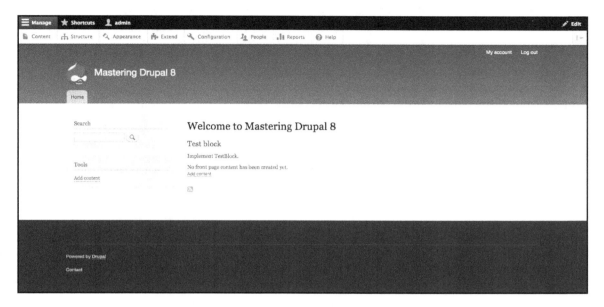

Annotations

An annotation is metadata that can be added to a file, class, function, or variable. These can be used to add information describing plugins without having to write a separate function. In Drupal 7, in order to expose a block, you needed to implement at least two hooks: `hook_block_info` to describe the block, give it a label, a machine name, describe caching, and so on; and then at least `hook_block_view` to render it. The same file that contains the plugin implementation also contains the metadata about it. It's encoded as a PHP docblock on the class itself. You can see that above the class declaration in our `TestBlock.php` file.

```
/**
 * Provides a 'TestBlock' block.
 *
 * @Block(
 * id = "test_block",
 * admin_label = @Translation("Test block"),
 * )
 */
```

As of PHP 5.1, the PHP Reflection API has allowed runtime inspection of multi-line doc comments (also called `T_DOC_COMMENTS`) using the `ReflectionClass::getDocComments` method. One important note is that only doc comments, that is, ones that begin with `/**`, are retrieved. Any comments that are normal multi-line comments (`T_COMMENT`) that begin with a single asterisk like `/*` are not stored in the opcode cache.

Symfony uses annotations to provide essential metadata to various handlers, though at the moment, Drupal only uses them for plugins. For instance, the `@Block` declaration invokes and attaches the `\Drupal\Core\Block\Annotation\Block` class, which defines the elements that can be used in the annotation:

- `admin_label`: The label that is shown in the administrative UI
- **Category**: The group that the plugin appears under in the administrative UI
- **Derivative**: It allows a plugin to be shown as and act like multiple plugins when the functionality is the same, for example, menu blocks

From a plugin object you can call `PluginInspectionInterface::getPluginDefinition` to retrieve the array that contains the annotation data. Looking at our new block plugin, it extends `BlockBase`, which implements `BlockPluginInterface`, which extends `PluginInspectionInterface`. So, to get the machine name of a block entity, you would do the following:

```
$machine_name = $block->getPlugin()->getPluginDefinition()['id'];
```

Anatomy of a plugin manager

A **plugin manager** is a service that defines how a plugin is discovered and annotated. Let's look at how the block plugin manager is set up. First, the service for it is defined, like other core services, in the `core.services.yml file`. You see:

```
plugin.manager.block:
  class: Drupal\Core\Block\BlockManager
  parent: default_plugin_manager
```

This declares the service by a unique name, `plugin.manager.block`, and defines the class name and the parent service, in this case `default_plugin_manager`, which was defined earlier as being the `DefaultPluginManager` class. Most of the work of the plugin manager is done inside the constructor. Looking at the `BlockManager::__construct function`, we have:

```
public function __construct(\Traversable $namespaces, CacheBackendInterface
$cache_backend, ModuleHandlerInterface $module_handler)
{
        parent::__construct('Plugin/Block', $namespaces, $module_handler,
        'Drupal\Core\Block\BlockPluginInterface',
        'Drupal\Core\Block\Annotation\Block'); $this->alterInfo('block');
        $this->setCacheBackend($cache_backend, 'block_plugins');
}
```

A lot of the work is handled by the parent, the `DefaultPluginManager`. It gets the path to use to detect new plugins, in this case plugin/Block--which is how our `TestBlock` is discovered--then the list of namespaces for Drupal and the module handler for Drupal. The next two define the interface that the plugin is expected to implement and the annotation class that is used to process the plugin's metadata. After this definition, it adds the hook that can be used to alter the `plugin: alterInfo('block')` becomes `hook_block_alter`. Finally, the plugins are cached to ensure Drupal doesn't have to go scanning for block plugins on each request.

Working with dependency injection

Dependency injection is an example of an inversion of control software design pattern. Inversion of control is a principle that involves having a generic and reusable framework to make calls and delegate to more custom code. In Drupal 7, an example of this is the menu system. A request comes in and is matched to a route and then Drupal loads the module file and calls the appropriate function. Dependency injection specifically allows you to define when your class needs a dependency and have those needs fulfilled by the system.

When creating new functionality in Drupal 8, you write your dependencies into your class constructor and, when the system creates your class, they are passed into it.

A key advantage to using dependency injection is that you do not have to know how to instantiate the services that your class depends on. Take, for example, a simple database connection. In order to connect to the database you need the appropriate driver, username, password, port, database name, or schema, and so on. These, in turn, could be stored in configuration files, in environment variables, or some other data storage. But when you want to use a database connection, you don't care about any of these implementation details. You ask for a database connection and one is provided.

Dependency injection also simplifies the process of testing. Dependency injection allows a developer to override the versions of services provided by the system with custom ones. This is often used to provide mock services that return pre-defined outcomes so you can easily test your logic. Imagine you were building a module that sent email and you wanted to test it without, of course, actually sending an email. You could create a class that implemented the `MailManagerInterface` and, instead of sending the email, allow your test to verify that it would have been sent.

The other side of the dependency injection coin is the service locator. There are times when you don't know specifically which functionality you'll need when you write your class. For example, Drupal 8 has built-in support for serialization to and from YAML, JSON, and basic PHP serialization. Suppose you wanted to take the `TestBlock` plugin from earlier and have to output its configuration to one of those three formats, depending on which one an administrator had selected. You could write that like:

```
protected $serializer; public function __construct($configuration,
$plugin_id, $plugin_definition, Json $json_serializer, Yaml
$yaml_serializer, PhpSerialize $php_serializer)
{
      parent::__construct($configuration, $plugin_id,
      $plugin_definition); switch ($configuration['serializer'])
      {
            case 'json': $this->serializer = $json_serializer; break;
            case 'yaml': $this->serializer = $yaml_serializer; break;
            case 'php': $this->serializer = $php_serializer; break;
      }
}
```

There are a couple of downsides to this approach. The first is that it could require Drupal to instantiate serializers that are never used. The second is that it makes it difficult to extend if you wanted to added additional serializers: you'd have to add them to the constructor signature and then to the switch statement.

Alternatively, you could load the Service Container and request the serialization method you want by the machine name. So, that would look like:

```
protected $serializer; public function __construct($configuration,
$plugin_id, $plugin_definition)
{
        parent::__construct($configuration, $plugin_id,
        $plugin_definition); $this->serializer = \Drupal::getContainer()
        ->get('serialization.' + $this->configuration['serializer']);
}
```

Services

We've talked a lot about services without really discussing what they are. In Drupal 8, a service is a PHP object that performs some sort of global task. That means they are separated from the specifics of *why* that task would need to be performed and be able to concentrate solely on *how* to perform that task. The services exposed by Drupal 8 core can be found in `/core/core.services.yml`. If you need functionality from the Drupal 8 system, either from core or contrib, you'll be requesting services. From interacting with the database, to making HTTP calls to external systems, to interacting with the cache, all of those are encapsulated in services. Using dependency injection, all you need to do is declare your dependency on them in your own code and then make use of them when your class is instantiated.

In most cases, services are singletons and stateless. The service container instantiates the service when necessary, stores that object, and provides it whenever requested. Services can be configured to be regenerated every time they are requested or for every request or sub-request.

Creating your own service

When creating your own service, the first step is to declare it to the system through your module's `{module}.services.yml` file. Imagine that we wanted to create a new block to display information from the Weather Underground's API. We could put all of the logic to connect to their API within the block itself, but that would defeat the purpose of modularity. So, first, we have to create a Weather Underground service.

This is another job for the Drupal Console. Run `drupal generate:service` and start answering some prompts.

```
[vagrant@localhost public]$ drupal generate:service

// Welcome to the Drupal service generator
Enter the module name [ctools]:
> mastering_drupal_8

Enter the service name [mastering_drupal_8.default]:
> mastering_drupal_8.weather_underground

Enter the Class name [DefaultService]:
> WeatherUnderground

Create an interface (yes/no) [yes]:
> no


Do you want to load services from the container (yes/no) [no]:
> yes


Type the service name or use keyup or keydown.
This is optional, press enter to continue

Enter your service [ ]:
> http_client
Enter your service [ ]:
>

Do you confirm generation? (yes/no) [yes]:
>

Generated or updated files
Site path: /vagrant/public
1 - modules/custom/mastering_drupal_8/mastering_drupal_8.services.yml
2 - modules/custom/mastering_drupal_8/src/WeatherUnderground.php
// cache:rebuild

Rebuilding cache(s), wait a moment please.

 [OK] Done clearing cache(s).
```

Services definition file

Now you have a `mastering_drupal_8.services.yml file` with:

```
services:
  mastering_drupal_8.weather_underground:
  class: Drupal\mastering_drupal_8\WeatherUnderground
  arguments: ["@http_client"]
```

The first two lines are pretty simple: we give our service a name, namespace it to our module, and set the class that is used to instantiate the service. That third line defines the arguments that are injected into the service. In this case, since we're going to be making calls to an external API, we need to have an HTTP client. Those two attributes, class, and arguments, are the most common metadata in the `services.yml` file.

Other, less common, options include:

abstract

Allows you to define a service that cannot be directly injected but serves as a parent class for other services.

alias

Defines an alternate name that can be used to access the service.

calls

Functions on the services that are called after it is instantiated. These can be used to set additional options on the service, especially ones that might not be required. For instance, on the `url_generator` service it has specific dependencies on the non-bubbling URL Generator Service as well as a `Renderer` service.

```
url_generator:
  class: Drupal\Core\Render\MetadataBubblingUrlGenerator
  arguments: ['@url_generator.non_bubbling', '@renderer']
  calls:
  - [setContext, ['@?router.request_context']]
```

If you look at the `UrlGenerator` class--the one that's created for the `url_generator.non_bubbling` service--you'll see that it creates its own `RequestContext`. However, if there is a current `RequestContext` for the Router, we'd want to use that instead of a more generic one. Since you could use this service in a context where there wasn't an active Router, you wouldn't want to make it part of the arguments array.

configurator

This defines a callable service and function name that are invoked after the service is instantiated to set up an element of it. An example of this are some of the services exposed on the new HTTP client, Guzzle:

```
http_handler_stack:
  class: GuzzleHttp\HandlerStack
  public: false
  factory: GuzzleHttp\HandlerStack::create
  configurator: ['@http_handler_stack_configurator', configure]
http_handler_stack_configurator:
```

```
class: Drupal\Core\Http\HandlerStackConfigurator
public: false
arguments: ['@service_container']
```

When Drupal goes to instantiate the `http_handler_stack  service`, it first creates the `GuzzleHttp\HandlerStack` object, then retrieves the `http_handler_stack_configurator` service, instantiating it as necessary. It then calls the `configure()` function on that object passing the `HandlerStack` object to it.

Using a configurator allows you to decouple the configuration of a service from the service implementation itself. In the case of Guzzle, the configurator is responsible for loading any middleware and adding it to the `HandlerStack`. This allows the `HandlerStack` to allow runtime definition of middleware, as well having it defined when instantiated.

factory

The Service Container has a great deal of flexibility when it comes to instantiating your service. Sometimes, however, this does not provide everything necessary to construct the service. When you need more specific control over this process, you can define a factory to instantiate the service. There are two ways to define this factory. First, you can define a `factory` service and define the function on that service to invoke:

```
http_client:
  class: GuzzleHttp\Client
  factory: http_client_factory:fromOptions
```

In this case, the class defined by the `http_client_factory` service has a member function, `fromOptions()`, that returns a `GuzzleHttp\Client` object.

The other option is to define the `factory` as a static function:

```
http_handler_stack:
  class: GuzzleHttp\HandlerStack
  public: false
  factory: GuzzleHttp\HandlerStack::create
  configurator: ['@http_handler_stack_configurator', configure]
```

To instantiate an `http_handler_stack` service, the static function on the `GuzzleHttp\HandlerStack` class will be invoked.

parent

Defines the parent to the service, which is almost always paired with abstract services. This is implemented in the service as either normal inheritance or as a trait. For instance:

```
entity.manager:
  class: Drupal\Core\Entity\EntityManager
  parent: container.trait
```

defines the `Drupal\Core\Entity\EntityManager` class, which uses the `Symfony\Component\DependencyInjection\ContainerAwareTrait`.

properties

In addition to the arguments and calls, you can also set public fields on the service class directly. The properties metadata is a hash of attributes and references to other services. For instance, if you had a service class like:

```
class MyService {
  public $database;
}
```

You could define the metadata like:

```
test.my_service:
  properties:
  value: '@database'
```

There are some fairly significant disadvantages to doing this, however. The first is that the Service Container will set the value on instantiation; there is no other control on when that value could be set. It could be changed at any point in the object's lifetime and there is no way to track this. The other is, there is no way to hint the class property. In other ways of injecting dependencies, the class or interface can be explicitly defined in the signature, which prevents invalid assignment. With public attributes, there is no such safety.

The most common use case for this behavior is when using a third-party library that expects dependencies to be added using public properties.

public

Marks the service as either public or private. Private services may only be used as arguments to other services, they cannot be injected into plugins. Set to `false` to mark the service as private. If you create an alias for a private service, it can still be accessed through the alias.

scope

This attribute defines how long the instance of the service is used by the Service Container. With the default value, "container," the Service Container always uses the same instance of the service. Other options include "prototype", which ensures the Service Container creates a fresh copy of the service for every request, and "request" ,which means the Service Container will create a new copy for every request or sub-request. Using "request" means that the service cannot be used in contexts where there is no request, namely the CLI.

tags

Tags are used to mark services for certain purposes. Various services use this tag in order to discover services. An example of this is how file streams are used. For example, the `public://` stream is defined with:

```
stream_wrapper.public:
  class: Drupal\Core\StreamWrapper\PublicStream
  tags:
  { name: stream_wrapper, scheme: public }
```

To add another file stream to Drupal you would create a service that implemented `Drupal\Core\StreamWrapper\StreamWrapperInterface` and then add the `stream_wrapper` tag to it, along with defining the scheme.

Service implementation

The Drupal Console has also created the initial stub of the service file at
`/modules/custom/mastering_drupal_8/src/WeatherUnderground.php`.

```php
1   <?php
2
3   /**
4    * @file
5    * Contains \Drupal\mastering_drupal_8\WeatherUnderground.
6    */
7
8   namespace Drupal\mastering_drupal_8;
9
10  use GuzzleHttp\Client;
11
12  /**
13   * Class WeatherUnderground.
14   *
15   * @package Drupal\mastering_drupal_8
16   */
17  class WeatherUnderground {
18
19    /**
20     * GuzzleHttp\Client definition.
21     *
22     * @var GuzzleHttp\Client
23     */
24    protected $http_client;
25    /**
26     * Constructor.
27     */
28    public function __construct(Client $http_client) {
29      $this->http_client = $http_client;
30    }
31
32  }
```

At this point, we can start implementing the Weather Underground API.

```php
/**
 * Returns information about current hurricanes and tropical storms.
 *
 * @return ResponseInterface
 */
public function getCurrentHurricane() {
  return $this->http_client->get('http://api.wunderground.com/api/{key}/currenthurricane/view.json');
}
```

Using your service

Creating the block to display this new information is a another call to Drupal's generate:plugin:block, except this time, we're going to tell it to use a service and provide the mastering_drupal_8.weather_underground service.

```
[vagrant@localhost public]$ drupal generate:plugin:block

// Welcome to the Drupal Plugin Block generator
Enter the module name [ctools]:
> mastering_drupal_8

Plugin class name [DefaultBlock]:
> CurrentHurricanes

Plugin label [Current hurricanes]:
>

Plugin id [current_hurricanes]:
>

Theme region to render Plugin Block [ ]:
>

Do you want to load services from the container (yes/no) [no]:
> yes


Type the service name or use keyup or keydown.
This is optional, press enter to continue

Enter your service [ ]:
> mastering_drupal_8.weather_underground
Enter your service [ ]:
>

You can add input fields to create special configurations in the block.
This is optional, press enter to continue

Do you want to generate a form structure? (yes/no) [yes]:
> no


Do you confirm generation? (yes/no) [yes]:
>

Generated or updated files
 Site path: /vagrant/public
 1 - modules/custom/mastering_drupal_8/src/Plugin/Block/CurrentHurricanes.php
// cache:rebuild

Rebuilding cache(s), wait a moment please.


 [OK] Done clearing cache(s).
```

Adding it to the **Content** region through the block administrative pages causes the default text to appear.

Then, we can wire up the block to the service in the `build()` function and output a list of any current hurricanes.

```
/**
 * {@inheritdoc}
 */
public function build() {
  $current_hurricanes = json_decode($this->mastering_drupal_8_weather_underground->getCurrentHurricane()->getBody());
  $build = [];

  $build['list'] = [
    '#theme' => 'item_list',
    '#items' => [],
  ];

  foreach ($current_hurricanes->currenthurricane as $hurricane) {
    $build['list']['#items'][] = $hurricane->stormName_Nice;
  }

  if (0 === sizeof($current_hurricanes->currenthurricane)) {
    $build['list']['#items'][] = 'None';
  }

  return $build;
}
```

One thing you'll notice in the code of our new `CurrentHurricanes` block is the addition of the static `create()` method. This static factory method is what provides the constructor with dependencies. In order to add new dependencies to a plugin you need to add them to both the constructor signature as well as the `create()` method.

Permissions

Adding permissions specific to your module has been moved from the Drupal 7 `hook_permissions` to a `{module}.permissions.yml` file. That file contains an element for each permission, along with the human-readable name and description. If we wanted to add a new permission for our module, we would create a `mastering_drupal_8.permissions.yml` file like:

```
access test content:
  title: Access test content
  restrict access: TRUE
  description: Whether a user can access test content
```

You can also add an array for `permission_callback` array that contains a list of callables that return an array in the same format as the YAML file. For instance, in `node.permissions.yml`, there is:

```
permission_callbacks:
  - \Drupal\node\NodePermissions::nodeTypePermissions
```

The function `nodeTypePermissions` on the `NodePermissions` class returns an array of permissions with the human-readable title keyed by the appropriate machine name.

Routing and menus

A core design principle in software development is the separation of concerns. Each piece of information that affects the operation of the system is separated into a distinct section. In Drupal 7, a notable violator of that principle was `hook_menu`. It controlled routing, how a URI was mapped to the section of code that would handle the request, menu links, and local tasks, all using a specialized array with 23 different attributes. In Drupal 8 routing, menus and related items have all been separated out into their own components and configuration.

Basic routing

A route is a way for Drupal to determine which system should be responsible for returning content to a request. For example, when it receives a request for /node, Drupal is able to match this to the home page and return the current list of content. Routes are defined in the {module}.routing.yml file inside the module directory. At its most basic, that file looks like:

```
mastering_drupal_8.test_page:
 path: 'mastering_drupal_8/test'
 defaults:
 _controller:
 '\Drupal\mastering_drupal_8\Controller\TestPageController::test'
 requirements:
 _permission: 'access content'
```

You have a name for the route, namespaced by the module that contains it. Within the route, other required elements are: path, the URL for the route; defaults, the default properties of the route; and requirements, the conditions that must be fulfilled to grant access to the route.

The most common element in defaults is the controller, which provides a callable string, typically in the format class::function. A basic controller for that route would look like:

```
class TestPageController extends ControllerBase {
 /**
 * Test.
 *
 * @return string
 * Return Test string.
 */
 public function test() {
 return [
 '#type' => 'markup',
 '#markup' => $this->t("Test")
 ];
 }
}
```

The controller extends ControllerBase and has a public function that matches the function in the routing file that returns a renderable array. The function can also return the Symfony\Component\HttpFoundation\Response object. Response objects will be sent directly and no theming or blocks will be added.

Display methods

In addition to using a controller, there are other display methods that can be specified under defaults in your routing file.

_form

Used when the route returns a form. The value should be a class that implements `Drupal\Core\Form\FormInterface`.

_form: 'Drupal\user\Form\UserLoginForm'

_entity_view

This is used to display an entity. The value should be the entity type and display mode:

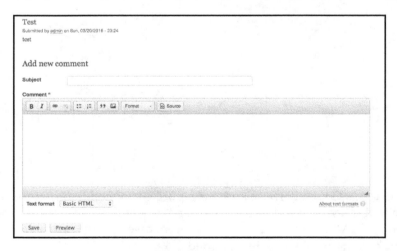

_entity_view: 'node.full'

_entity_list

This is used to display a list of entities using the appropriate EntityListController. The value should be the name of the entity:

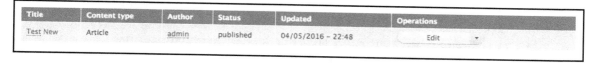

_entity_list: 'node'

_entity_form

This is used to display an edit form for an entity. The value should be the name of the entity:

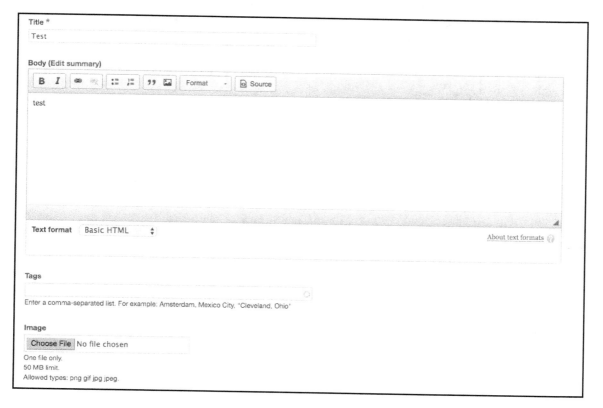

_entity_form: node.default

There are also some optional parameters that may be added in the defaults section of the route.

- `_title`: The page title of the route
- `_title_context`: Any additional information for the title sent to the `t()` function
- `_title_page_callback`: A PHP callable, typically in the format `class::function`, which returns the page title for the route

Handling arguments

When you define a route URL, you can add parameters by name to be sent to the display method. These parameters are wrapped in braces, for example, `/node/add/{node_type}`. The values passed in via the URL are passed to the controller by name, so the name of the variable in the controller function needs to be the same name as the parameter in the URL. The order of the parameters in the function signature doesn't matter, only that they are named the same.

So, if we changed the route URL to `mastering_drupal_8/test/{message}`, we would change the controller function to:

```
public function test($message) {
 return [
 '#type' => 'markup',
 '#markup' => $this->t("Test: " . $message),
 ];
}
```

Named parameters are not sanitized by default. You need to sanitize them in your controller before using them. Named parameters are also required initially. In our example above, if you don't provide a value for the message, you will receive a 404 Page Not Found error. You add attributes matching the parameter name in the defaults section of the routing YAML file. For example:

```
mastering_drupal_8.test_page_message:
 path: 'mastering_drupal_8/message/{message}'
 defaults:
 _controller:
 '\Drupal\mastering_drupal_8\Controller\TestPageController::testMessage'
 message: 'foo'
 requirements:
 _access: 'TRUE'
```

If the named parameter is the name of an entity, it will be loaded prior to it being sent to the controller. Changing the routing YAML file to:

```
mastering_drupal_8.test_page_node:
 path: 'mastering_drupal_8/node/{node}'
 defaults:
 _controller:
 '\Drupal\mastering_drupal_8\Controller\TestPageController::testNode'
 requirements:
 _access: 'TRUE'
```

Would change the controller function to:

```
public function test(NodeInterface $node) {
 return [
 '#type' => 'markup',
 '#markup' => $this->t("Test: " . $node->getTitle()),
 ];
}
```

When using the entity lookup parameter, if the entity fails to load, Drupal will return a **404 Page Not Found error**. Your code will be guaranteed to receive an actual entity interface.

Requirements checking

The **requirements** section of the route defines the criteria that must be satisfied in order to match the route or to be granted access to the route.

Route matching

Some elements in the requirements section provide additional matching criteria for the route. If they fail to match a request, they will return a **404 Not Found error**. You can add multiple matching criteria to the route and all that is needed to succeed in order for the route to match.

_module_dependencies

The name of one or more modules that are required to be enabled to serve this request. Multiple modules can be specified using either a , (comma) or + (plus) separator. Using a comma will match for any of the modules; where as the plus will require all of the modules. For example, _module_dependencies: 'node+search' requires that both the node and search modules are enabled.

_method

The name of one or more HTTP verbs to restrict access to. Multiple verbs can be concatenated with the | (pipe) character. So, to restrict access to only GET, you would use _method: GET.

Parameter matching

You can add optional tests for any of the parameters in the route. For each parameter, you can add a regular expression that's checked before matching the route. For example, the route for the node revisions is:

```
entity.node.version_history:
 path: '/node/{node}/revisions'
 defaults:
 _title: 'Revisions'
 _controller: '\Drupal\node\Controller\NodeController::revisionOverview'
 requirements:
 _access_node_revision: 'view'
 node: \d+
 options:
 _node_operation_route: TRUE
```

Under requirements, you see the attribute for node with the regular expression \d+. This ensures that /node/1/revisions gets matched, while /node/foo/revisions doesn't.

Access tests

Other elements under the requirements section control whether a given user has access to the route once it has been matched. You can add multiple elements and they must all succeed in order to provide access. The default action is to deny access, so if you do not provide any criteria, access will be denied.

_permission

The machine name of one or more permissions to check against. You can specify multiple permissions to use by separating them with either a , (comma) or a + (plus) symbol. Using a comma indicates that all of the permission checks must succeed; the plus indicates that any must succeed. For instance _permission: 'access content,access user profiles' requires the user to have the permission for "access content" and the permission for "access user profiles".

_role

The name of one or more Drupal roles. You can add multiple roles, separating them using a , or + sign with the same and or checking as permissions.

_access

Sets absolute values for permissions. For instance, using `_access: 'TRUE'` ensures the route is accessible by all requests. Note that the value must be a string that evaluates to a PHP Boolean value, so it must be enclosed in quotations.

_entity_access

Verifies when the entity ID is part of the route you can check against specific actions on the entity. For example, if you have an argument for `{node}`, you could specify `_entity_access: 'node.view'` to ensure the user had access to display the node.

_csrf_token

Verifies that a valid CSRF token has been submitted with the request. Any route that performs actions or operations that do not use a form callback should use a CSRF token to prevent replay attacks. In order for the token to be added correctly, the URL must be generated using the `url_generator` service rather than a manually constructed path.

Dynamic routes

The simplest way to provide routes is to define them in your module's routing YAML file. Not all routes can be known ahead of time and specified this way. By adding a `route_callbacks` entry in your routing YAML file as an array, callables that return a list of routes. For example adding:

```
route_callbacks:
  - '\Drupal\mastering_drupal_8\Routing\TestRoutes::routes'
```

If we were to create the same route as above, that file would look like:

```
/**
 * Defines dynamic routes.
 */
class TestRoutes {
  /**
   * {@inheritdoc}
   */
```

```
 public function routes() {
 $routes = array();
 // Declares a single route under the name
 'mastering_drupal_8.test_page'.
 // Returns an array of Route objects.
 $routes['mastering_drupal_8.test_page'] = new Route(
 // Path to attach this route to:
 '/mastering_drupal_8/test',
 // Route defaults:
 array(
 '_controller' =>
 '\Drupal\mastering_drupal_8\Controller\TestPageController::test',
 ),
 // Route requirements:
 array(
 '_access' => 'TRUE',
 )
 );
 return $routes;
 }
}
```

Alternatively, you can return the routes using a `RouteCollection` object.

```
/**
 * @file
 * Contains \Drupal\mastering_drupal_8\Routing\TestRoutes.
 */
namespace Drupal\mastering_drupal_8\Routing;
use Symfony\Component\Routing\Route;
use Symfony\Component\Routing\RouteCollection;
/**
 * Defines dynamic routes.
 */
class TestRoutes {
 /**
 * {@inheritdoc}
 */
 public function routes() {
 $routes = new RouteCollection();
 // Declares a single route under the name
 'mastering_drupal_8.test_page'.
 // Returns an array of Route objects.
 $route = new Route(
 // Path to attach this route to:
 '/mastering_drupal_8/test',
 // Route defaults:
 array(
```

```
  '_controller' =>
'\Drupal\mastering_drupal_8\Controller\TestPageController::test',
  ),
  // Route requirements:
  array(
  '_access' => 'TRUE',
  )
  );
  $routes->add('mastering_drupal_8.test_page', $route);
  return $routes;
  }
}
```

Going through this process for a simple route to a controller is unnecessary. It is much simpler in most cases to just add the route to a routing YAML file. However, for cases like Views or Image where the routes are dependent on other factors, it allows the creation of those routes with specific URLs and access criteria.

Menu links

Menu links have been moved out into a separate YAML file. To create menu links, add a {module}.links.menu.yml file in the root directory of your module. To create a menu link for the test page we created earlier, you would make a mastering_drupal_8.links.menu.yml file that looks like:

```
mastering_drupal_8.test_page:
  title: 'Test'
  description: 'Test page'
  route_name: mastering_drupal_8.test_page
  weight: 100
  menu_name: main
```

For each menu link element, you have the following attributes:

- **title**: Title shown in the menu link
- **description**: Title attribute for the menu link
- route_name: Machine name of menu route
- **weight**: Determines the order of the menu links; higher weight links appear later
- menu_name: Machine name of the menu that the link is shown in
- **parent**: Machine name of the menu link that is the parent in the menu tree

One thing to note is that you cannot create a menu link to a route with named parameters that do not have defaults.

You are also able to create menu links dynamically. For example, the Views menu links YAML file looks like:

```
views_view:
  class: Drupal\views\Plugin\Menu\ViewsMenuLink
  form_class: Drupal\views\Plugin\Menu\Form\ViewsMenuLinkForm
  deriver: \Drupal\views\Plugin\Derivative\ViewsMenuLink
```

The deriver class extends `\Drupal\Component\Plugin\Derivative\DeriverBase` and the `getDerivativeDefinitions()` function returns an array in the same format as the menu links YAML element.

Local tasks

Local tasks generate tabs on pages and are defined in a `{module}.links.task.yml` file in the root directory of your module. In this file, you have two or more local task declarations like:

```
mastering_drupal_8.test_page:
  title: 'Test'
  route_name: mastering_drupal_8.test_page_messag
  base_route: mastering_drupal_8.test_page
  weight: 1
mastering_drupal_8.test_2:
  title: 'Test 2'
  route_name: mastering_drupal_8.test_page_2
  base_route: mastering_drupal_8.test_page
  weight: 2
```

For each local task element, you have the following attributes:

- **title**: Title shown in the tab
- `route_name`: Machine name of the route that the tab directs to
- `base_route`: Machine name of the route that the tab is shown on
- **weight**: Determines the order of the tabs; higher weight links appear later

The local task, where the `route_name` matches the `base_route`, is the default local task that is active when the user visits the route.

Like menu links, you are able to create local tasks dynamically by adding a deriver to the local tasks `YAML` file. The `getDerivativeDefinitions()` function returns an array in the same format as the local tasks YAML element.

Local actions

Local tasks generate tabs on pages and are defined in a `{module}.links.action.yml` file in the root directory of your module. In this file, you have two or more local task declarations like:

```
mastering_drupal_8.test:
  route_name: mastering_drupal_8.test_page
  title: 'Test'
  appears_on:
  - mastering_drupal_8.test_page
```

For each local action element, you have the following attributes:

- `route_name`: Machine name of the route that the local action directs to
- **title**: Title shown on the local action
- **weight**: Determines the order of the local actions; higher weight links appear later
- `appears_on`: Array of routes that the local action is displayed on

The local task, where the `route_name` matches the `base_route`, is the default local task that is active when the user visits the route.

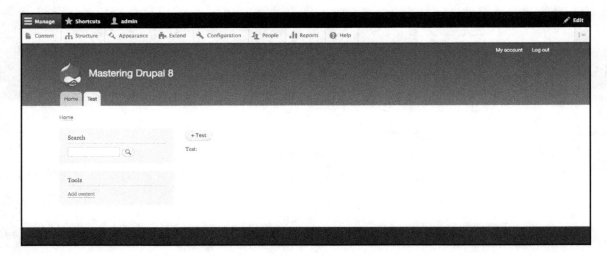

Like menu links, you are able to create local actions dynamically by adding a deriver to the local actions `YAML` file. The `getDerivativeDefinitions()` function returns an array in the same format as the local tasks YAML element.

Contextual links

Contextual links allow the user to perform actions directly on a particular entity or other portion of the site. Adding one is done by creating a `{module}.links.contextual.yml` file in the root directory of your module. In order to add a contextual link for the `mastering_drupal_8` module, it would look like:

```
mastering_drupal_8:
  title: 'Test'
  route_name: 'mastering_drupal_8.test_page_block'
  group: 'block'
```

For each contextual link element, you have the following attributes:

- **title**: Title of the link in the contextual link area
- `route_name`: Machine name of the route that the contextual link directs to
- **group**: Area the contextual link appears in for example, "block," "menu," and so on

- **weight**: Determines the order of the contextual links; higher weight links appear later

The contextual link route will receive information about the entity or other item that the contextual link was triggered on. For example, if our route is `mastering_drupal_8/test/{block}`, it would be injected with the block name to be passed to our controller.

Events and hooks

In Drupal 8, there are two methods of responding to interacting with the system and other modules. The first is the normal hook system that is the same as previous versions of Drupal. The second is the event system using the Symfony EventDispatcher. The EventDispatcher system is still new to Drupal, so there aren't many places in Drupal that can use it and you'll find yourself using hooks for a lot of things still. You can see a list of the ones available at `https://api.drupal.org/api/drupal/core!core.api.php/group/events/8`. But the EventDispatcher is definitely the future of interacting with the Drupal system.

Using the EventDispatcher

An event listener is first and foremost just another type of service. This gives you the advantage of being able to isolate your event listener and use dependency injection. This gives you an ease of unit testing that the normal hook system cannot provide. You can create an event listener manually or use the Drupal Console to do by it by running `drupal generate:event:subscriber` and following the prompts:

```
[vagrant@localhost public]$ drupal generate:event:subscriber
 Enter the module name [ctools]:
 > mastering_drupal_8

 Enter the service name [mastering_drupal_8.default]:
 > mastering_drupal_8.event_subscriber

 Class name [DefaultSubscriber]:
 > MasteringDrupal8EventSubscriber


Type the event name or use keyup or keydown.
This is optional, press enter to continue

 Enter event name [ ]:
 > kernel.terminate

 Callback function name to handle event [kernel_terminate]:
 > onTerminate

 Enter event name [ ]:
 >
 Do you want to load services from the container (yes/no) [no]:
 >


 Do you confirm generation? (yes/no) [yes]:
 >

Generated or updated files
 Site path: /vagrant/public
 1 - modules/custom/mastering_drupal_8/src/EventSubscriber/MasteringDrupal8EventSubscriber.php
 2 - modules/custom/mastering_drupal_8/mastering_drupal_8.services.yml
 // cache:rebuild

 Rebuilding cache(s), wait a moment please.

 [OK] Done clearing cache(s).
```

The Drupal console updated the `mastering_drupal_8.services.yml` file to add the new service with the following:

```
mastering_drupal_8.event_subscriber:
  class:
Drupal\mastering_drupal_8\EventSubscriber\MasteringDrupal8EventSubscriber
  arguments: []
  tags:
  - { name: event_subscriber }
```

The `event_subscriber` tag is what marks this service as an event listener. In your event listener, you need to implement a static `getSubscribedEvents()` function that returns an array of event names with corresponding functions. Each event handler receives a `Symfony\Component\EventDispatcher\Event` object or subclass, which contains information about the event. This event object event allows you to cancel the event in the same way that you can for JavaScript events.

```php
namespace Drupal\mastering_drupal_8\EventSubscriber;

use Symfony\Component\EventDispatcher\EventSubscriberInterface;
use Symfony\Component\EventDispatcher\Event;

/**
 * Class MasteringDrupal8EventSubscriber.
 *
 * @package Drupal\mastering_drupal_8
 */
class MasteringDrupal8EventSubscriber implements EventSubscriberInterface {

  /**
   * Constructor.
   */
  public function __construct() {

  }

  /**
   * {@inheritdoc}
   */
  static function getSubscribedEvents() {
    $events['kernel.terminate'] = ['onTerminate'];

    return $events;
  }

  /**
   * This method is called whenever the kernel.terminate event is
   * dispatched.
   *
   * @param GetResponseEvent $event
   */
  public function onTerminate(Event $event) {
    drupal_set_message('Event kernel.terminate thrown by Subscriber in module mastering_drupal_8.', 'status', TRUE);
  }

}
```

Summary

In this chapter we have gone over a lot of new ground. We started with the tools that you will want to use to create new modules and components, and then moved on to how to use those to add new capabilities to your Drupal site. This included:

- Creating a new module
- Understanding the plugin system and creating a new block
- Working with the dependency injection container and creating a new service
- Exploring the new menu system and creating custom menu routers, links, and local tasks
- Learning about the new Event system and how to receive and dispatch events.

These tasks will form the basis of almost all custom development in Drupal. With these under your belt, you are ready to add new behaviors and customize every part of your Drupal site.

In the next chapter, we will be going through the Form API. We will learn how to create custom forms to capture and store information.

11
Working with Forms and the Form API

Forms are a critical part of any web application. They provide a mechanism for users to interact with Drupal. Adding forms is a fundamental part of creating a new functionality for Drupal; it ensures that administrators can configure it as well as provide the ability to capture information from other users. In this chapter, we will be covering the following topics:

- How to create and use your own forms
- The new Form API types
- Adding AJAX to a form

Creating and managing forms

In this section, let's learn how to create new forms and manage them.

Creating a new form

In Drupal 7, a form was a function that returned an array containing nested elements from the Form API. Then, you would add appropriate _validate and _submit functions to handle verifying the submission and to handle the completed form in a simple case that would look as follows:

```
function my_module_my_form($form, &$form_state)
  $form['first'] = array(
    '#type' => 'textfield',
    '#title' => t('First name'),
    '#required' => TRUE,
  );
  $form['last'] = array(
    '#type' => 'textfield',
    '#title' => t('Last name'),
    '#required' => TRUE,
  );
  $form['submit'] = array(
    '#type' => 'submit',
    '#value' => 'Submit',
  );

  return $form;
}

function my_module_my_form_validate($form, &$form_state) {
  // Handle form validation
}

function my_module_my_form_submit($form, &$form_state) {
  // Handle form submission
}
```

Like many of the changes in Drupal 8, this convention has been replaced by an explicit class hierarchy. Forms are classes that implement \Drupal\Core\FormInterface or extend \Drupal\Core\Form\FormBase. Like other components in Drupal 8, the simplest way of creating a form is to use Drupal Console by running drupal generate:form. For our new forms, we'll be adding them to the Mastering Drupal 8 custom module that we built in Chapter 10, *Extending Drupal*.

```
[vagrant@localhost public]$ drupal generate:form

// Welcome to the Drupal form generator
Enter the module name [ctools]:
> mastering_drupal_8

Enter the Form Class name [DefaultForm]:
> TestForm

Enter the Form id [test_form]:
>


Do you want to load services from the container (yes/no) [no]:
>

Do you want to generate a form structure? (yes/no) [yes]:
>

Type [ ]:
> textfield

Input label:
> First name

Input machine name [first_name]:
>

Maximum amount of characters [64]:
>

Width of the textfield (in characters) [64]:
>

Description [ ]:
>

Default value [ ]:
>

Weight for input item [0]:
>
```

Generating a form using Drupal Console

While the structure of the form is different from the Drupal 7 example, it still has all the information needed. Instead of form ID being the name of the function that returns the Form API array, it's explicitly returned in the getFormId function. The Form API array is returned by the buildForm function. Form submission is implemented in the submitForm function, and optional validation occurs with the validateForm function. So, to have a form like the Drupal 7 example from earlier, it will look like this:

```
class TestForm extends FormBase {

  /**
   * {@inheritdoc}
   */
  public function getFormId() {
```

```
      return 'test_form';
   }

   /**
    * {@inheritdoc}
    */
   public function buildForm(array $form, FormStateInterface $form_state) {
      $form['first_name'] = array(
         '#type' => 'textfield',
         '#title' => $this->t('First name'),
         '#maxlength' => 64,
         '#size' => 64,
      );
      $form['last_name'] = array(
         '#type' => 'textfield',
         '#title' => $this->t('Last name'),
         '#maxlength' => 64,
         '#size' => 64,
      );
      $form['submit'] = array(
         '#type' => 'submit',
         '#value => $this->t('Submit'),
      );

      return $form;
   }

   /**
    * {@inheritdoc}
    */
   public function submitForm(array &$form, FormStateInterface $form_state)
   {

   }
}
```

In addition to the Form class, Drupal Console also creates a menu router in the module. By default, it uses the machine name of the module and the first part of the form machine name. So, for our test form, this becomes /mastering_drupal_8/form/test. You can see this router in the mastering_drupal_8.routing.yml file, where it looks as follows:

```
mastering_drupal_8.test_form:
   path: '/mastering_drupal_8/form/test'
   defaults:
      _form: '\Drupal\mastering_drupal_8\Form\TestForm'
      _title: 'TestForm'
   requirements:
      _access: 'TRUE'
```

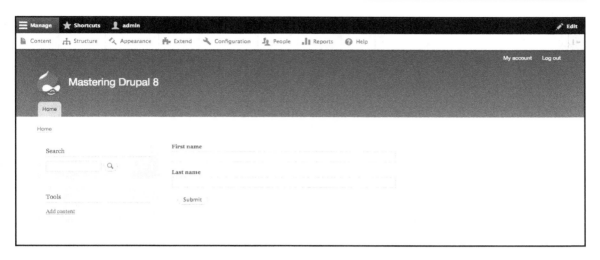

Form displayed on the website

One area that hasn't changed significantly from Drupal 7 is the actual structure of the form elements array. While Symfony has its own API to define forms, the decision was made to keep the Drupal Form API's structure the same in Drupal 8. As backward compatibility was not guaranteed with Symfony Forms in 2.3, any further changes to the Drupal Form API were deferred to Drupal 9.

Using FormState

Beyond separating each Form into separate classes, another significant change is the introduction of `FormStateInterface`. In Drupal 7, the `$form_state` variable that was passed to the various form functions was a simple array. However, in Drupal 8, in addition to getting the values from the previous form actions, the `FormStateInterface` is used to set form errors. In Drupal 7, if you needed to indicate an error with a form field, you would call the following:

```
Form_set_error('first_name', t('The first name is invalid'));
```

In Drupal 8, this looks like this:

```
$form_state->setErrorByName('first_name', $this->t('The first name is invalid'));
```

The `FormStateInterface` has some other nice convenience functions, especially around checking to see whether a form element has data. You can easily check for the existence of a value using `FormStateInterface::isValueEmpty` as well as pass a default value to `FormStateInterface::getValue`. Moving to functions to return values does have one side effect that takes some getting used to. Previously, you would get nested values by just traversing the appropriate array in the `$form_state` array, for example `$form_state['values']['nested']['value']`. In order to get the same value from the `FormStateInterface`, you pass an array to `getValue`, for example `$form_state->getValue(array('nested', 'value'))`.

Other form types

In addition to the `FormBase` class, there are two other built-in types of form: `ConfirmFormBase` and `ConfigFormBase`. In order to create a form of these types, you would use Drupal Console to create the form and then change the class to extend the appropriate `FormBase` class. You would use the `ConfirmFormBase` class to verify the user intended to perform an action. In Drupal 7, this was handled using the `confirm_form` function; in Drupal 8, you create your form class and extend the `ConfirmFormBase` class. When you extend `ConfirmFormBase`, you will be implementing `ConfirmFormInterface`, which contains some functions that are not implemented on the base class. At the very least, you need to write the `getCancelUrl` function, which returns a URL object to navigate to if the user clicks on the **Cancel** button, and `getQuestion`, which provides the text shown on the form. A basic form would look like this:

```
class TestConfirmForm extends ConfirmFormBase {

  /**
   * {@inheritdoc}
   */
  public function getFormId() {
    return 'test_confirm_form';
  }

  /**
   * {@inheritdoc}
   */
  public function getQuestion() {
    return $this->t('Are you sure you want to proceed?');
  }

  /**
   * {@inheritdoc}
```

```
  */
  public function getCancelUrl() {
    return new Url('<front>');
  }

  /**
   * {@inheritdoc}
   */
  public function submitForm(array &$form, FormStateInterface $form_state)
  {
    $form_state->setRedirectUrl($this->getCancelUrl());
  }
}
```

As with any form, you also need to implement `submitForm` and `getFormId`. If you created the form using Drupal Console, it will again add the menu router for the form. Otherwise, you will need to add your own to the `mastering_drupal_8.routing.yml` file. This should look as follows:

```
mastering_drupal_8.test_confirm_form:
  path: '/mastering_drupal_8/form/test_confirm'
  defaults:
    _form: '\Drupal\mastering_drupal_8\Form\TestConfirmForm'
    _title: 'TestConfirmForm'
  requirements:
    _access: 'TRUE'
```

You can now view your form at `/mastering_drupal_8/form/test_confirm`:

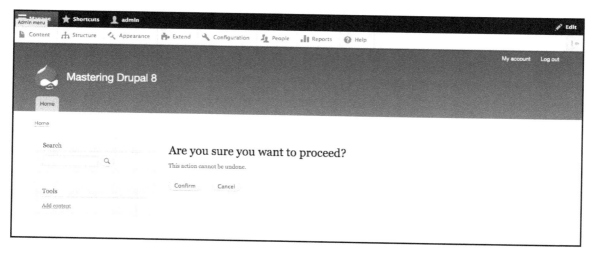

Confirmation form

The `ConfigFormBase` is used to assist in saving configuration settings. It serves as a replacement for the `system_settings_form` Drupal 7 function that was used to wrap a form in order to save it to the variables table. In Drupal 8, the `ConfigFormBase` class does a little bit less for you; specifically, it does not handle the saving of the configuration. So, instead of having to manipulate the submitted data in a validate function in Drupal 7, you can alter it within the `submitForm` function. Once you are ready, you will call `$this->config()->set()` to set the configuration and save it to the database. The other function that you need to implement is `getEditableConfigNames`, which returns an array of configuration object names modified by the form in an array. A basic example that allows the user to edit some configuration settings will look like this:

```
class TestConfigForm extends ConfigFormBase {

  /**
   * {@inheritdoc}
   */
  public function getFormId() {
    return 'test_config_form';
  }

  /**
   * {@inheritdoc}
   */
  protected function getEditableConfigNames() {
    return ['mastering_drupal_8.settings'];
  }

  /**
   * {@inheritdoc}
   */
  public function buildForm(array $form, FormStateInterface $form_state) {
    $config = $this->config('mastering_drupal_8.settings');
    $form['name'] = array(
      '#type' => 'textfield',
      '#title' => $this->t('Name'),
      '#default_value' => $config->get('name'),
    );

    return parent::buildForm($form, $form_state);
  }

  /**
   * {@inheritdoc}
   */
  public function submitForm(array &$form, FormStateInterface $form_state)
  {
```

```
    $this->config('mastering_drupal_8.settings')
      ->set('name', $form_state->getValue('name'))
      ->save();

    parent::submitForm($form, $form_state);
  }
}
```

If you created the form using Drupal Console, it will again add the menu router to the form. Otherwise, you will need to add your own to the `mastering_drupal_8.routing.yml` file. This should look like this:

```
mastering_drupal_8.test_config_form:
  path: '/mastering_drupal_8/form/test_config'
  defaults:
    _form: '\Drupal\mastering_drupal_8\Form\TestConfigForm'
    _title: 'TestConfigForm'
  requirements:
    _access: 'TRUE'
```

You can now view your form at `/mastering_drupal_8/form/test_config`:

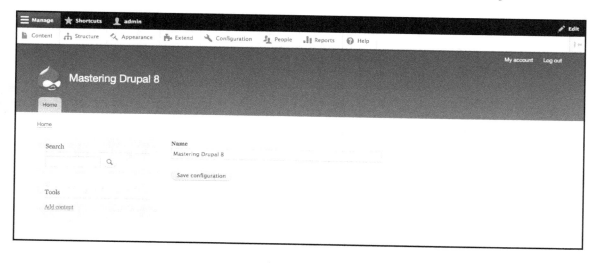

Configuration form

After you click on the **Save configuration** button, you can go to the **Configuration synchronization administrative** section and export it to copy to another site:

Configuration export screen

Exploring the Form API

The structure of the Form API elements returned by the buildForm function is almost completely the same as it was in Drupal 7. The attributes for the form elements are generally identical. One parameter that has changed is #attached, which is used to add libraries, arbitrary JavaScript, HTML head links and tags, and so on. For example, if you wanted to ensure that the backbone was loaded with the configuration form earlier, you would attach it to a form element like this:

```
public function buildForm(array $form, FormStateInterface $form_state) {
  $config = $this->config('mastering_drupal_8.settings');
  $form['name'] = array(
    '#type' => 'textfield',
    '#title' => $this->t('Name'),
    '#default_value' => $config->get('name'),
    '#attached' => array(
      'library' => array('core/backbone')
```

```
    )
  );

  return parent::buildForm($form, $form_state);
}
```

One attribute that was added was `#cache`, to enable customization of the cache contexts, tags, and max-age attributes. If the form varies by request context, such as language, or depends on modifiable information, such as a node or other entity, or is only valid for a limited time, you might edit these attributes. So, if the configuration form was expected to change based on the user's language, you will add the cache attribute as follows:

```
public function buildForm(array $form, FormStateInterface $form_state) {
  $config = $this->config('mastering_drupal_8.settings');
  $form['name'] = array(
    '#type' => 'textfield',
    '#title' => $this->t('Name'),
    '#default_value' => $config->get('name'),
    '#attached' => array(
      'library' => array('core/backbone')
    ),
    '#cache' => array(
      'contexts' => ['language'],
    ),
  );

  return parent::buildForm($form, $form_state);
}
```

New Form API types

All the Form API types from Drupal 7 continue to exist in Drupal 8. In addition, types based on new HTML 5 components have been added. This includes the following:

- **tel**: For telephone numbers
- **email**: For email addresses
- **number**: For numeric values
- **date**: For dates
- **search**: For searching
- **range**: For values that should be within a range; it can be rendered as a slider

The tel, email, number, and search types extend the text field type and can use any attributes that apply to it as well.

The Form API in Drupal 8 has been integrated with the generic render array. This allows renderable elements to be included natively in the form. In addition, several new types have been added.

Color

The color type allows users to select a color using a variety of methods, including lists of web-safe colors, **CMYK Sliders**, picking from a spectrum of colors, and even selection by colored pencil. Consider the following example:

```
$form['color'] = array(
    '#type' => 'color',
    '#title' => $this->t('Value'),
);
```

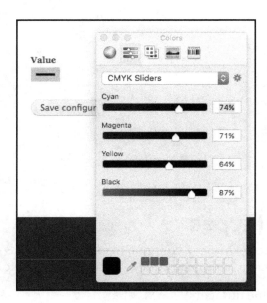

Color type

Details

The details type provides a collapsible area around other elements, similar to a fieldset. Fieldsets can only be used around form elements, whereas the details type can be used outside of them. Take a look at this example:

```
$form['name'] = array(
  '#type' => 'details',
  '#title' => $this->t('Name')
);
$form['name']['value'] = array(
  '#type' => 'textfield',
  '#title' => $this->t('Value'),
);
```

Detail type

Dropbutton

The dropbutton type displays a set of links as drop-down buttons. The links can be themed separately from other links by creating a links--dropbutton.html.twig file, and you can also add a #subtype attribute to make it even more specific. For example, if you add '#subtype' => 'foo', the template suggestions will go:

- links--dropbutton--foo.html.twig
- links--dropbutton.html.twig
- links.html.twig

Consider this example:

```
$form['test'] = array(
  '#type' => 'dropbutton',
  '#links' => array(
    'action_one' => array(
      'title' => $this->t('Action 1'),
      'url' => new Url('<front>'),
    ),
    'action_two' => array(
```

```
        'title' => $this->t('Action 2'),
        'url' => new Url('<front>'),
    ),
  ),
);
```

Action 1
Action 2

Dropbutton type

HTML tag

The `html_tag` type allows you to easily add arbitrary HTML tags within the Form API structure. Where you would have to use the markup type in Drupal 7, you will specify your own HTML in the text in Drupal 8; this allows you to easily separate out the tag from the content. Take into consideration the following example:

```
$form['tag'] = array(
  '#type' => 'html_tag',
  '#tag' => 'h1',
  '#value' => $this->t('Mastering Drupal 8'),
);
```

Mastering Drupal 8

HTML tag type

Language select

The `language_select` type provides a dropdown that allows the user to select a system language. The `#languages` attribute determines which set of system languages to use and can be the following:

- `LanguageInterface::STATE_CONFIGURABLE`: A list of any configured languages on the site
- `LanguageInterface::STATE_LOCKED`: The languages that are used solely by the system, but not an actual language, that is, **Not specified** and **Not applicable**
- `LanguageInterface::STATE_ALL`: Both the configurable and locked languages

Note that you need to have the Language module enabled for this form type to be displayed. Consider the following example:

```
$form['langcode'] = array(
    '#type' => 'language_select',
    '#title' => $this->t('Language'),
    '#languages' => LanguageInterface::STATE_ALL,
);
```

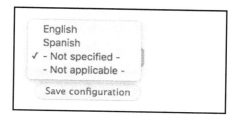

Language select type

Link

As a result of using the render arrays natively within forms, you can easily place arbitrary links in a form using the `link` type. Take into consideration the following example:

```
$form['link'] = array(
    '#type' => 'link',
    '#title' => $this->t('Mastering Drupal 8'),
    '#url' => new Url('<front>'),
);
```

Link type

More link

Similarly to the link type, you can now add one more link directly in the form using the `more_link` type. You can provide an optional `#title` attribute to control the text of the link. If no `#title` attribute is provided, it will default to **More**. Consider the following example:

```
$form['more_link'] = array(
    '#type' => 'more_link',
    '#title' => $this->t('See more'),
    '#url' => new Url('<front>'),
);
```

More link type

Pager

Pagers can be easily added to forms using the pager type. You can provide the following optional attributes:

- `#element`: The pager ID to use if you need to distinguish between multiple pagers on the screen; it defaults to `0`
- `#parameters`: An associative array of query parameters to append to each link of the pager
- `#quantity`: The maximum number of links to display; it defaults to `9`
- `#tags`: Text to use for the **First**, **Previous**, **Next**, and **Last** links
- `#route_name`: The name of the route to use for the URLs; it defaults to `<none>`, which uses the current route

Consider this example:

```
// Create dummy pager
pager_default_initialize(100, 10);
$form['pager'] = array(
  '#type' => 'pager',
);
```

| 1 | 2 | 3 | 4 | 5 | 6 | 7 | 8 | 9 | ... | Next › | Last » |

Pager type

Path element

The path type provides a textbox that captures and validates a path within the system. You can set the `#convert_path` attribute to either `PathElement::CONVERT_NONE` to return the string value that was entered, `PathElement::CONVERT_ROUTE` to return an array containing the route name and parameters, or `PathElement::CONVERT_URL` to return a URL object in the `FormState`. You can also disable the path validation by setting the `#validate_path` attribute to `FALSE`. The path type inherits from the `textfield` type and can use any attributes that apply to it as well. Take this example into consideration:

```
$form['path'] = array(
  '#type' => 'path',
  '#title' => $this->t('Path'),
);
```

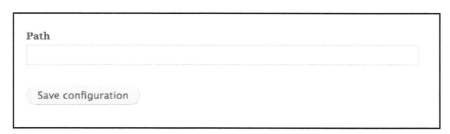

Path

Save configuration

Path type

Table select

The `tableselect` type creates a table with checkboxes or radio buttons to allow a user to select either single or multiple rows within a table. You need to provide the `#header` attribute as an associative array of columns and `#options` as an array of values, each containing an associative array mapping a value to the key of the `#header` column. In addition, you can provide the following optional attributes:

- `#empty`: The value to display if the table has no options
- `#multiple`: Tells whether a user is able to select multiple values; it defaults to TRUE
- `#js_select`: Tells whether a **select all** checkbox should appear in the header, it defaults to TRUE

Consider this example:

```
$form['table'] = array(
  '#type' => 'tableselect',
  '#header' => [
    'column_one' => $this->t('Column one'),
    'column_two' => $this->t('Column two')
  ],
  '#options' => [
    [
      'column_one' => $this->t('Row'),
      'column_two' => $this->t('One') ,
    ],
    [
      'column_one' => $this->t('Row'),
      'column_two' => $this->t('Two'),
    ],
    [
      'column_one' => $this->t('Row'),
      'column_two' => $this->t('Three'),
    ],
    [
      'column_one' => $this->t('Row'),
      'column_two' => $this->t('Four'),
    ],
    [
      'column_one' => $this->t('Row'),
      'column_two' => $this->t('Five'),
    ],
  ],
);
```

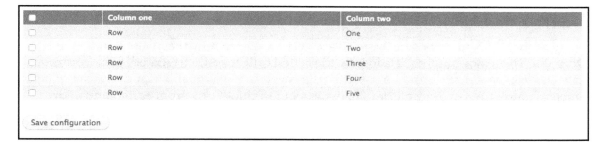

Table select type

URL

The URL type provides a textbox that allows the user to enter a URL and validates it for correctness. The URL type inherits from the `textfield` type and can use any attributes that apply to it as well. Let's look at an example:

```
$form['path'] = array(
  '#type' => 'url',
  '#title' => $this->t('Url'),
);
```

URL type with validation error

Using AJAX

Many of the AJAX functions in Drupal 8 are very similar to how they were handled in Drupal 7. The major difference is in how the actual callbacks are triggered. Since forms are now classes, the `#submit` and `#ajax` attributes need to have callable values instead of just function names. As an example, let's take the configuration form from earlier and allow users to add multiple URLs. The first thing we do is to construct the wrapper around our list of URLs:

```php
public function buildForm(array $form, FormStateInterface $form_state) {
  $config = $this->config('mastering_drupal_8.settings');
  $form['vals'] = array(
    '#type' => 'details',
    '#title' => $this->t('Rows'),
    '#open' => TRUE,
  );
  // Wrapper around rows
  $form['vals']['rows'] = array(
    '#type' => 'item',
    '#tree' => TRUE,
    '#prefix' => '<div id="rows__replace">',
    '#suffix' => '</div>',
  );
  return parent::buildForm($form, $form_state);
}
```

The next thing we need to do is to get the current number of URLs and ensure that we have that many input elements. So here we add the following where we define the row wrapper:

```php
$count = $form_state->getValue('count', 1);
for ($i = 0; $i < $count; $i++) {
  // Make sure we don't overwrite existing rows
  if (!isset($form['vals']['rows'][$i])) {
    $form['vals']['rows'][$i] = array(
      '#type' => 'url',
      '#title' => $this->t('URL %num', [ '%num' => $i ]),
    );
  }
}
$form['count'] = array(
  '#type' => 'value',
  '#value' => $count,
);
```

We create the new URL rows in the wrapper and store the current number of rows in the `FormState`. We want to be careful not to replace the existing form elements because that will remove the values attached to them. The next step is to add the actual AJAX submit button. So, we add the count value as follows:

```
$form['add'] = array(
  '#type' => 'submit',
  '#name' => 'add',
  '#value' => $this->t('Add row'),
  '#submit' => [ [ $this, 'addRow' ] ],
  '#ajax' => [
    'callback' => [ $this, 'ajaxCallback' ],
    'wrapper' => 'rows__replace',
    'effect' => 'fade'
  ]
);
```

Note that we are using the callable syntax for `#submit` as well as the callback attribute in `#ajax`; this will ensure that the function will be called on the current object. The next step is to get the other functions in place. So, in the current form class, we'll add the following functions:

```
/**
 * Increments the row count
 */
public function addRow(array &$form, FormStateInterface &$form_state) {
  $count = $form_state->getValue('count', 1);
  $count += 1;
  $form_state->setValue('count', $count);
  $form_state->setRebuild(TRUE);
}
/**
 * Returns the array of row elements
 */
public function ajaxCallback(array &$form, FormStateInterface &$form_state)
{
  return $form['vals']['rows'];
}
```

The `addRow` function increments the count value and then triggers a rebuild of the form, which ensures that `buildForm` is run again with the new count. Then finally, `ajaxCallback` is called, which returns the fragment of the form to be serialized and sent back to the browser to replace the previous form section. Now you have a form that starts with one row, but allows you to add any number of new rows by clicking on an **Add row** button:

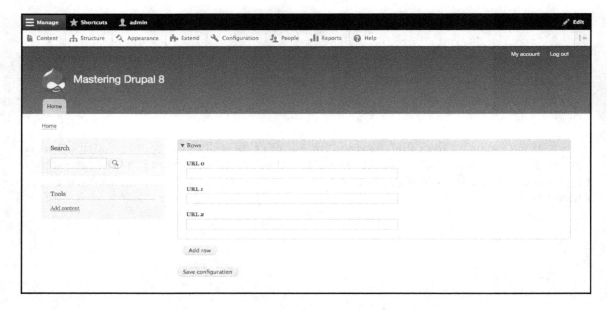

Form with AJAX button

Summary

In this chapter, we covered creating our own custom forms. We started with a confirmation form to verify user actions. Next, we created our own configuration form and stored the entered information in the Configuration API.

Then, we looked at all the new types in the Form API in Drupal 8. These include both new HTML 5-based form elements as well as new interface elements used in Drupal 8, such as the Drop button.

Finally, we learned how to create a form that can be submitted via AJAX and how to change the form on the browser without a full-page load.

12

RESTful Services

Back in 2012 Dries wrote a blog post declaring that the future was a "RESTful Drupal." In all previous versions of Drupal there were competing methods of implementing REST APIs in Drupal: services, RESTWS and RESTful were the more popular ones in contrib. This lead to other modules having to target one implementation or another in order to work. You could end up finding the functionality you wanted to leverage already built, but using a different set of APIs than you had already implemented. The goal of the Drupal 8's Web Services Initiative was to consolidate the basic REST functionality and allow Drupal to serve as the content repository for any number of clients, and not just the Drupal interface. This allows Drupal to expose content and functionality to anything from mobile applications, other CMS and platforms, and single-page applications. In this chapter we will be covering:

- An overview of REST and HTTP verbs
- Enabling core modules and customizing permissions
- Exposing content using Views
- Creating, updating and deleting content via the REST interface
- Authenticating against the REST API
- Creating your own REST plugins

Overview of REST

REST (Representational State Transfer) is described in the original dissertation as an *"architectural style for distributed hypermedia systems."* There are several key features of a REST API:

- It separates the client representation from the server data
- It is stateless
- It is cacheable

- It relies on a uniform interface, generally HTTP verbs
- It leverages a decoupled, layered system

Many people consider any API that uses a **Universal Resource Indicator** (**URI**) style to be REST by comparing it against other protocols like SOAP, AMF, or CORBA. REST, however, is specific to acting on resources using the correct HTTP verb. If you are performing some other action on the system, it's a **Remote Procedure Call** (**RPC**). The following table uses some examples to compare the two styles:

Operation	RPC style	REST style
Login	POST /login	POST /session
Logout	GET /logout	DELETE /session/id
Create user	POST /addUser	POST /user
Update a node	POST /updateNode	PATCH /node/id

With traditional REST architecture, you don't login, you create a new session resource; you don't logout, you delete your current session. This encourages consistency because you have a limited number of resources and a limited number of operations on them from the HTTP verbs.

REST in Drupal 8

For all the good intentions in including a REST server natively in Drupal 8, many aspects of it come across as incomplete and rushed. The most noticeable is in the differences between the URIs used to request resources. One of the hallmarks of a good REST interface is consistency, that there are essentially only two URIs and four actions. For example:

- To retrieve a list of users you would make a GET request to `/user`
- To create a new user you would make a POST request to `/user`
- To retrieve information about a specific user with an ID of 1 you would make a GET request to `/user/1`
- To update that user you would make a PUT or PATCH request to `/user/1`
- To delete that user you would make a DELETE request to `/user/1`

Unfortunately, in Drupal, you have `/user/1` for GET, PATCH and DELETE, but then `/entity/user` for POST, and the URI to list resources needs to be created by the user, and has to be on a separate URI. There are further issues with the authentication methods that are available in core: inconsistent use of HAL and issues with content negotiation and serialization that require knowledge of a large number of idiosyncrasies. We'll discuss these other issues in more detail in other sections in this chapter.

HTTP verbs

As we've described previously, REST relies on the idea of interacting with resources. The HTTP protocol has a number of what are called verbs, or methods, used to interact with remote resources. For the purpose of REST, we use POST, GET, PATCH and DELETE which map to the basic **CRUD** operations of Create, Read, Update and Delete. Each of these verbs has specific meanings and properties:

Verb	Description	Properties
GET	Reads a resource	Safe, idempotent and cacheable
POST	Creates a resource or trigger a data-handling process	Not safe, idempotent or cacheable
PATCH	Updates specified fields in a resource	Idempotent, but not safe or cacheable
DELETE	Deletes a resource	Idempotent, but not safe or cacheable

Safe operations are ones that are "read-only": idempotent operations are ones where the effects on the system from performing multiple identical requests are the same as performing only a single one.

HAL JSON

The default serialization method for the Drupal 8 REST API is **HAL JSON (Hypertext Application Language JavaScript Object Notation)**. HAL is a format for expressing actions and relationships between resources. It adds additional attributes to allow exploration and traversal of your API from within the API response itself.

The following screenshot explains the `_links` object:

When we examine the results of a simple node query, the first element we see in the response is the `_links` object. This contains URLs that can be used to traverse the API and retrieve other data. You'll notice that it contains a link to the author of both the node as well as the node revision. These can be understood in a generic way without the interface needing to construct the URL from other information in the response. HAL also defines the idea of embedded resources.

Embedded resources are intended to reduce the amount of traffic to the API by having important information about a related resource contained within the response. For example, a node is associated with a user, so information about that user would be embedded within the response for the node. Likewise, Taxonomy terms, images, or any other sort of related entity could be exposed in this way. Unfortunately, while Drupal does include these embedded entities, it only exposes the URL and type. There has been discussion about better exposure of embedded resources since September 2013 and, right now, they are targeting Drupal 8.4, for more information see `https://www.drupal.org/node/2100637`.

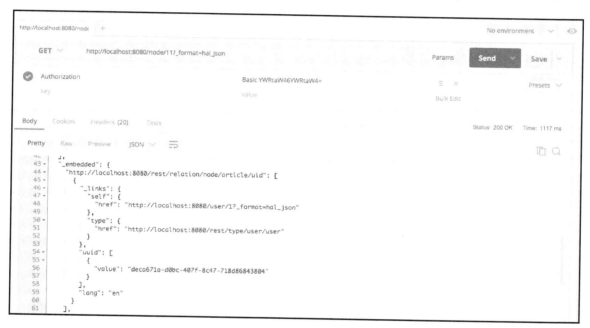

Enabling core modules and customizing permissions

Since the core REST module is included in Drupal 8 core, enabling it is simply a matter of going to the **Extend** page, selecting the checkbox next to **RESTful Web Services** and clicking the **Install** button. If you want to enable HAL JSON you'll also want to select the **HAL** module and the **HTTP Basic Authentication** module.

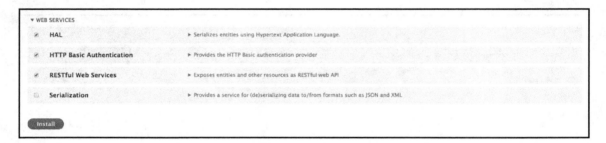

You can also enable it by running `drush pm-enable rest hal basic_auth`. Note that, if you are running PHP 5.6, you need to set `always_populate_raw_post_data` to `-1` in your `php.ini` file; it cannot be set using `ini_set`. For more information, see `https://www.drupal.org/node/2456025`.

The core REST module allows access to the REST interface but it doesn't make configuring it simple. If you want to configure access to specific entities, specific verbs, change serialization methods, or change the authentication methods allowed, you need to create and import a `rest.settings.yml` file. For example, if you wanted to allow GET operations on nodes that output JSON and support either basic HTTP authentication or cookies, you'd need to create a YAML file like the following:

```
resources:
  'entity:node':
    GET:
      supported_formats:
        - json
      # Support both the core provided auth protocols.
      supported_auth:
        - cookie
        - http_basic
```

You'd then import it using Configuration Management. Alternatively, you could install the REST UI module (restui) and configure it through the user interface. To download and install that module, you can run `drush dl restui` and then `drush pm-enable restui`. The REST UI module adds the permission "Administer rest resources" that grants access to alter how the system exposes content via REST.

The core REST module exposes permissions for each verb for each resource. By default, the node interface is enabled so there are permissions for "Access DELETE on Content resource", "Access GET on Content resource", and so on. This allows you to be extremely granular with what operations you expose on your system.

Exposing content using Views

As we've noted previously, Drupal 8 does not have a default method for listing content. The simplest way of adding this capability is to define a REST resource list using Views. To demonstrate this, we'll create a simple resource that lists nodes that a given user is listed as the author. The first step is to go to **Structure** | **Views** and click the **Add new view** button. Give the View a name, select the checkbox for **Provide a REST export**, and enter the path for the resource. In this case, since it extends the user information, it would be `user/%/posts`. When you have that in place, click the **Save and edit** button.

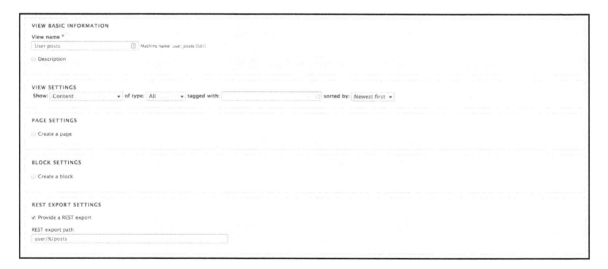

Since this View depends on filtering the nodes based on the author, we need to add the appropriate Relationship. So expand the **Advanced** field set, and click to **Add** a Relationship. Scroll down until you see the checkbox for **User**, select that, and then click **Apply (all displays)**. Since we only want nodes for a given user, it's safe to select **Require this relationship** on the next dialog and then click **Apply (all displays)**.

Next we need to capture the user ID from the URL and use that to power our listing. You'll click to **Add** a contextual filter and then scroll until you find the checkbox for **User ID**. Select that and click the **Apply (all displays)** button.

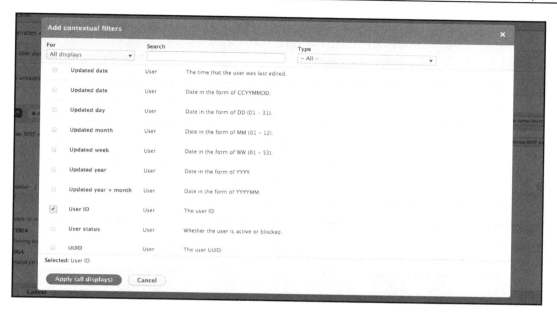

Views should automatically associate the contextual filter with the user relationship you added, so you should only need to select the **Provide default value** for the **Default actions** and select **Content ID from URL** for **Type**.

Click the **Apply (all displays)** button and then the **Save** button and you can then navigate to `localhost/user/1/posts?_format=hal_json` and see the output of nodes that were authored by UID 1. The default output from the View is the full entity output, the same as you would get by requesting `/node/{nid}?_format=hal_json`, but you can also change the output to Fields and manually select which fields are sent.

There are some unfortunate limitations with using Views to output lists of contents. While the output of each entity through Views adheres to the HAL specification, the overall list does not. The only output is an array of entities, and it does not provide any `_links` object to allow traversal or any other information about the list. In particular, it does not list the total number of entities found by the View. While the View does support paging through the use of the page query attribute, there is no way for a client to know how many pages of information there might be. Often these are presented in the `_links` object as URLs for the next, previous, first and last pages of information. Discussion about the lack of pagination has been in progress since September, 2013 and there is no current resolution or target for release. For more information, see `https://www.drupal.org/node/2099281`.

Using RESTful endpoints

The URLs to access the REST API for GET, PATCH and DELETE are the same as if you were trying to view the page on the website. For example if you have a node with an NID of 1, you can view it in your browser at `/node/1`, but it will render the node using its display mode, run it through the appropriate templates and wrap it with all of the other regions you may have defined. In order to get the API you need to provide the `_format` request parameter. So in order to access the same node through the API in HAL JSON format you would use `/node/1?_format=hal_json`.

If you are using POST, PATCH, or DELETE with an authentication method other than HTTP basic authentication, you will need to provide the X-CSRF-Token request header to prevent request forgery attacks. You need to request a CSRF token at `/rest/session/token`.

We'll be demonstrating each of the REST API calls available in Drupal core. For each one, we'll provide cURL commands to test. Reading the output from that can be a little challenging, so we recommend using another product to help test as well. We'll also be using an extension for Chrome named Postman which allows you to set authorization, cookies, and other headers, and easily examine the results.

Displaying content

When you want to get the API representation of content, you need to make a GET request to the appropriate resource. For example, if you have a node with an NID of 1, you would make a GET request to /node/1?_format=hal_json. You will need to provide some authentication parameters unless you have changed your permissions to allow anonymous access to GET requests for nodes. To test this with cURL, you would make the following request:

```
curl --request GET --user myusername:mypassword --header 'Accept:
application/hal+json' http://localhost/node/1?_format=hal_json
```

The response will contain all the fields for the node, along with the links to the author of the node and entity bundle.

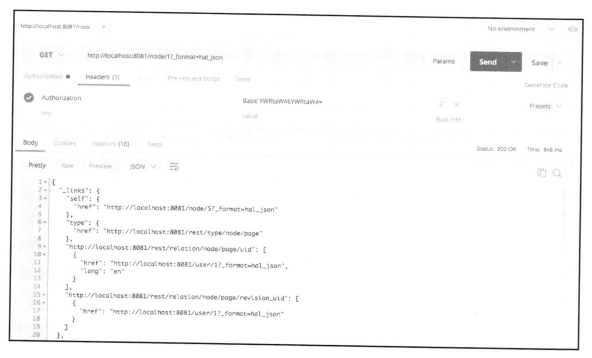

Unsafe methods and CSRF protection

As a security method to prevent **Cross-Site Request Forgery** 9s (**CSRF**) attacks, Drupal 8 requires a special X-CSRF-Token header to be passed when making a non-safe method. This includes any request that is not read-only, including POST, PATCH, and DELETE. The token can be retrieved by making a GET request to /session/token. This token is specific to the current session, so if the user were to log in or log out, a new session token would need to be requested.

Creating content

When creating content, you have a slightly different URI to other API requests. The URI is /entity/{type}, so, to create a new node, you would make a POST request to /entity/node. When sending a POST request, you provide the type of data provided using the Content-Type header. So, to create a new node using HAL JSON, there would be a Content-Type: application/hal+json header in your request. To test this using cURL you would make the following request:

```
curl --include --request POST --user myusername:mypassword --header
'Content-type: application/hal+json'
http://localhost/entity/node?_format=hal_json --data-binary
'{"_links":{"type":{"href":"http://localhost:8080/rest/type/node/article"}}
,"title":[{"value":"Example node
title"}],"type":[{"target_id":"article"}]}'
```

When you send the request using HAL JSON you need to provide the type of the new entity using _links. This is provided in the form of a URL which needs to match the hostname and protocol of the web server itself. For example, if you are running Varnish or some other reverse proxy on port 80 and the web server on port 8080, the link to the entity type and bundle needs to be on port 8080 as well. If the request is successful, you will receive a 201 Created response that contains a Location header, which contains the URL to the new node. In Drupal 8.1.0 or higher the response will be a 200 OK response with the serialized version of the entity, the same as you would receive if you made a GET request.

Updating content

Updating a node involves a PATCH request to the URI of the entity. So, if we were going to update the node we just created, you would make a PATCH request to /node/10. The headers and data are similar to those you send for creating a node. When updating a node, you only need to send the information that you want to change. There is also some information that you cannot send since they it be changed; for instance, you cannot submit the **UUID** (**Universally Unique Identifier**) attribute even if it is the same value. Sending that in the PATCH request will return a **403 Forbidden** response. There are also some pieces of information that must be sent; for instance, you must submit the entity type and bundle even though you cannot change this on a node. The entity type and bundle is required because the data must be deserialized before it can be passed to the REST controller.

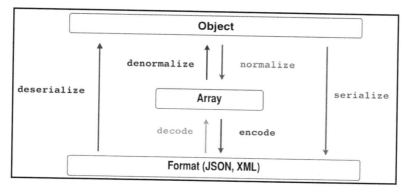

To test this using cURL, you would make the following request:

```
curl --include --request PATCH --user myusername:mypassword --header
'Content-type: application/hal+json'
http://localhost/node/[nid]--data-binary
'{"_links":{"type":{"href":"http://localhost:8080/rest/type/node/article"}}
,"title":[{"value":"Example node title
UPDATED!"}],"type":[{"target_id":"article"}]}'
```

You'd replace the `[nid]` with a real node ID of an article on your site. If the request is successful you will receive a **204 No Content** response. In Drupal 8.1.0 or higher, the response will be a **200 OK** response with the serialized version of the updated entity.

Deleting content

Deleting content via the REST API is very simple. All that is necessary is make a DELETE request to the URI of the entity. So, to delete the node we have just created would require a DELETE request to `/node/10`. To test this using cURL you would make the following request:

```
curl --include --request DELETE --user myusername:mypassword
http://localhost/node/[nid]
```

You do not need to add either the `_format` query attribute or provide the Content-Type header since there is no data sent and no serialization necessary. If the request is successful, you will receive a **204 Completed** response.

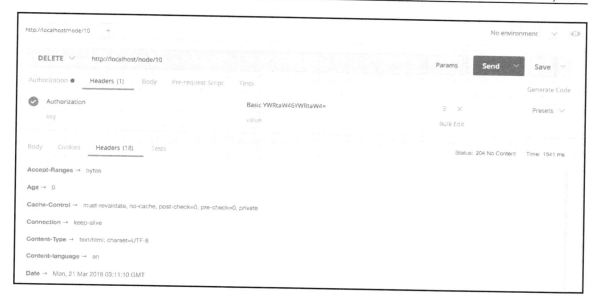

Authenticating an application as a Drupal user

When you access Drupal pages, your browser passes a cookie that is used to identify the current user. This ensures that Drupal is able to determine whether you are logged in or not and what your roles are, and then determine whether you have the permission to perform certain actions.

Core methods

Drupal 8 core contains two methods of authenticating a user when making an API request:

- **Basic authentication**: The username and password of a valid account are passed in the request header. Note that this does not create a session in Drupal. The REST module is able to check permissions for operations, but other modules that expect to have a valid user session will not work as intended. This includes Views, so any Views that check either roles or permissions will fail with a **403 Forbidden** response when using HTTP authentication.

- **Cookies**: The user session cookie is passed with the request in the same way that a normal page request would be. If the application using the REST API relies on the user logging in using the normal /user/login process, this will work without any changes. If the REST client needs to do so directly, it can make a POST request to /user/login?_format=json and pass the username and password as a JSON object like {name: "name", "pass": "password"}. If successful, the response will contain information about the user as well as the CSRF token to use for all authenticated requests. For example:

```
{
"current_user": {
"uid": 1,
"roles": ["authenticated"],
"name": "username"
},
"csrf_token": "abc123",
"logout_token": "def123"
}
```

When logging out, the logout token must be sent in the GET request. For example, /user/logout?_format=json&token=def123. The application will need to keep track of the logout_token because any attempt to login again with the same credentials will return a **403 Forbidden** until either a successful logout request is sent or the session expires or is deleted.

Contrib methods

There are a number of contributed modules that add to additional authentication methods. There are modules that allow OAuth2 logins, OAuth bearer tokens, IP matching and JSON Web Tokens. The OAuth and Simple OAuth modules allow you to generate tokens that can be used to simulate a session that can be used to test for roles and permissions.

Creating REST resources

When creating a REST interface for your Drupal 8 site, you can use the core methods on various entities like node and create Views. You also have the option to extend the platform to create your own plugins. This allows you to get around some of the challenges presented earlier in this chapter.

Using parameters

The simplest way to get started with a new REST plugin is to use the Drupal console to create the stub of a resource that extends ResourceBase. Start by typing `drupal generate:plugin:rest:resource` and then answer the prompts. We'll be recreating the functionality from the User Posts View from earlier in this chapter within the Mastering Drupal 8 module from previous chapters.

```
[vagrant@localhost public]$ drupal generate:plugin:rest:resource

// Welcome to the Drupal Plugin Rest Resource generator
Enter the module name [entity_rest_extra]:
> mastering_drupal_8

Enter the plugin rest resource name [DefaultRestResource]:
> UserPostsResource

Enter the plugin rest resource id [user_posts_resource]:
>

Enter the plugin rest resource label [User posts resource]:
>

Enter the plugin rest resource url:
> user/{user}/posts

Please select what REST States implement in your resource (GET is selected by default):
  [0] GET
  [1] PUT
  [2] POST
  [3] DELETE
  [4] PATCH
  [5] HEAD
  [6] OPTIONS
> 0


Do you confirm generation? (yes/no) [yes]:
>

Generated or updated files
 Site path: /vagrant/public
 1 - modules/custom/mastering_drupal_8/src/Plugin/rest/resource/UserPostsResource.php
// cache:rebuild

Rebuilding cache(s), wait a moment please.

[OK] Done clearing cache(s).
```

Once you've done that, you'll have a `UserPostsResource.php` in `src/Plugin/rest/resource` of the `mastering_drupal_8` module. Once you create this and rebuild the cache you'll need to enable it at **Configuration | REST**. At first, this new REST resource doesn't do very much; it just prints out "Implement REST State GET!" when you go to `localhost/user/1/posts?_format=hal_json`. In fact, it doesn't even get the user ID correctly, so you need to change the signature of the `get()` function to do that. So, the first thing you need to do is change the signature to public function `get($user)`. Now that we have the user ID, we need to get the nodes authored by the user and output them. Within the `get()` function, replace what's in there with:

```
// Load all nodes authored by the user
$nids = \Drupal::entityQuery('node')
  ->condition('uid', $user)
  ->sort('created', 'ASC')
  ->execute();

// Load the nodes
$nodes = Node::loadMultiple($nids);

return new ResourceResponse($nodes);
```

You will also have to add use `Drupal\node\Entity\Node;` at the top of the file, so you can use `Node::loadMultiple`. Now, when you rebuild the cache and return to `localhost/user/1/posts?_format=hal_json`, you'll see a list of nodes very much like what you received.

Now we'll want to take it further to get rid of some of the issues we had with the Views approach. The first thing we need to do is add pagination so we can handle cases where a user might have a large number of nodes. At the top of the `get()` function add:

```
$page = \Drupal::request()->query->has('page') ?
\Drupal::request()->query->get('page') : 0;
```

Then we need to edit the query itself to use the pager. So change that to:

```
// Load all nodes authored by the user
$nids = \Drupal::entityQuery('node')
  ->condition('uid', $user)
  ->sort('created', 'ASC')
  ->pager()
  ->execute();
```

Perform a quick cache rebuild and now you can go to
`localhost/user/1/posts?_format=hal_json&page=0` and you'll see the same list as
before. Now go to `localhost/user/1/posts?_format=hal_json&page=1` and you see
exactly the same list as you did on the previous page. In fact, no matter what you put in for
the page query parameter, you get the same output. One of the major enhancements in
Drupal 8 is in the caching system. REST resources vary, based on attributes defined for the
route and by the output format, but nothing else. Since we want the output to differ based
on the page, this isn't going to work. Since the `ResourceResponse` implements the
`CacheableResponseInterface`, we can add a new cache context to prevent this issue.
Instead of just returning a new `ResourceResponse`, add the following:

```
$response = new ResourceResponse($nodes);
// Add URL cache context
 $metadata = new CacheableMetadata();
 $metadata->addCacheContexts([ 'url' ]);
 $response->addCacheableDependency($metadata);
return $response;
```

You will also need to add use `Drupal\Core\Cache\CacheableMetadata;` at the top of the
file to pull in that namespace. Now, when you change the page in the query parameters,
you'll get different results. The Cache Context of `'url'` is pretty broad; if you wanted to,
you could narrow it by using `'url.query_args'`, to just consider the query parameters, or
even `'url.query_args:page'`, to bring it down to just the page query parameter. At this
point, your function should look like this.

```
/**
 * Responds to GET requests.
 *
 * Returns a list of bundles for specified entity.
 *
 * @throws \Symfony\Component\HttpKernel\Exception\HttpException Throws exception expected.
 */
public function get($user) {
  $page = \Drupal::request()->query->has('page') ? \Drupal::request()->query->get('page') : 0;

  // Load all nodes authored by the user
  $nids = \Drupal::entityQuery('node')
    ->condition('uid', $user)
    ->sort('created', 'ASC')
    ->pager()
    ->execute();

  // Load the nodes
  $nodes = Node::loadMultiple($nids);

  $response = new ResourceResponse($nodes);

  // Add URL cache context
  $metadata = new CacheableMetadata();
  $metadata->addCacheContexts([ 'url' ]);
  $response->addCacheableDependency($metadata);

  return $response;
}
```

As we noted, at the moment this code isn't doing anything that the Views version of it wasn't. Since we're controlling the output, we have complete freedom to add additional information. A critical one would be a count of how many nodes are authored by this user, regardless of the number being output from this response. To do that we'll need to add a count query:

```
// Get count of all nodes authored by the user
 $count = \Drupal::entityQuery('node')
   ->condition('uid', $user)
   ->count()
   ->execute();
 $pages = floor($count / 10);
```

Now that we have the count, we need to add it to the response. So instead of just returning the array of nodes, we'll add an attribute for total:

```
$response = new ResourceResponse([ 'total' => $count, 'posts' =>
array_values($nodes) ]);
```

Test this by going to various pages and, seeing that regardless of how many nodes are shown, it always has the `'count'` attribute. Okay, that's a good step toward making it more useful, but we're still lacking some of what makes HAL really useful: the links. We'll want to have the self link, of course, but also basic navigation like start, last, next, and prev. Since these are pretty much the same, we'll first need a function to generate those links:

```
/**
  * Returns a link to the Resource for a given user and page
  *
  * @param number $user
  * @param number $page
  *
  * @return string
  */
protected function getPagerLink($user = 0, $page = 0) {
    return URL::fromRoute('rest.user_posts_resource.GET.hal_json',
      [ 'user' => $user, 'page' => $page ], [ 'absolute' => TRUE])
    ->setRouteParameter('_format', 'hal_json')
    ->toString(TRUE)
    ->getGeneratedUrl();
  }
```

This function will generate a link back to this REST resource for a given user ID and page. Of course, we also need to add the use `Drupal\Core\URL;` to our namespace declaration. Next we'll construct the links:

```
$links = [
    'self' => [ 'href' => $this->getPagerLink($user, $page) ],
    'start' => [ 'href' => $this->getPagerLink($user, 0) ],
    'last' => [ 'href' => $this->getPagerLink($user, $pages) ],
  ];
if (0 < $page) {
    $links['prev'] = [ 'href' => $this->getPagerLink($user,
      ($page - 1)) ];
  }
if (0 < $pages && $page != $pages) {
    $links['next'] = [ 'href' => $this->getPagerLink($user,
      ($page + 1)) ];
  }
```

We'll then add them to the `ResourceResponse` by replacing the declaration with:

```
$response = new ResourceResponse([
    '_links' => $links,
    'total' => $count,
    'posts' => array_values($nodes)
  ]);
```

Now when you visit `localhost/user/1/posts?_format=hal_json` you will have links that allow you to traverse through the results page by page as well as skipping to the start or end of the list.

At this point your function will look like this:

```php
/**
 * Responds to GET requests.
 *
 * Returns a list of bundles for specified entity.
 *
 * @throws \Symfony\Component\HttpKernel\Exception\HttpException
 *   Throws exception expected.
 */
public function get($user) {
  $page = \Drupal::request()->query->has('page') ? \Drupal::request()->query->get('page') : 0;

  // Get count of all nodes authored by the user
  $count = \Drupal::entityQuery('node')
    ->condition('uid', $user)
    ->count()
    ->execute();

  $pages = floor($count / 10);

  // Load all nodes authored by the user
  $nids = \Drupal::entityQuery('node')
    ->condition('uid', $user)
    ->sort('created', 'ASC')
    ->pager()
    ->execute();

  // Load the nodes
  $nodes = (sizeof($nids)) ? Node::loadMultiple($nids) : [];

  $links = [
    'self' => [ 'href' => $this->getPagerLink($user, $page) ],
    'start' => [ 'href' => $this->getPagerLink($user, 0) ],
    'last' => [ 'href' => $this->getPagerLink($user, $pages) ],
  ];

  if (0 < $page) {
    $links['prev'] = [ 'href' => $this->getPagerLink($user, ($page - 1)) ];
  }
  if (0 < $pages && $page != $pages) {
    $links['next'] = [ 'href' => $this->getPagerLink($user, ($page + 1)) ];
  }

  $response = new ResourceResponse([
    '_links' => $links,
    'total' => $count,
    'posts' => array_values($nodes)
  ]);

  // Add URL cache context
  $metadata = new CacheableMetadata();
  $metadata->addCacheContexts([ 'url.query_args:page' ]);
  $response->addCacheableDependency($metadata);

  return $response;
}
```

Using the current user

The REST resource that we just created works, but it is pretty naive. At the moment, it doesn't make any attempt to ensure that the requesting user has permissions to view any of the content. The first part of that is making sure that we don't show any content that is unpublished and that the requesting user might not have access to. When our REST resource is called, we have access to the `currentUser` attribute. This `AccountProxy` is the user that is provided from the appropriate authentication methods enabled on the endpoint. We need this since, as we discussed earlier, we can't rely on there being an actual user session. So let's create a function to check to see if the requesting user is able to see unpublished content:

```
/**
 * Returns whether the provided user should be able to see un-published
content
 *
 * @param \Drupal\user\Entity\User $user
 *
 * @return Boolean
 */
protected function canSeeUnpublished($user) {
  $filter_unpublished = TRUE;
  // If user can bypass node access don't filter by published
  if ($this->currentUser->hasPermission('bypass node access')) {
    $filter_unpublished = FALSE;
  }
    // If there are node access
  else if (count(\Drupal::moduleHandler()
  ->getImplementations('node_grants'))
      && node_access_view_all_nodes($this->currentUser)) {
    $filter_unpublished = FALSE;
  }
  // If current user and can view own unpublished content
  else if ($user->id() == $this->currentUser->id()
      && $this->currentUser->hasPermission('view own unpublished
content')) {
    $filter_unpublished = FALSE;
  }
  return !$filter_unpublished;
}
```

There are a number of conditions that could allow a user to view unpublished content. The first is that they have permissions to "bypass all access restrictions", the next is if there is a module that implements `node_grants` and this user is granted the ability to view all nodes, and lastly, if the requesting user is the same as the requested user and they have permissions to "view own unpublished content." If any of these is correct, we need to return that we should not filter unpublished content. We then need to rewrite the queries to make use of that information. While we're at it, we will add the query tags and metadata to ensure that any queries we run also check against node access rules and are executed as the requesting user:

```
$filter_unpublished = !$this->canSeeUnpublished($request_user);
// Get count of all nodes authored by the user
 $count_query = \Drupal::entityQuery('node')
    ->condition('uid', $user);
if ($filter_unpublished) {
    $count_query->condition('status', 1);
 }
$count_query->count()
    ->addTag('node_access')
    ->addMetaData('op', 'view')
    ->addMetaData('account', $this->currentUser->getAccount());
$count = $count_query->execute();
// Load all nodes authored by the user
 $node_query = \Drupal::entityQuery('node')
    ->condition('uid', $user);
if ($filter_unpublished) {
    $node_query->condition('status', 1);
 }
$node_query->sort('created', 'ASC')
    ->pager()
    ->addTag('node_access')
    ->addMetaData('op', 'view')
    ->addMetaData('account', $this->currentUser->getAccount());
$nids = $node_query->execute();
```

Now you can test un-publishing a node and then testing `localhost/user/1/posts?_format=hal_json` logged in, as the administrator as well as not logged in and see how the count of nodes changes. If you haven't done so already, ensure that anonymous users are able to access "Access GET on User posts resource resource" in the permissions list. Your `get()` function should look like this.

```php
/**
 * Responds to GET requests.
 *
 * Returns a list of bundles for specified entity.
 *
 * @throws \Symfony\Component\HttpKernel\Exception\HttpException Throws exception expected.
 */
public function get($user) {
  $page = \Drupal::request()->query->has('page') ? \Drupal::request()->query->get('page') : 0;

  // Load the user being requested
  $request_user = User::load($user);

  $filter_unpublished = !$this->canSeeUnpublished($request_user);

  // Get count of all nodes authored by the user
  $count_query = \Drupal::entityQuery('node')
    ->condition('uid', $user);

  if ($filter_unpublished) {
    $count_query->condition('status', 1);
  }

  $count_query->count()
    ->addTag('node_access')
    ->addMetaData('op', 'view')
    ->addMetaData('account', $this->currentUser->getAccount());

  $count = $count_query->execute();

  // Load all nodes authored by the user
  $node_query = \Drupal::entityQuery('node')
    ->condition('uid', $user);

  if ($filter_unpublished) {
    $node_query->condition('status', 1);
  }

  $node_query->sort('created', 'ASC')
    ->pager()
    ->addTag('node_access')
    ->addMetaData('op', 'view')
    ->addMetaData('account', $this->currentUser->getAccount());

  $nids = $node_query->execute();

  // Load the nodes
  $nodes = Node::loadMultiple($nids);

  $links = [
    'self' => [ 'href' => $this->getPagerLink($user, $page) ],
    'start' => [ 'href' => $this->getPagerLink($user, 0) ],
    'last' => [ 'href' => $this->getPagerLink($user, (ceil($count / 10) - 1)) ],
  ];

  $response = new ResourceResponse([
    'links' => $links,
    'total' => $count,
    'posts' => array_values($nodes)
  ]);

  // Add URL cache context
  $metadata = new CacheableMetadata();
  $metadata->addCacheContexts([ 'url.query_args:page' ]);
  $response->addCacheableDependency($metadata);

  return $response;
}
```

Only one thing remains to properly secure our new REST endpoint. We should ensure that the requesting user has permissions to view the user they are trying to get information about. This is a simple matter of adding the following test after we load the user:

```
// Ensure the requesting user is able to view the requested user
$entity_access = $request_user->access('view',
  $this->currentUser, TRUE);
if (!$entity_access->isAllowed()) {
  throw new AccessDeniedHttpException();
}
```

This will ensure that only users with permission to view the requested users will see their posts. We also need to add the result of the access test to the cache context to ensure that, if that permission changes, our page is invalidated correctly. That's a simple matter of adding the following code at the bottom of the function before we return the response:

```
$response->addCacheableDependency($entity_access);
```

Now we have a robust way of retrieving all nodes authored by a given user. It has pagination and allows traversal through the API. It also has security in place to ensure that the user who requests the list is able to view the user in question, as well as all nodes that might be returned. It also respects all the authentication methods available in both core and contrib. In the end, your get () function should look like this:

```
public function get($user) {
  $page = \Drupal::request()->query->has('page') ? \Drupal::request()->query->get('page') : 0;

  // Load the user being requested
  $request_user = User::load($user);

  // Ensure the requesting user is able to view the requested user
  $entity_access = $request_user->access('view', $this->currentUser, TRUE);
  if (!$entity_access->isAllowed()) {
    throw new AccessDeniedHttpException();
  }

  $filter_unpublished = !$this->canSeeUnpublished($request_user);

  // Get count of all nodes authored by the user
  $count_query = \Drupal::entityQuery('node')
    ->condition('uid', $user);

  if ($filter_unpublished) {
    $count_query->condition('status', 1);
  }

  $count_query->count()
    ->addTag('node_access')
    ->addMetaData('op', 'view')
    ->addMetaData('account', $this->currentUser->getAccount());

  $count = $count_query->execute();

  // Load all nodes authored by the user
  $node_query = \Drupal::entityQuery('node')
    ->condition('uid', $user);

  if ($filter_unpublished) {
    $node_query->condition('status', 1);
  }

  $node_query->sort('created', 'ASC')
    ->pager()
    ->addTag('node_access')
    ->addMetaData('op', 'view')
    ->addMetaData('account', $this->currentUser->getAccount());

  $nids = $node_query->execute();

  // Load the nodes
  $nodes = Node::loadMultiple($nids);

  $links = [
    'self' => [ 'href' => $this->getPagerLink($user, $page) ],
    'start' => [ 'href' => $this->getPagerLink($user, 0) ],
    'last' => [ 'href' => $this->getPagerLink($user, (ceil($count / 10) - 1)) ],
  ];

  $response = new ResourceResponse([
    'links' => $links,
    'total' => $count,
    'posts' => array_values($nodes)
  ]);

  // Add URL cache context
  $metadata = new CacheableMetadata();
  $metadata->addCacheContexts([ 'url.query_args:page' ]);
  $response->addCacheableDependency($metadata);
  $response->addCacheableDependency($entity_access);

  return $response;
}
```

Summary

Drupal 8 promised an API-first approach. Having the REST API in core means that you no longer have to find the right contributed module to serve your content up to single-age applications or other sites. In this chapter, we learned how to:

- Create basic lists of content with Views
- Create a custom REST plugin to handle custom integrations
- Properly secure and cache your REST endpoint

In the next chapter we will be looking at the multilingual interface in Drupal 8 and how to translate content and localize configuration within your site.

13
Multilingual Capabilities

It has been said at a number of conferences that the multilingual capabilities in Drupal 8 core are more capable than Drupal 7 with all the appropriate contributed modules installed. Drupal 8 now ships with a standard way of translating content, translating configuration, and translating the user interface. The easiest way to get started with Drupal 8's multilingual capabilities is to begin with the Drupal 8 multilingual demo distribution available at `https://www.drupal.org/project/multilingual_demo`. This will install all of the appropriate modules, as well as creating some initial content so you can get a feel of how to set up and use them.

In this chapter, we will be covering the following topics:

- Enabling core multilingual modules
- Installing and configuring languages
- Adding language detection
- Working with language switching blocks
- Translating content
- Translating the Drupal admin UI
- Using the multilingual API

Enabling core multilingual modules

Unlike previous versions of Drupal, everything that you need to start translating your website is available in four modules in core.

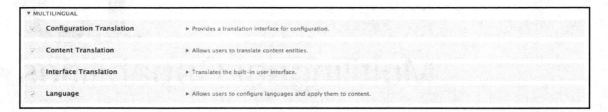

Multilingual modules

Language

The **Language module** provides the base functionality used by all of the other multilingual modules. Language allows site administrators to select the languages available on the site and configure how the language is selected and applied to the content. This includes:

- Selecting the languages available on the site
- Selecting a default language for users and other content
- Selecting how language is detected for a request
- Selecting a user interface language for a user

Interface Translation

The **Interface Translation** module allows site administrators to translate the interface of the Drupal site. This includes:

- Translating messages, labels, and administrative menu items
- Importing translation sets
- Exporting translation sets

Content Translation

The **Content Translation** module allows users to translate individual entities. These include users, node, taxonomy terms, blocks, and so on. This includes:

- Selecting which entity types can be translated
- Selecting which bundles can be translated
- Selecting which fields can be translated
- Selecting the default language for bundles

Configuration Translation

The **Configuration Translation** module allows configuration elements to be translated and exported. This includes:

- Translating field labels and descriptions
- Translating bundle names and descriptions
- Translating text used in Views

Installing and configuring languages

After installing the appropriate modules, the next step is to enable the languages you wish to have on the site. Select **Configuration** and then **Languages** from the menu bar or navigate to `/admin/config/regional/language`.

This page shows the currently installed languages, which one is currently set as the default, and how many interface strings have been translated for that language:

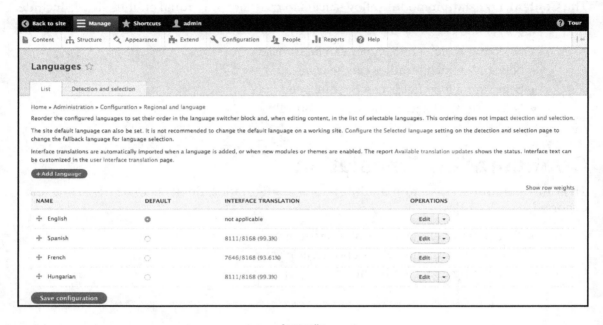

Language list

To add another language to the site, click on the button labeled **Add language** and select the language from the dropdown.

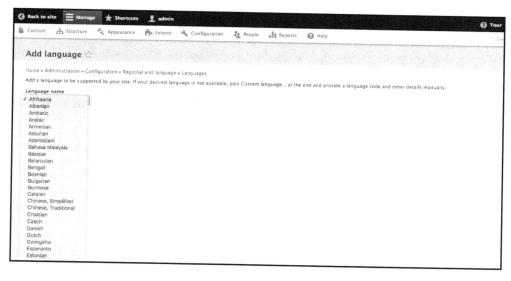

Add language page

There are 93 languages directly available from the list. In addition to those, you can select **Custom language...** from the list and enter a W3C language tag, the name of the language, and whether text is displayed left-to-right or right-to-left.

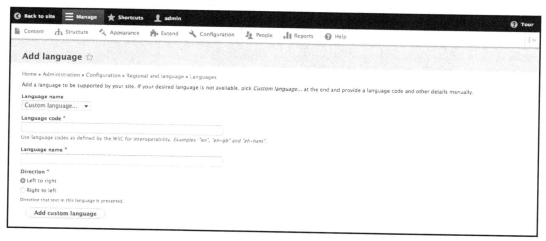

Add custom language

Adding language detection

Now that we have added languages, we need to have a process to identify which language a given request uses. From the **Languages** page, select the **Detection and selection** tab to configure these settings. There are a number of different options available to select. Starting from the detection method at the top, Drupal will attempt each enabled method until one returns a value.

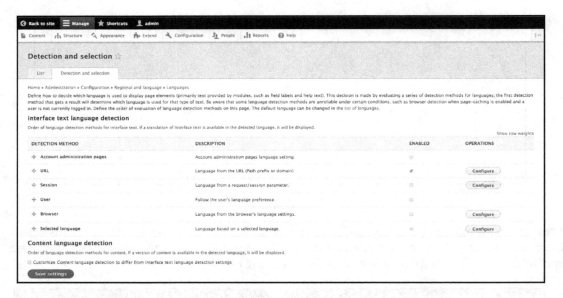

Language detection settings

Account administration pages

If **Account administration pages** is selected, then each user will see an option to choose which language is used to display the administrative section. There is an option for **No preference**, which will move on to the next language detection method. This language will be used on any routes that have the attribute `_admin_route`.

User language settings

URL

If URL is selected, you are able to use either a path prefix or subdomain to be checked for the current language. The default configuration is to use a path prefix that corresponds to the code for the language, with the site default language used if no prefix is provided. For example, `/node/1` would display the English version of the site and `/es/node/1` would display the Spanish version of it. If subdomain is selected, the URL `es.example.com/node/1` would retrieve the Spanish version of the site.

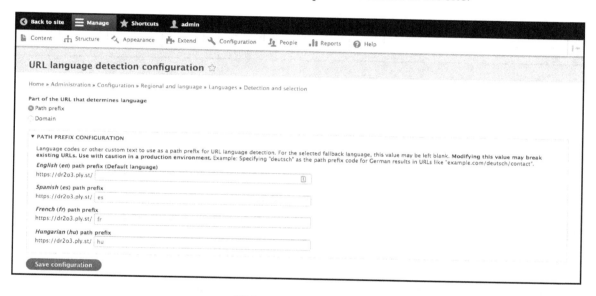

URL language detection configuration

Session

If **Session** is selected, you are able to configure a session or query parameter to be checked for the current language. This means that if a query parameter is passed on any request, it defaults to language, and that page is returned in that language.

In addition, it stores that language so, as the user moves around the site, the language is maintained.

Session language detection configuration

User

If User is selected, the language selected for a user's profile will be checked for the current language.

Browser

If Browser is selected, the `Accept-Language` request header will be checked for the current language. The configuration screen allows you to map language and locale tags defined by the **World Wide Web Consortium** (**W3C**) to languages installed on the site. For more information about the language tag specification, go to `https://www.w3.org/TR/ltli/`. Text entered for the language code is compared to the value from the browser after converting both to lowercase to avoid case issues.

Browser language detection configuration

Selected language

If **Selected language** is selected, a specific language is used for the current language. Since this always returns a value, it defaults to the last detection method in the chain. The Selected language method cannot be disabled, which guarantees that a language is always present for the request.

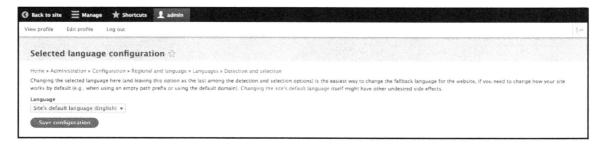

Selected language configuration

Content language detection

By default, the methods used to determine the interface language will also be used to determine the content language. Selecting the checkbox labeled **Customize Content language detection** allows you to specify different methods and order to determine how the content language is determined.

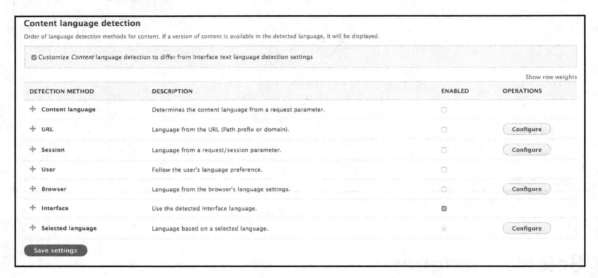

Content language detection

Working with language switching blocks

The Language module provides a block that can be used to switch the current interface and content language. By default, the language switching block allows the user to change to any language present in the system, but this can also be configured to restrict the options to specific languages. If the checkbox for **Customize Content language detection** has been selected, you must select whether the block uses the interface or content configuration.

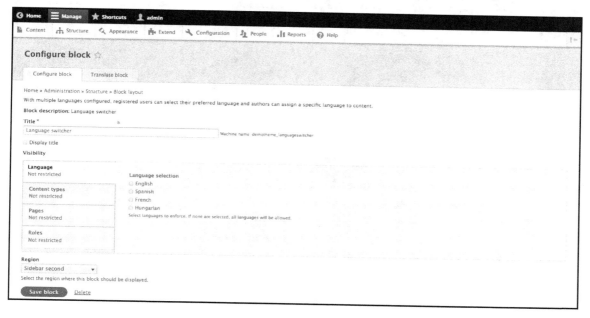

Language switcher block configuration

The block will output each language translated into the target language. For example, Spanish is output as **Español** no matter which language the user is currently in. The link for each language is generated using the first enabled detection method that alters the URL. This means that only URL and Session provide links. For example, if URL is placed first, the link for Spanish will look like /es and if Session is it would be /?language=es. If neither **URL** or **Session** are selected, then the language switching block will not be displayed.

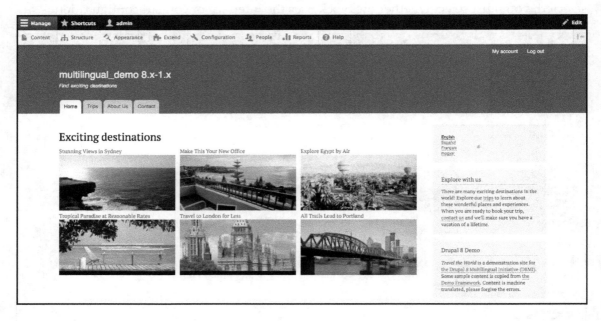

Language switching block

Translating content

With languages and detection set up, the next step is to translate content. If the content type is marked as translatable in the language configuration, you are able to update how the default language is selected either on that page or on the **Edit Basic page content type** page. The default setting is to use the site's default language, but you can also use a fixed language, the current interface language, or the author's preferred language. You can also allow the selection of the language on the form used to create or edit a node.

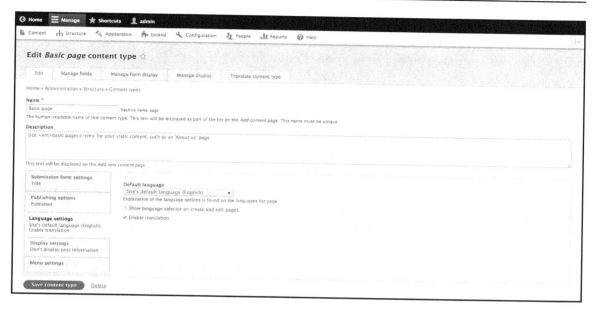

Content type edit screen with language settings

Once a translatable entity has been created, a new tab will appear for users with permissions to translate content. Clicking on the **Translate** tab shows a list of languages enabled on the site, and either the version of the entity translated into that language or the option to translate the entity.

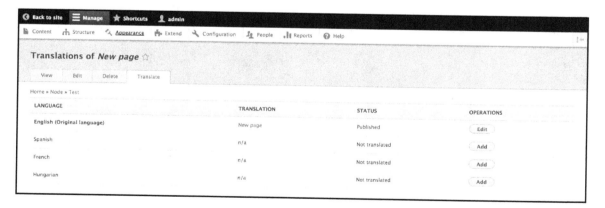

Node translation page

Clicking on the button to **Add** a translation takes you to an edit screen to provide the translation for the entity. This form is shown in the designated language's interface, but only if the URL language detection method is enabled.

Translating the Drupal admin UI

When you enable a language for the first time, translation files from `localize.drupal.org` are downloaded. Depending on the language, these may cover a large portion of strings in the Drupal admin UI, but there are likely to be some texts that are not translated. In addition, any text custom-created for the current site would need to be translated. The interface to translate these strings can be found by going to **Configuration**, then **User interface translation**, or by navigating to `/admin/config/regional/translate`.

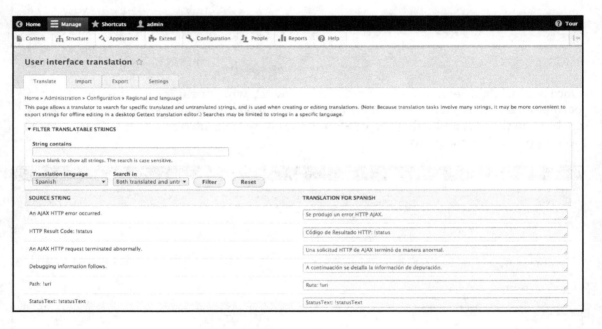

User interface translation page

On the **User interface translation** form, you can view all strings in the system, as well as locating ones that need translation into a particular language. You can select the appropriate language, select whether to see untranslated strings, translated strings, or all, and optionally provide text to be matched from the primary site language. For example, when selecting Spanish as the language, only untranslated strings and entering the search text of "path" finds any strings in English containing the word "path" that need to be translated. The text can be entered into the text areas on that page and then will appear in the appropriate location for Spanish users.

Using the multilingual API

When you have content in custom code, it needs to be output using specific functions and other methods to ensure it can be translated through the administrative UI. How this is exposed depends on the manner it is embedded in the code.

PHP code

Like Drupal 7, there are still the `t()` and `format_plural()` functions. However, the functionality behind these relies on the `TranslationManager` class. This means that it can be dependency injected into any Drupal 8 services, controllers, plugins, and so on. This is the preferred mechanism for translating text in PHP, and many base plugin classes in Drupal already implement functions that delegate to the `TranslationManager`.

One thing to be aware of is that the mechanism that discovers translatable strings relies on the functions being called, named `t()` and `formatPlural()`. So, while the actual method to translate content is `TranslationManager::translate()`, the following will not be picked up by `localize.drupal.org`:

```
$this->stringTranslation->translate('Something');
```

In addition to the function names, using variables in calls to the translation functions also prevents the strings from being discovered. So, writing code like this:

```
t($variable)
$this->t($first . ' word ' . $last);
```

Will prevent it from being able to be extracted and translated by the community. If you need to use a variable, you should use variable substitution, like this:

```
$this->t('@first word @last', [ '@first' => $first, '@last' => $last ]);
```

JavaScript

Like Drupal 7, there are functions available on the global Drupal object to translate or format plural values. When writing JavaScript, text wrapped in `Drupal.t` and `Drupal.formatPlural` provide functionality similar to `t()` and `format_plural()` in PHP.

YML files

Some attributes in various `YAML` files are automatically translated. These include:

- Module name and description in `.info.yml` files
- Menu router title in the `_title` attribute in `.routing.yml` files
- Menu link title in the `title` attribute in `.links.action.yml`, `.links.task.yml` and `.links.contextual.yml` files

Annotations

Classes that use annotations to provide information used to register also need to be able to be translated. Since annotations are not code or Twig templates, they need an alternate mechanism to define translatable text. For example:

```
/**
 * Defines the file entity class.
 *
 * @EntityType(
 *   id = "file",
 *   label = @Translation("File"),
 *   ....
 */
class File {
}
```

This runs any text within the `@Translation` wrapper through the `t()` function.

Twig templates

Content in Twig templates can translate content either in small sets by using the `t` or `trans` filter, or the `{% trans %}` block. For instance, you can run text through the translate function using either of the following:

```
{{ 'Hello world' | t }}
{{ 'Hello world' | trans }}
```

Placing output within a `{% trans %}` block runs text through the translation function, including handling variables. For example:

```
{% trans %}
  Submitted by {{ author.username }} on {{ node.created }}
{% endtrans %}
```

This is the same as running `t('Submitted by @username on @created')` and passing the appropriate variables. The default variable handling is to escape the values, but you are also able to avoid this escaping or wrapping it in an <em> tag by using filters. For example:

```
{% trans %}
  Submitted by {{ author.username | passthrough }} on {{ node.created |
passthrough }}
{% endtrans %}
```

This is the same as running `t('Submitted by !username on !created')`. Similarly:

```
{% trans %}
  Submitted by {{ author.username | placeholder }} on {{ node.created |
placeholder }}
{% endtrans %}
```

This is the same as running `t('Submitted by %username on %created')`.

Summary

With just these core modules, you are now ready to completely translate a Drupal 8 site. This includes all the content, but also the interface and any configuration as well. In addition, we've learned the following:

- How to translate text within your own custom modules
- How to translate text in Twig templates

Next, we will be learning how to manage site configuration and transfer it between different environments.

14
Configuration Management

Once you move beyond making all of your changes on the live site, it becomes imperative that there is some way of moving your changes between different versions of the site. In Drupal 7 and earlier, the Features module was used, but many modules either implemented their own incompatible way to export configuration or simply stored it in a way that couldn't easily be pulled out by Features. Having a standard mechanism to store configuration and to import and export it in the core is one of the most anticipated changes in Drupal 8. It was also the very first initiative announced for Drupal 8. In this chapter, we will be covering:

- How configuration is stored in Drupal 8
- Exploring the user interface for managing configuration in Drupal 8
- How to use the Configuration API in your own custom modules
- Exporting and importing individual configuration items
- Exporting and importing the whole site's configuration
- A configuration workflow using Drush
- Using configuration management with multilingual sites

Configuration Management files

Because the **Configuration Management** (**CM**) system needs to be able to store anything that any contrib module might want to keep track of, the storage mechanism is a lot different from what you may have seen in Features.

File format

Configuration values are stored in YAML files. Each set of configuration values is stored in a separate file for each configuration object. This means each View, entity bundle, field, permission, and so on is in a separate file. This helps limit the risk of conflicts when merging configuration, as well as making it evident from the filename which configuration the values inside apply to.

Schema

All exportable configuration is defined by a **schema**. For example, basic information about the site, including the name, email address, slogan, and so on are exported to a system.site.yml file. This is defined by system.schema.yml in core/modules/system/config/schema. It contains the definition of the exports, such as the following:

```
system.site:
  type: config_object
  label: 'Site information'
  mapping:
    uuid:
      type: string
      label: 'Site UUID'
    name:
      type: label
      label: 'Site name'
    mail:
      type: email
      label: 'Email address'
    [...]
```

These schemas are used for the following reasons:

- To identify translatable strings that can be discovered by localize.drupal.org
- To discover labels and other properties when translating configuration
- To describe the actual information being stored in the exported configuration and to ensure it can be validated
- To allow automatic typecasting of values to ensure that only actual changes are shown rather than changes in type

When developing a new custom module, you can use `drupal.org/project/config_inspector` to help debug your schema as well as to test any custom exports.

Each element of the schema can have the following properties:

- **type**: The data type of the element
- **label**: The label shown on the interface
- **translatable**: Whether the configuration element can be translated
- **nullable**: Whether the value can be empty; the default is false

The data types supported in the schema are:

- Scalar values
- Mapping
- Sequence
- Reusable types
- Dynamic type references

Scalar values

The basic types that can be associated with a configuration element are:

- Boolean
- email
- integer
- float
- string
- uri

There are other data types defined that are aliases for string. These include:

- path
- text
- date_format
- color_hex

This is done to provide hinting to allow additional validation to the exported data.

These will be output in the configuration YAML and then retrieved and converted to the appropriate type in Drupal. This avoids some of the possible confusion in YAML by ensuring that the value 0 is converted to either the Boolean FALSE or the integer 0 as appropriate.

Mapping

Mappings are a way of constructing more complicated data types by allowing nested key-value pairs. For example, from the same system.site block from earlier:

```
page:
  type: mapping
  label: 'Pages'
  mapping:
    403:
      type: path
      label: 'Default 403 (access denied) page'
    404:
      type: path
      label: 'Default 404 (not found) page'
    front:
      type: path
      label: 'Default front page'
```

When the type is set to mapping, the schema expects one or more children defined under the mapping attribute. These could potentially be mappings as well, allowing for arbitrary nesting depth.

Sequence

A **sequence** is an array of zero or more elements of a given type. For example, the system.schema.yaml defines a configuration object system.mail that contains:

```
system.mail:
  type: config_object
  label: 'Mail system'
  mapping:
    interface:
      type: sequence
      label: 'Interfaces'
      sequence:
        type: string
        label: 'Interface'
```

The export would contain an attribute called **interface** containing an array of elements that would be treated as strings. Any type can be used in the sequence, including scalar and complex types.

Reusable types

A configuration schema can contain not only configuration objects, but also complex defined types. For example, in the `core.data_types.schema.yml` file there is:

```
# Mail text with subject and body parts.
mail:
  type: mapping
  label: 'Mail'
  mapping:
    subject:
      type: label
      label: 'Subject'
    body:
      type: text
      label: 'Body'
```

This allows any other configuration schema to define its type as `Mail` and have it interpreted as that mapping without having to repeat it.

Dynamic type references

Sometimes the configuration value being exported is not static and can depend on the data being exported itself. Two areas where this occurs are with image styles where the attributes for the effects depend on the type of effect, and Views where the values for plugins depend on the plugin type. Variables from the export can be combined to form the data type for the element. These variables are enclosed in `[]` brackets and follow one of the following rules:

- `[value]` where value is an attribute of current element; for example, `views.field.[table]-[field]` would construct the type based on the attributes of `table` and `field` found in the mapping
- `[%key]` refers to the key of the current element
- `[%parent]` refers to the parent of the current element and is usually combined with an attribute; for example, `views.display[%parent.display_plugin]` would construct the type based on the `display_plugin` attribute of the current element's parent

A comprehensive example can be seen in the initial image styles; for example, in `image.style.large.yml` in `core/modules/image/config/install` you have:

```
langcode: en
status: true
dependencies: {  }
name: large
label: 'Large (480×480)'
effects:
  ddd73aa7-4bd6-4c85-b600-bdf2b1628d1d:
    uuid: ddd73aa7-4bd6-4c85-b600-bdf2b1628d1d
    id: image_scale
    weight: 0
    data:
      width: 480
      height: 480
      upscale: false
```

This is governed by the schema defined in `image.schema.yml`:

```
image.style.*:
  type: config_entity
  label: 'Image style'
  mapping:
    name:
      type: string
    label:
      type: label
      label: 'Label'
    effects:
      type: sequence
      sequence:
        type: mapping
        mapping:
          id:
            type: string
          data:
            type: image.effect.[%parent.id]
          weight:
            type: integer
          uuid:
            type: string
```

You see that effects are a sequence, where the data attribute type depends on the value of the `id` attribute of the parent. So, when parsing the large image style effects data, it goes up one level to the UUID and then the `id` value, which is `image_scale`, and uses the type `image.effect.image_scale`.

Override system

Configuration in Drupal is stored in the database and can be imported from and exported to the filesystem. But there are times when it is necessary to apply a set of changes to the existing configuration outside of this system. A common reason is to set attributes on a specific environment. In Drupal 7, there was the `global $conf` variable, which could be manipulated in the `settings.php` file to provide this functionality.

A major challenge with the approach in Drupal 7 is that any overrides could not be distinguished from other settings. From the point of view of a configuration form, there was no distinction between attributes coming from the database or from the override. This means that if the configuration form were submitted, it would save the override to the database. In Drupal 8, these overrides are maintained as a layer on top of the existing configuration and it does not use them on configuration forms.

In Drupal 8, the `$conf` variable has been renamed `$config` and can still be set from the `settings.php` file, using the same nested array syntax as Drupal 7. For example, to get the system maintenance message, you would use this:

```
$message = \Drupal::config('system.maintenance')->get('message');
```

If you wanted to override that, you would override it using this:

```
$config['system.maintenance']['message'] = 'The site is down.';
```

Additional levels can be traversed using nested array keys. If you need access to `$config` outside of the `settings.php` file you need to first declare it using `global $config`.

Differences between configuration and state

In Drupal 7 and earlier, system configuration and state were commingled in the `variables` table. In addition to the new Configuration API, Drupal 8 added the State API. This should be used for settings that are:

- Specific to an individual environment and should not be deployed between environments
- Can be reset without adverse consequences

This encompasses items such as the last cron run timestamp, CSRF tokens, and so on. Typical uses include:

- Getting a state variable:

```
$val = \Drupal::state()->get('key');
```

- Setting a state variable:

```
\Drupal::state()->set('key', 'value');
```

- Deleting a state variable:

```
\Drupal::state()->delete('key');
```

Using the Config object

The Config object is the primary interface to interact with the system configuration. You retrieve the Config object by calling the `config()` function like so:

```
$config = \Drupal::config('system.site');
```

This method returns a `\Drupal\Core\Config\ImmutableConfig` object that can only be used to read the configuration. If you need to modify the configuration, you can use the `config.factory` service, like so:

```
$config = \Drupal::service('config.factory')->getEditable('system.site');
```

To read attributes of the Config object, you can use the `get()` function, like:

```
$name = \Drupal::config('system.site')->get('name');
```

When retrieving nested configuration values, you can retrieve the full array of values using the `get()` function. For example, calling:

```
$pages = \Drupal::config('system.site')->get('page');
```

Will return an array with each value from the mapping, like so:

```
[
  '403'   => 'url',
  '404'   => 'url',
  'front' => 'url',
]
```

If you want to retrieve a nested value, you can specify the path to the value separated by periods. If you wanted to get the path to the **404 page**, you could run:

```
$page_404 = \Drupal::config('system.site')->get('page.404');
```

The mutable Config objects have additional functions to `set()`, `clear()` and `delete()` configuration. Both `set()` and `clear()` can traverse nested configuration using periods like `get()`. The `delete()` function is used to remove whole configuration sections, for example:

```
// Set 404 page
\Drupal::service('config.factory')->getEditable('system.site')->set('page.4
04', 'new url');

// Clear 404 page setting
\Drupal::service('config.factory')->getEditable('system.site')->clear('page
.404');

// Delete all system.site configuration
\Drupal::service('config.factory')->getEditable('system.site')->delete();
```

Once you have modified the Config object, you need to call `save()` to persist the change. These functions each return the Config object so you can chain multiple operations after each other. For example:

```
\Drupal::service('config.factory').getEditable('system.site')->set('page.40
4', 'new url')->set('page.403', 'new url')->save();
```

Configuration interface

Drupal 8 provides an interface to interact with the configuration. You can import, export, and synchronize through the administrative interface by navigating to **Configuration** and then **Configuration synchronization** from the menu bar.

Synchronize configuration

The first tab, labeled **Synchronize**, allows you to see the state of any configuration that has been exported to the filesystem and compare it to the configuration currently in the database. Each configuration item that contains a difference is listed, along with a button to show the differences.

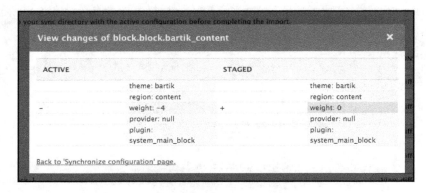

Synchronize configuration screen

Clicking on the **View differences** button opens up a dialog that shows the differences between the configuration in the synchronization directory and what is in the database.

Differences dialog

Once you have verified each change, you can click the button labeled **Import all** to set the current database configuration to the files in the synchronization directory.

Exporting single configuration

If you need to export only a single configuration item, you can click the tab labeled **Export** and then the secondary tab labeled **Single item**. From there, you can select the configuration object and item. Doing so outputs the current value to the text area and allows you to copy and paste it to either a file or another site. The system will also print the name of the file following to the text area to assist in creating a file to contain the configuration.

Export single configuration item

Importing single configuration

Once you have exported a configuration item from one environment, or you have settings from another source, you can import that directly into the site by clicking on the tab labeled **Import** and then the secondary tab labeled **Single item**. You would select the configuration object and enter the item name, and then paste the configuration directly into the text area.

Clicking the button labeled **Import** will insert it into the database.

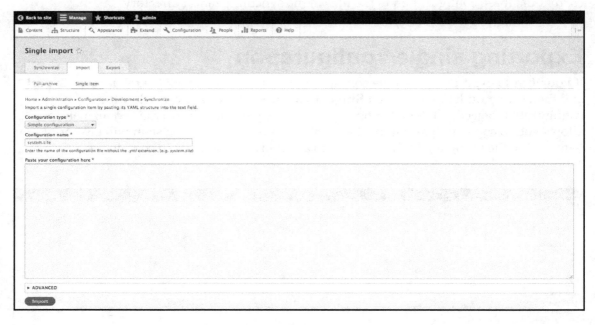

Import single configuration item

Exporting whole site configuration

The Configuration interface allows you to export all configuration items on the site to an archive file. Selecting the **Export** tab takes you to a form with a button labeled **Export**. Clicking on that button downloads a file that contains all site configuration.

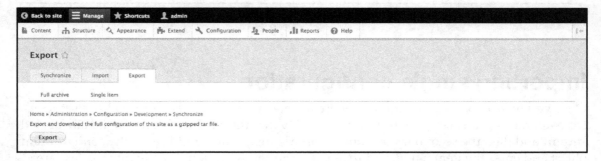

Export site configuration

Importing whole site configuration

The archive file generated from exporting all site configuration can be uploaded and then imported directly into the site. Selecting the **Import** tab takes you to a form with file upload control. Selecting a previously exported file and clicking the button labeled **Upload** will import all configuration items in the export. Like other import methods, any configuration on the site not present in the uploaded archive will be deleted.

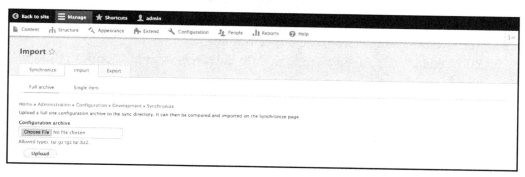

Import site configuration

Configuration workflow with Drush

In addition to using the interface to import and export configuration, it can also be triggered through Drush. The following commands are available:

- `drush config-export`: Exports all site configuration to the `synchronization` folder.

- `drush config-import`: Imports all site configuration from the `synchronization` folder. By default, this will delete any configuration on the system that is not present in the `synchronization` folder; you can provide the `--partial` flag to avoid this behavior.

- `drush config-pull`: Exports configuration from one remote site and copies it to another; for example, `drush config-pull @live @self` will export all configuration on the site at the `@live alias` and copy the files down to the current site.

- `drush config-list`: Lists all configuration objects on the site.

- `drush config-set`: Directly sets a configuration value in the database.

- `drush config-get`: Returns the value of a configuration object.

- `drush config-edit`: Opens the system editor, for example `nano` or `vim`, for the provided configuration object and then imports the value when it closes.

To transfer site configuration from one site to another, you would perform the following actions:

1. Make changes to site configuration.
2. Run `drush config-export` to update the synchronized configuration.
3. Commit file changes to the version control system.
4. Retrieve file changes from the target system.
5. Run `drush config-import` to update the target system's configuration to match.

Configuration and multilingual sites

The Configuration API allows for each value to be translated into each site language. These translations can be added in a few different ways.

Configuration forms

Any form that extends `ConfigFormBase` will display a tab that allows users to translate the configuration elements.

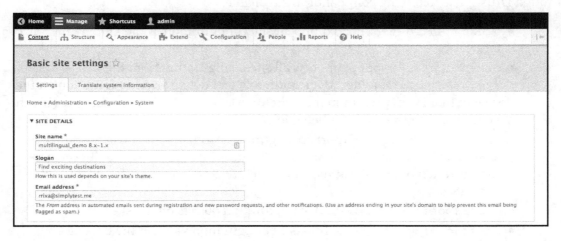

Translate configuration tab

Clicking on the tab shows a list of system languages with buttons to **Add**, **Edit**, and **Delete** translations for the form.

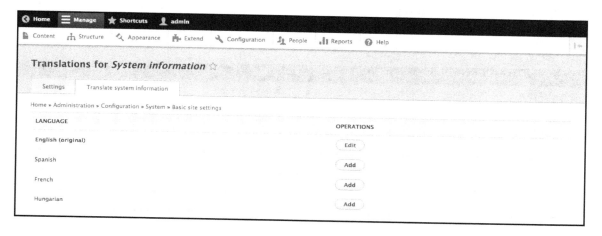

Language selection form

Selecting to **Add** or **Edit** the configuration in the language displays a form to allow translations. This form is built using the Configuration schema for the configuration names declared by the underlying configuration form.

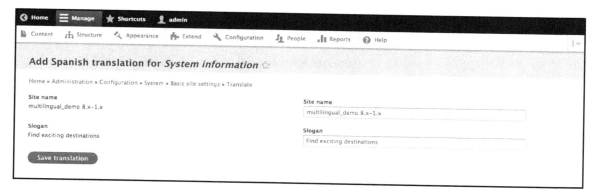

Form translation

Configuration translation

All of the configuration elements can be accessed for translation by selecting **Configuration** and then **Configuration translation** from the menu bar, or by navigating to `admin/config/regional/config-translation`.

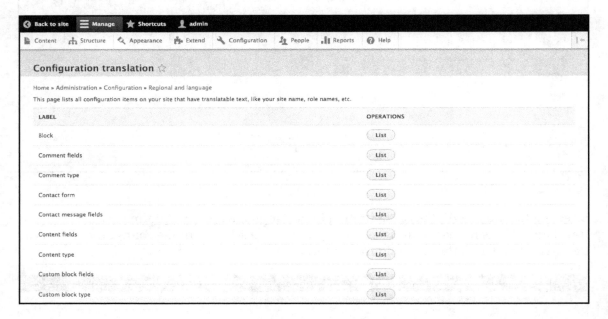

Configuration translation list

Each configuration object or type is displayed in a list with a button to either **Translate** the object or list the objects of that type. For instance, clicking on **List** next to **Block** shows a list of all Blocks with the ability to translate the values for each one.

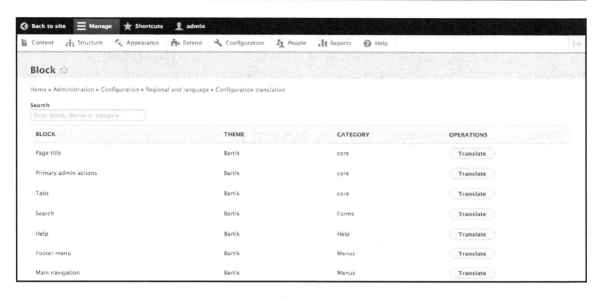

List of Blocks to translate

After clicking the **Translate** button next to the **Block**, you are able to **Add**, **Edit**, or **Delete** translations for any text elements exposed by the Block.

Language selection for Block

User interface translation

Each configuration text element is also exposed under the general **User interface translation** page. Select **Configuration** and then **User interface translation**, or navigate to `admin/config/regional/translate` to see the form. From there, you can browse or search for the original language string and enter the translated text.

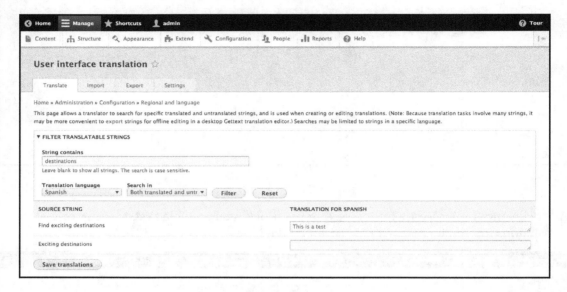

User interface translation

Summary

Managing, storing, and moving the configuration is a critical need for almost any site. We started with learning the intricacies of the configuration files and schemas and how to create our own. From there, we looked at how to load and store our own configuration and override it for particular environments.

Next, we worked on exporting and importing a configuration. We went through how to do that through the web interface, as well as through Drush. Finally, we learned how to use the configuration system on a multilingual site.

In the next chapter, you will be learning how to migrate a site from an earlier version of Drupal to Drupal 8. We will be using the migration steps built into Drupal 8 core and then customizing the process with your own custom code.

15
Site Migration

Like previous versions, Drupal 8 ships with a method for upgrading from previous versions of Drupal. In addition, it contains the underlying functionality from the migrate API to allow importing data from other sources as well. In this chapter, we will be covering:

- Exploring core options for migration
- Customizing the migration
- Enhancing migrations with contributed modules
- Using Drush to manage migrations

Enabling core modules to migrate content

Drupal 8 comes with a set of modules in core to help migrate content from previous versions of Drupal. You can enable these modules by selecting **Extend** from the administrative menu:

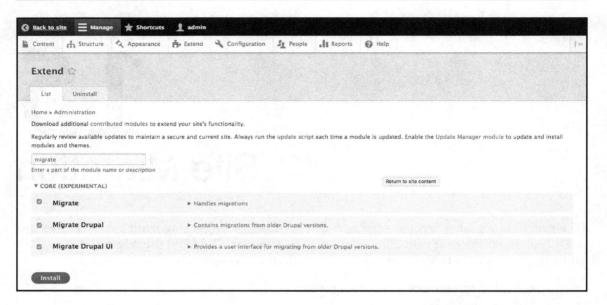

Core migration modules

These modules perform the following functions:

- **Migrate**: It installs the core migration API
- **Migrate Drupal**: It installs helper classes to assist in migrating Drupal 7 and earlier sites to Drupal 8
- **Migrate Drupal UI**: It adds a user interface

Using Drupal 8's Migrate to handle migrations

Once the Migrate modules are installed, you can navigate to **Configuration** and then **Drupal Upgrade** to begin the migration process:

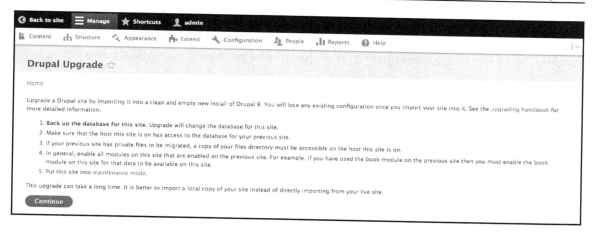

Starting Drupal migration process

The first step is to select the source for the migration. Enter the credentials for a database that the current site has access to and optionally provide the path to files that are part of the source site. After this has been entered, click the button labeled **Review upgrade**:

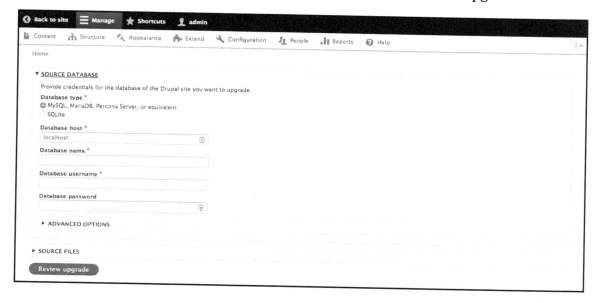

Migration source form

The Migrate module will scan the modules that were installed in the source site and look for `\Drupal\migrate\ProcessPluginBase` plugins that are valid for that module. First, the modules from the migration source that do not have a matching path will be listed:

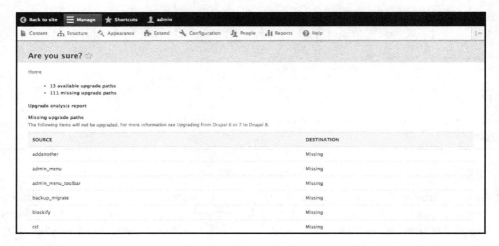

Missing upgrade paths

Next, each module that has an upgrade path is listed. Verify that the list matches your expectation and then click the button labeled **Perform upgrade**:

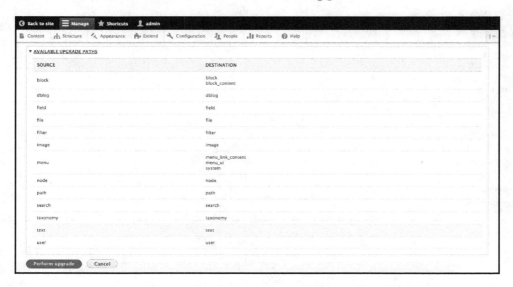

Available upgrade paths

After the upgrade process completes, you will be directed back to the home page displaying the results:

Migration result

The migration modules will bring over all the entities in the source database. This includes all nodes, vocabularies and terms, and users:

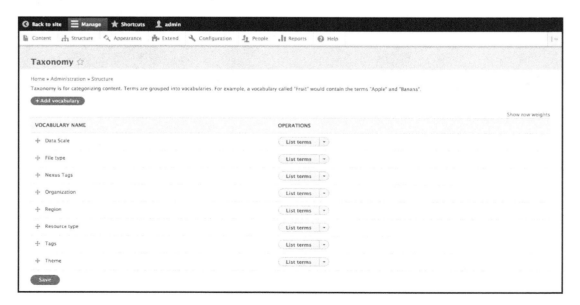

Migrated vocabularies

The migration modules will also bring over each entity type, bundle, and field that can be recognized:

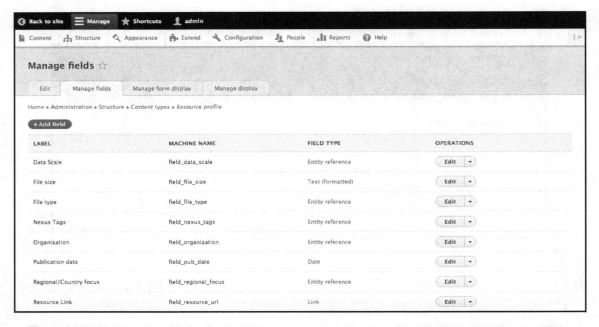

Migrated content type

Extending migrations with contributed modules

Drupal 8 core contains the basic migration framework adapted from Drupal 7, but not all of it. The functionality included in Drupal 8 supports upgrading from Drupal 6 and 7 from a database only. There are additional capabilities that are available in contrib:

- **Migrate Plus**: The Migrate Plus module adds a large part of the Migrate framework functionality. This includes creating migration processes in code and adding Configuration Entities to persist settings to remote systems. It also adds plugins to load data from JSON and XML files.
- **Migrate Tools**: The Migrate Tools module adds Drush commands to manage migrations. These include running migrations, checking their status and rolling them back as necessary. There is also a UI to view migrations, but as of Drupal 8.1.3, it is not completely functional.

Building a migration process

The Migrate Plus module also comes with some examples of how to build and manage migrations. Once you download the Migrate Plus module using `drush dl migrate_plus`, the examples are available in `modules/contrib/migrate_plus/migrate_example`.

The first step is creating a migration group, which is found in the `config/install` directory for the module for the Configuration Entity to be created when the module is installed. The migration group has basic attributes for a machine name, label, description, and source description:

```
id: beer
label: Beer Imports
description: A few simple beer-related imports, to demonstrate how to
implement migrations.
source_type: Custom tables
shared_configuration:
    key: default
```

Once you have the migration group defined, you would add individual migrations to it:

```
# Migration configuration for beer content.
id: beer_node
label: Beers of the world
migration_group: beer
source:
  plugin: beer_node
destination:
  plugin: entity:node
process:
  type:
    plugin: default_value
    default_value: migrate_example_beer
  title: name
  nid: bid
  uid:
    plugin: migration
    migration: beer_user
    source: aid
  sticky:
    plugin: default_value
    default_value: 0
  field_migrate_example_country: countries
  field_migrate_example_beer_style:
    plugin: migration
    migration: beer_term
    source: terms
```

```
    'body/value': body
    'body/summary': excerpt
migration_dependencies:
  required:
    - beer_term
    - beer_user
```

In the configuration definition, it defines the migration group that it is part of, the source migration plugin, the target entity that will be created or updated, and then how values from the source are mapped to it. For example, the field title in the node will be populated from the `name` attribute from the migration plugin. In addition to basic mappings, you can also add different plugins to process the result. These include:

- `Callback`: It triggers a callable with the value
- `Concat`: It concatenates an array of values
- `DefaultValue`: It sets a default value for missing values
- `Explode`: It converts a delimited string into an array of values
- `Extract`: It returns a single value from an array
- `Flatten`: It flattens a nested array to a single depth
- `Get`: It applies a regular expression to the value
- `MachineName`: It constructs a machine name from a value
- `SkipOnEmpty`: It skips the current field or row if the value is empty
- `SkipRowIfNotSet`: It skips the current row if the value is empty
- `StaticMap`: It maps the value to another value

Creating a migration source

A migration source provides the initial rows that are passed to any registered processors and then ultimately to the destination entity. Drupal 8 core provides a `SqlBase` class that serves as the base class for migrations that read from the database. The `migrate_example` module contains the following:

```php
<?php

/**
 * @file
 * Contains
 * \Drupal\migrate_example\Plugin\migrate\source\BeerNode.
 */

namespace Drupal\migrate_example\Plugin\migrate\source;
```

```
use Drupal\migrate\Plugin\migrate\source\SqlBase;
use Drupal\migrate\Row;

/**
 * Source plugin for beer content.
 *
 * @MigrateSource(
 *   id = "beer_node"
 * )
 */
class BeerNode extends SqlBase {

  /**
   * {@inheritdoc}
   */
  public function query() {
    /**
     * An important point to note is that your query *must* return
     * a single row for each item to be imported. Here we might be
     * tempted to add a join to migrate_example_beer_topic_node in
     * our query, to pull in the relationships to our categories.
     * Doing this would cause the query to return multiple rows
     * for a given node, once per related value, thus processing
     * the same node multiple times, each time with only one of
     * the multiple values that should be imported. To avoid that,
     * we simply query the base node data here, and pull in the
     * relationships in prepareRow() below.
     */
    $query = $this->select('migrate_example_beer_node', 'b')
      ->fields('b', ['bid', 'name', 'body', 'excerpt', 'aid',
                'countries', 'image', 'image_alt', 'image_title',
                'image_description']);
    return $query;
  }

  /**
   * {@inheritdoc}
   */
  public function fields() {
    $fields = [
      'bid' => $this->t('Beer ID'),
      'name' => $this->t('Name of beer'),
      'body' => $this->t('Full description of the beer'),
      'excerpt' => $this->t('Abstract for this beer'),
      'aid' => $this->t('Account ID of the author'),
      'countries' => $this->t('Countries of origin. Multiple values,
delimited by pipe'),
      'image' => $this->t('Image path'),
```

```
      'image_alt' => $this->t('Image ALT'),
      'image_title' => $this->t('Image title'),
      'image_description' => $this->t('Image description'),
      // Note that this field is not part of the query above - it
      // is populated by prepareRow() below. You should document
      // all source properties that are available for mapping
      // after prepareRow() is called.
      'terms' => $this->t('Applicable styles'),
    ];

    return $fields;
}

/**
 * {@inheritdoc}
 */
public function getIds() {
    return [
      'bid' => [
        'type' => 'integer',
        'alias' => 'b',
      ],
    ];
}

/**
 * {@inheritdoc}
 */
public function prepareRow(Row $row) {
    /**
     * As explained above, we need to pull the style relationships
     * into our source row here, as an array of 'style' values
     * (the unique ID for the beer_term migration).
     */
    $terms = $this->select('migrate_example_beer_topic_node',
            'bt')
            ->fields('bt', ['style'])
            ->condition('bid', $row->getSourceProperty('bid'))
            ->execute()
            ->fetchCol();
    $row->setSourceProperty('terms', $terms);

    // As we did for favorite beers in the user migration, we need
    // to explode the multi-value country names.
    if ($value = $row->getSourceProperty('countries')) {
      $row->setSourceProperty('countries', explode('|', $value));
    }
    return parent::prepareRow($row);
```

```
      }
  }
```

A migration source implements `\Drupal\migrate\Plugin\MigrateSourceInterface`, which specifies the following functions:

- `fields()`: It returns an array of fields that are present in each row
- `getIds()`: It returns an array of fields that uniquely identify each row
- `prepareRow()`: It returns the modified row prior to being passed to the processors; if `FALSE` is returned, the row is skipped

Creating a migration processor

A migration processor extends the `\Drupal\migrate\ProcessPluginBase` class. It expects to implement the `transform()` function and return the result based on the configuration provided. For example:

```php
<?php

namespace Drupal\migrate\Plugin\migrate\process;

use Drupal\migrate\MigrateException;
use Drupal\migrate\MigrateExecutableInterface;
use Drupal\migrate\ProcessPluginBase;
use Drupal\migrate\Row;

/**
 * Concatenates the strings in the current value.
 *
 * @MigrateProcessPlugin(
 *   id = "concat",
 *   handle_multiples = TRUE
 * )
 */
class Concat extends ProcessPluginBase {

  /**
   * {@inheritdoc}
   *
   * Concatenates the strings in the current value.
   */
  public function transform($value, MigrateExecutableInterface
$migrate_executable, Row $row, $destination_property) {
    if (is_array($value)) {
```

```
      $delimiter = isset($this->configuration['delimiter']) ?
$this->configuration['delimiter'] : '';
      return implode($delimiter, $value);
    }
    else {
      throw new MigrateException(sprintf('%s is not an array',
var_export($value, TRUE)));
    }
  }
}
```

The `transform()` function receives the value from the migration source, a `\Drupal\migrate\MigrateExecutableInterface` that defines how the migration is being triggered, the migration source row, and the property on the destination entity. Processors implement the `\Drupal\migrate\Plugin\MigrateProcessInterface`, which specifies the following functions:

- `transform()`: It returns the modified value
- `multiple()`: It returns whether the value is treated as a scalar value or an array; the implementation in the `ProcessPluginBase` class returns `FALSE`, which would be overridden in circumstances where the processor returns an array

Using Drush to manage migrations

With the `migrate_tools` module enabled, there are Drush tasks that allow you to run, view the status of, and roll back migrations. To view a list of migrations, you would run `drush migrate-status`, which will show a list of all registered migrations and their current status. Individual migrations or sets of migrations can be run using `drush migrate-import`, followed by a comma-separated list of migrations; an example is running `drush migrate-import d7_user, d7_user_role`. Once a set of migrations have been run, they can be rolled back by running `drush migrate-rollback`, followed by the list of migrations to roll back. Rolling back migrations will remove any entities or configurations they had created. For example, running `drush migrate-rollback d7_user` would remove any users created by the migration.

Summary

Starting with a clean installation of Drupal 8, you have the ability to migrate from Drupal 6 and Drupal 7. But Drupal 8 adopted the core of the migration module from Drupal 7, giving you the ability to customize these migrations and bring in content from other sources as well. With a few contributed modules and a little bit of custom code, you can import data from other databases as well as static files.

16
Debugging and Profiling

While developing on Drupal, it is important to be able to see what is going on under the hood. Drupal 8 has enhanced capabilities here over Drupal 7, in both debugging and profiling. In this chapter, we will be covering the following:

- First, we will explore the debugging functionality built into Drupal 8 core. This will allow us to examine information from the theme layer as well as looking at how Drupal processes content.
- Next, we will install the Devel module and use it to debug our custom modules.
- Finally, we will use the Web Profiler to ensure that our site is performing well.

Enabling core debugging

There are a number of steps you can take just within Drupal 8 that will help you diagnose problems in your site. If you have Drupal Console installed, you can enable many of these modules by running `drupal site:mode dev`. Many of the debugging settings are controlled in the `/sites/default/services.yml` file.

If there isn't one already, you can copy the starting
`/sites/default/default.services.yml` file to the `services.yml` file to start with.

```
[vagrant@localhost default]$ drupal site:mode dev
Configuration name: system.performance
-------------------------- ---------------- ----------------
 Configuration key          Original Value   Override Value
-------------------------- ---------------- ----------------
 cache.page.use_internal    false            false
 css.preprocess             false            false
 css.gzip                   false            false
 js.preprocess              false            false
 js.gzip                    false            false
 response.gzip              false            false
-------------------------- ---------------- ----------------


Configuration name: views.settings
-------------------------------- ---------------- ----------------
 Configuration key                Original Value   Override Value
-------------------------------- ---------------- ----------------
 ui.show.sql_query.enabled        true             true
 ui.show.performance_statistics   true             true
-------------------------------- ---------------- ----------------


Configuration name: system.logging
------------------- ---------------- ----------------
 Configuration key   Original Value   Override Value
------------------- ---------------- ----------------
 error_level         all              all
------------------- ---------------- ----------------


 Services files /vagrant/public/sites/default/services.yml was overwritten


New services settings
-------------- -------------- -------
 Service        Parameter      Value
-------------- -------------- -------
 twig.config    auto_reload    true
 twig.config    cache          true
 twig.config    debug          true
-------------- -------------- -------

// settings:set

 [OK] Setting checked was set to true


// cache:rebuild

Rebuilding cache(s), wait a moment please.

 [OK] Done clearing cache(s).
```

Disabling caching

The first step is to start looking at how your code is running to ensure that caching is off. Otherwise, you may find yourself wondering why your errors appear only intermittently. You might want to start off by disabling both the dynamic page cache and render cache. If you have not done it already, you should enable the `settings.local.php` file by finding and uncommenting the line in the `default /sites/default/settings.php` file that has the following:

```
if (file_exists(__DIR__ . '/settings.local.php'))
{
        include __DIR__ . '/settings.local.php';
}
```

From there, add the following lines to your `/sites/default/settings.local.php` file:

```
$settings['cache']['bins']['dynamic_page_cache'] = 'cache.backend.null';
$settings['cache']['bins']['render'] = 'cache.backend.null';
```

Enabling Twig debugging

The Twig engine provides a number of options to assist with debugging. Enabling overall debugging adds comments around each Twig template, showing the theme hook and any template suggestions:

```
297  <!-- THEME DEBUG -->
298  <!-- THEME HOOK: 'region' -->
299  <!-- FILE NAME SUGGESTIONS:
300     x region--header.html.twig
301     * region.html.twig
302  -->
303  <!-- BEGIN OUTPUT from 'core/themes/bartik/templates/region--header.html.twig' -->
304    <div class="clearfix region region-header">
305
306
307  <!-- THEME DEBUG -->
308  <!-- THEME HOOK: 'block' -->
309  <!-- FILE NAME SUGGESTIONS:
310     * block--bartik-branding.html.twig
311     x block--system-branding-block.html.twig
312     * block--system.html.twig
313     * block.html.twig
314  -->
315  <!-- BEGIN OUTPUT from 'core/themes/bartik/templates/block--system-branding-block.html.twig' -->
316  <div id="block-bartik-branding" class="contextual-region clearfix site-branding block block-system block-system-branding-block">
317
318        <div data-contextual-id="block:block=bartik_branding:langcode=en"></div>
319          <a href="/" title="Home" rel="home" class="site-branding__logo">
320          <img src="/core/themes/bartik/logo.svg" alt="Home" />
321        </a>
322        <div class="site-branding__text">
323            <div class="site-branding__name">
324          <a href="/" title="Home" rel="home">Mastering Drupal 8</a>
325        </div>
326              </div>
327    </div>
328
329  <!-- END OUTPUT from 'core/themes/bartik/templates/block--system-branding-block.html.twig' -->
330
331
332    </div>
333
334  <!-- END OUTPUT from 'core/themes/bartik/templates/region--header.html.twig' -->
```

Turning on Twig debugging also enables some additional functions inside the Twig templates. Inside a Twig template, you can place `{{ dump(var) }}` to output the value of a given variable. If you have the **Kint** submodule from the Devel module enabled, you can also place `{{ kint() }}` in your template, which will display the full context available to the template, all variables, and theme hook suggestions.

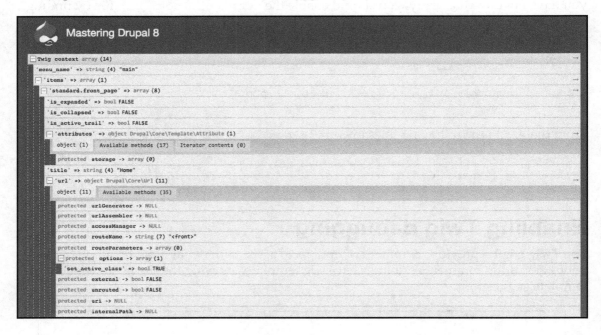

By default, Twig compiles templates into PHP code and stores that compiled PHP in cache directories. This makes rendering the Twig templates faster since that compilation process can be expensive, but it requires a full cache rebuild in order to see changes to the Twig templates. To enable this auto-reload process, edit your `/sites/default/services.yml` file, find the section for `twig.config`, and change `auto_reload: null` to `true`. If you have enabled Twig debugging, you can leave this as `null` and it will inherit from that setting. When auto-reload is enabled, it ensures that the Twig templates are re-compiled every time they are changed. It is recommended that you do disable the auto-reload functionality in production.

Debugging cache performance

A major source of performance enhancements in Drupal 8 is from the new system of cache contexts and tags. Normally these are used internally by Drupal to assemble the page from various cached items and not made visible outside the site. In order to debug effective cache clearing, you will need to have the cache tags and context exposed as response headers. Edit your `/sites/default/settings.yml` file and find the line that has `http.response.debug_cacheability_headers:  false` and change that to `true`.

Working with Devel and Kint

The **Devel** module continues to be a primary method of assisting developers to debug their code. One of the things that's new in the version for Drupal 8 is Kint replacing **Krumo** as the library used to output debugging information. Using Kint offers a number of improvements over Krumo. The most significant is the ability to see private attributes of objects. Kint uses the PHP Reflection API to get all information about an object, where Krumo used `get_object_vars()`.

Installing the Devel module

To install the Devel module on a new site, you can download it directly from `drupal.org/project/devel` or by running `drush dl devel`. From there you can run `drush pm-enable devel kint` to activate the Devel module and the Kint submodule on your site. You will need to grant the **Access kint** permission to any roles you want to see Kint debugging output.

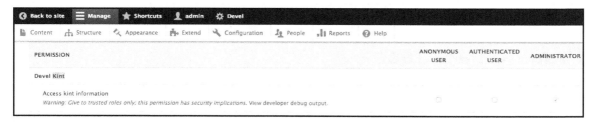

Printing variables

Debugging with an interactive debugger such as **Zend Debugger** or **Xdebug** is an extremely powerful way to dig deep into a Drupal site. Unfortunately, it can be time consuming to set up, may be difficult to use with some editors, and may not be available in your current environment. The Kint module has a very easy way to handle lightweight debugging by outputting variables. By adding a simple `kint($var)` statement, you can output the value for a variable to the screen. If the variable is an array, it will output each row; if it's an object, it will output all class variables and functions. For each class method, it will also read the PHPDoc block at the top of the function to give you some idea of what the function does. If you prefer to have the debugging happen through the message block, you can run `ksm($var)` instead, just like you had `dpm($var)` in earlier versions of Drupal.

Printing backtrace

In addition to outputting information about a single variable, you can also do a full stack trace using Kint. By adding a call to `ddebug_backtrace()` in your function, it will output a list of all functions leading to the current one. Kint will output this in two ways, one as a simple list of the functions showing the function name, file name, and line number.

Clicking on the plus sign next to **$input** will show the same list of functions, file name, and line number, but it also shows the class name of the callers along with all variables passed to those functions. These are displayed using Kint and allow you to drill down into arrays and objects just as if you had run `kint()` on them.

Using the Web Profiler

Symfony2 comes with the Web Profiler, a plugin that allows a developer to check how their application is performing. The Web Profiler collects information about each request made to the site and allows you to visualize it within the browser. The Web Profiler bundle isn't included in Drupal 8 by default but it can be installed as part of the Devel module.

Installing the Web Profiler module

The Web Profiler module is a submodule of the Devel module. When you download the Devel module, it becomes available and you can enable it either through the user interface or by running `drush pm-enable webprofiler`. There are some additional configuration steps you need to perform in order to use all of the functionality of the Web Profiler. First you will need two JavaScript libraries. You will need to download D3 (`https://d3js.org`) to `/libraries/d3` and download Highlight (`https://highlightjs.org`) to `/libraries/highlight`. Next you will need to add the following to your `/sites/default/settings.local.php` file:

```
$class_loader->addPsr4('Drupal\\webprofiler\\', [ __DIR__ .
'/../../modules/contrib/devel/webprofiler/src']);
$settings['container_base_class'] =
'\Drupal\webprofiler\DependencyInjection\TraceableContainer';
```

After enabling the Web Profiler module, each page you visit as a user with the `View webprofiler toolbar` permission will see a toolbar at the bottom of the page showing information such as the time to build the page, the number of database queries, and so on.

You can click on one of the areas of the toolbar to view more details from the page or you can navigate to **Reports | Webprofiler** to access details about specific URLs.

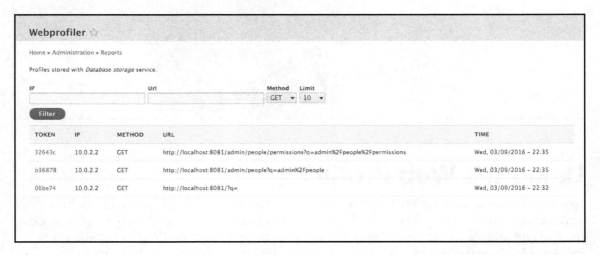

Request information

From the URL detail page, the second tab shows information about the request. This tab shows all information about the request including request and response headers, cookies, server parameters, query parameters, as well as routing parameters. That last one reveals some very important information about how Symfony handles the request. It shows the machine name of the route, and route parameters, as well as a link to the controller file. By default, the link is set to open in **Textmate**. This can be altered by navigating to **Configuration** | **Devel settings** | **Webprofiler** and opening up the **IDE Settings** fieldset. Files can be changed to open in PHPStorm 8 or higher by setting the IDE link to `phpstorm://open?file=@file&line=@line`.

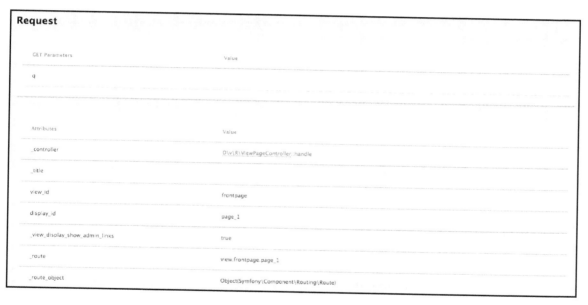

Processing timeline

From the URL detail page, the third tab shows a waterfall view of the how the page is built. This waterfall is similar to the one found in the DevTools in Google Chrome or the profiler in Firefox. The visualization shows the order in which the controllers, events, templates, and so on are executed, as well as how long they take to compile and run, and how much memory is being used at each step.

It can allow you to trace the path from the initial request coming through to the final rendering of the page and can help spot areas that may need to be optimized.

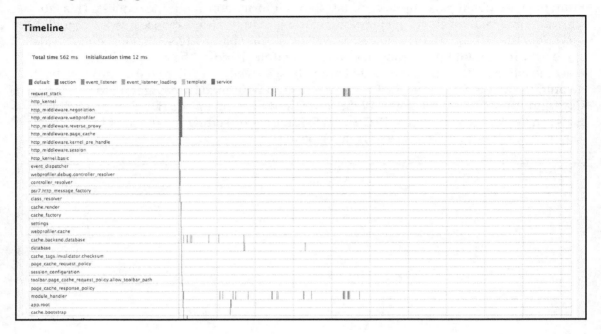

Performance timing

The next tab on the URL details page contains information about how long it took the browser to send the request, and receive and process the response. For the request, it shows the amount of time to do a DNS lookup as well as perform the TCP handshaking. Then, it shows the amount of time to receive the first byte from the site and how long the transfer of data took. Finally, it shows how long it took the browser to build and render the DOM elements.

Debugging queries

In Drupal 7, the Devel module could be toggled to display all database queries below the page. In the Web Profiler module, the **Database** tab shows these queries and allows you to filter, show the full query, and run an **EXPLAIN** on them.

Database

Caller
Caller   Query type   Any ▾   Slow queries   Any ▾   SWAP PLACEHOLDERS

```
SELECT session FROM sessions WHERE sid = :sid LIMIT 0, 1
```

Time: 0.34 ms   Caller: S\C\H\S\S\H\WriteCheckSessionHandler::read   Target: default

                                     EXPLAIN   INFO   SWAP PLACEHOLDERS

There are filters for Query types such as SELECT, INSERT, UPDATE, and so on, as well as whether the query is considered slow. For each query, you can see the values for each placeholder, as well as placing that value in the query to see what was presented to the database. You are also able to run the **EXPLAIN** command right from the interface and receive additional information about how the database processed the request.

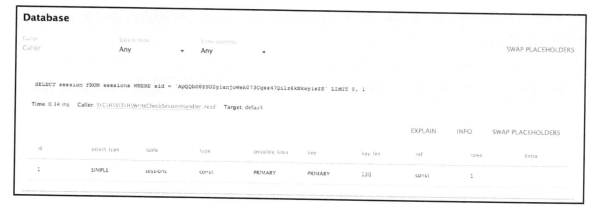

For each query, you will also see a link to open the file that contains the query using the URL format as the Request information. Clicking on the link will use the IDE link configured earlier to open the file directly in your editor of choice.

Debugging Views

Views is an important part of many Drupal sites and there are often multiple Views on a single page. The Views Web Profiler tab shows a list of all Views executed on a given page, along with information about how long it took to build the View, execute it, and then render the View. For each View, there is also a link that takes you directly to where you can edit the View.

name	display	build time	execute time	render time	Action
content	page_1	0.21 ms	0.01 ms	0.03 ms	Edit

Summary

With previous versions of Drupal, in order to get deep insights into what was going on, you would need to install tools like Xdebug or XHProf. Without those, you were limited to what you could do with printing variables to the screen using `print_r()`, `kpr()`, `dpm()` with the Devel module. First, we covered installing the Devel module and using the new Kint module. This allows us to view detailed information about the backtrace as well as any object or Twig template variable. Next, we went over how to use the Web Profiler bundle to get detailed information about each request. This includes:

- Information about the request and route
- The timeline of each component used in building the page
- A list of all queries run on the page

Index

CPSIA information can be obtained
at www.ICGtesting.com
Printed in the USA
LVHW101621070519
616954LV00007B/328/P